KW-370-054

# Cases in Total Quality Management

*To Susan and Norma*

LANCHESTER LIBRARY

```
3 8001 00228 6262
```

Lanchester Library

LANCHESTER LIBRARY, Coventry University
Gosford Street, Coventry CV1 5DD Telephone 024 7688 7555

WITHDRAWN

24 OCT 2004

2 6 NOV 2004        16 MAY 2006

1 3 JAN 2005

29 JAN 2005      3 0 SEP 2006

CANCELLED

1 0 MAY 2005    2 9 JAN 2007

24 APR 2006

−2 APR 2009

This book is due to be returned not later than the date and
time stamped above. Fines are charged on overdue books

# Cases in
# Total Quality Management

John S. Oakland

and

Leslie J. Porter

*European Centre for TQM,*
*University of Bradford Management Centre*

**B**UTTERWORTH
**H**EINEMANN

Butterworth-Heinemann
Linacre House, Jordan Hill, Oxford OX2 8DP
A division of Reed Educational and Professional Publishing Ltd

℞ A member of the Reed Elsevier plc group

OXFORD    BOSTON    JOHANNESBURG
MELBOURNE    NEW DELHI    SINGAPORE

First published 1994
Reprinted 1994, 1996, 1997

© John S. Oakland and Leslie J. Porter 1994

All rights reserved. No part of this publication
may be reproduced in any material form (including
photocopying or storing in any medium by electronic
means and whether or not transiently or incidentally
to some other use of this publication) without the
 written permission of the copyright holder except
in accordance with the provisions of the Copyright,
Designs and Patents Act 1988 or under the terms of a
licence issued by theCopyright Licensing Agency Ltd,
90 Tottenham Court Road, London, England W1P 9HE.
Applications for the copyright holder's written permission
to reproduce any part of this publication should be addressed
to the publishers

**British Library Cataloguing in Publication Data**
Oakland, John S.
   Cases in Total Quality Management
   I. Title II. Porter, Leslie J.
   658.5

Coventry University

ISBN 0 7506 1565 6

**Library of Congress Cataloguing in Publication Data**
Oakland, John S.
   Cases in Total Quality Management/by John S. Oakland and
   Leslie J. Porter.
   p.  cm.
   Includes index.
   ISBN 0 7506 1565 6
   1. Total quality management - Case studies. I. Porter, Leslie J.
   II. Title
   HD62.15.017          P O O 1658          93-34170
   658.5'62-dc20            19/3/98          CIP

Composition by Genesis Typesetting, Laser Quay, Rochester, Kent
Printed and bound in Great Britian by Athenaeum Press Ltd, Gateshead, Tyne & Wear

# Contents

# Preface

The literature on total quality management (TQM) has increased in volume substantially in recent years. There is, however, a shortage of good cases from 'ordinary' companies and organizations, yet business education and training are reliant upon the use of such cases. This lack of availability of suitable case material, particularly based on UK and European organizations, has in our opinion limited TQM training and education development.

This book contains a collection of 17 real cases which we have used and continue to use and develop in our own teaching. We hope that the nature of the cases and their variety will aid the study and comprehension of TQM at all levels, including undergraduate, postgraduate and executive development.

The cases are not from the usual stable of well-known TQM companies, such as Xerox, IBM, Milliken – the 80% Baldrige Award scorers! These cases describe organizations which are more likely to achieve Baldrige or European Quality Award scores of 40–60% and thereby should offer a closer relationship to the 'average' organization considering a change process such as TQM. Few of the organizations described would claim 'best practice' and one of the tasks in reading the cases should be to identify how the organization should move forward and improve.

The seventeen organizations form a heterogeneous mixture, in terms of size, business type, industry sector, and stage of TQM development, which should provide a learning opportunity for everyone. The cases are organized under the headings or parts of the TQM model presented in the second edition of John S. Oakland's book *Total Quality Management*. The first section presents selected highlights from this book as 'the essentials of TQM'. The second section gives some tips on reading, using and analysing the cases.

We would like collectively to thank our associated contributors – mentioned as appropriate in the cases or at the end of the cases – and all the students and managers who have participated in their discussions and development. Special thanks must go to Barbara Ward and Wendy Docherty for their work and support.

# The essentials of TQM

## Selected highlights from
### *Total Quality Management 2*
### by John S. Oakland.

## Part One   The foundations

### Understanding quality, competitiveness and processes

The reputation enjoyed by an organization is built by quality, reliability, delivery and price. Quality is the most important of these competitive weapons. Reputations for poor quality last for a long time, and the management of quality can be learned and used to improve reputation.

Quality is meeting the customer requirements, and this is not restricted to the functional characteristics of the product or service. Reliability is the ability of the product or service to continue to meet the customer's requirements over time. Organizations 'delight' the customer by consistently meeting customer requirements, and achieve a reputation for 'excellence'.

There exists throughout all organizations a series of internal suppliers and customers. These form the so-called quality chains, the core of company-wide quality improvement (CWQI). The internal customer – supplier relationships must be managed by interrogation using a set of questions at every interface. Measurement of capability is vital.

There are two distinct but interrelated aspects of quality, design and conformance to design. Quality of design is a measure of how well the product or service is designed to achieve the agreed requirements. Quality of conformance to design is the extent to which the product or service achieves the design. Organizations should assess how much time they spend doing the right things right.

Everything we do is a process, which is the transformation of a set of inputs into the desired outputs. In every organization there are some key, critical or business processes, which must be performed especially well if the mission and objectives are to be achieved. Processes should be managed through a strategy of *prevention*, rather than *detection*.

Quality control is the employment of activities and techniques to achieve and maintain the quality of a product, process or service. Quality assurance is the prevention of quality problems through planned and systematic activities.

Marketing establishes the true requirements for the product or service. These must be communicated properly throughout the organization in the form of specifications. The involvement of all members of an organization is a requirement of CWQI, which necessitates everyone working together at every interface to achieve perfection.

## Leadership and commitment to TQM

TQM is a comprehensive approach to improving competitiveness, effectiveness and flexibility through planning, organizing and understanding each activity, and involving each individual at each level. It is useful in all types of organizations. TQM ensures that management adopt a strategic overview of quality and focus on prevention, not detection of problems. It often requires a mind-set change to break down existing barriers.

TQM must start at the top where serious commitment to quality must be demonstrated. Middle management also have a key role to play in communicating the message. Every chief executive must accept the responsibility for commitment to a quality policy which deals with the organization for quality, the customer needs, the ability of the organization, supplied materials and services, education and training, and review of the management systems for never-ending improvement.

The culture of an organization is formed by the beliefs, behaviours, norms, dominant values, rules and the climate in the organization. Any organization needs a vision framework that comprises its guiding philosophy, core values and beliefs, a purpose, and a mission. Effective leadership starts with the chief executive's vision and develops into a strategy for implementation.

To be effective leaders, top management must develop the following: clear beliefs and objectives in the form of a mission statement; clear and effective strategies and supporting plans; the critical success factors and critical processes; the appropriate management structure; and employee participation through empowerment and the PDCA (plan–do–check–act) cycle.

The effectiveness of an organization then depends on the extent to which people perform their roles and move towards the common goals and objectives. TQM is concerned very much with moving the focus of control from outside individuals to within, so that everyone is accountable for their own performance.

TQM is the key to effective leadership through: commitment to constant improvement, a right-first-time philosophy, training people to understand customer–supplier relationships, not buying on price alone, managing systems improvement, modern supervision and training, managing processes through teamwork and improved communications, elimination of barriers and fear, constant education and expert development, and a systematic approach to TQM implementation.

The core of TQM is the customer–supplier relationship, where the processes must be managed. The 'soft' outcomes of TQM – the culture, communications and commitment – provide the foundation for the TQM model. The process core must be surrounded by the 'hard' management necessities of systems, tools and teams. This model provides a framework against which an organization's progress towards TQM can be examined. It also provides a useful framework for the analysis of the case studies in this book.

# Part Two    The role of the quality system

## Policy and systems

An appropriate documented quality system will enable the objectives set out in the quality policy to be accomplished. The International Standards Organization (ISO) 9000 series sets out methods by which a system can be implemented to ensure that the specified requirements are met.

A quality system may be defined as an assembly of components such as the organizational structure, responsibilities, procedures, processes and resources. Quality systems should apply to and interact with all activities of the organization. The activities are generally processing, communicating and controlling. These should be documented in the form of a quality manual. The system should follow the PDCA cycle, through documentation, implementation, audit and review.

The general categories of ISO-based standards include: management responsibility, quality system, contract review, design control, document control, purchasing, customer-supplied products or services, identification and traceability, process control, checking/measuring/inspecting of incoming materials or services, measuring/inspection/test equipment, inspection/test status, non-conforming products or services, corrective action, protection of product or service quality, quality records, quality system audits and reviews, training, servicing and statistical techniques.

Senior management in all types of industry should take responsibility for the adoption and documentation of the appropriate quality system in their organization.

## Documentation and assessment

The quality manual is the document in which it is explained how the organization carries out the quality policy. It should be no longer than 25–30 pages. The quality manual should reflect the type and level of quality system, and refer to the standard being used as the framework.

The quality system should be a living thing, not a bureaucracy or paperwork model, and this requires the involvement of everyone. It can be difficult sometimes for people to change, to accept and adopt new procedures. Small organizations may see formalized quality system documentation as unnecessary or costly, but often find that certain customers or contracts may be retained only by compliance or registration. One solution to this problem is for a group of small organizations to share a professional quality manager on an internal/external consultancy basis.

In using a consultant for quality system advice, select one who does not offer a standard package. A good advisory project covers four phases: initial or terms of reference; interim report and action plan; final report and draft quality manual; and audit.

There are two major elements of error or defect prevention: checking the system, and error/defect investigations and follow-up. A good-quality system will not function without adequate audits and reviews. Audits make sure the actual methods are adhering to documented procedures. Reviews ensure the system achieves the desired effect. System assessment by internal audit and review is known as first-party, by external customer is second-party, and by an independent organization is third-party certification. For the latter to be of real value the certification body must itself be recognized.

One of the most famous and widely used frameworks for TQM self-assessment is the Malcolm Baldrige National Quality Award (MBNQA) in the USA. The MBNQA criteria are built on 10 core values and concepts which are embodied on a framework of seven first-level categories: leadership (driver), information and analyses, strategic quality planning, human resource development and management, management of process quality (system), quality and operational results (measure of focus), and customer focus and satisfaction (goal). These are comparable with the 10 categories of the Japanese Deming Prize, and the nine components of the European Quality Award (EQA), categorized as *enablers* and *results*.

The various award criteria provide rational bases against which to measure progress towards TQM in organizations. The 'motors' driving an organization towards its mission must be linked to its five stakeholders: customers, employees, suppliers (determinants), and shareholders, community (resultants).

To the foundation framework of the customer–supplier chain, processes and the 'soft' outcomes of TQM, must be added the first hard management necessity – a quality system based on a good international standard.

# Part Three   The tools and the improvement cycle

## Measurement and benchmarking

Traditional performance measures based on cost accounting information provide little to support TQM, because they do not map process performance and improvements seen by the customer. Measurement is important in identifying opportunities, and comparing performance internally and externally. Measures, typically non-financial, are used in process control and performance improvement.

In TQM measurement, the strategic objectives will be converted into desired standards of performance, and metrics developed. This separation of process performance and process management is important, since it determines the type of questions to be asked, e.g. how much, how many versus what, where, why? Process owners should be involved in defining the performance measures that must reflect customer requirements.

Benchmarking measures an organization's operations, products and services against those of its competitors. It establishes targets, priorities and operations, leading to competitive advantage. There are four basic types of benchmarking: internal, competitive, functional and generic. The evolution of benchmarking in an organization is likely to progress through four focuses towards continuous improvement.

## The costs of quality

A competitive product or service based on a balance between quality and cost factors is the principal goal of responsible management. The analysis of quality-related costs provides a method of assessing the overall effectiveness of the management of quality and of determining problem areas, opportunities, savings and action priorities.

Total quality costs may be categorized into prevention, appraisal, internal failure and external failure costs: the P–A–F model. Prevention costs are associated with doing it right the first time, appraisal costs with checking it is right, and failure costs with getting it wrong. When quality awareness in an organization is low, the total quality-related costs are high, the failure costs predominating. After an initial rise in costs, mainly through the investment in training and appraisal, increasing investment in prevention causes failure, appraisal and total costs to fall.

In manufacturing industries the costs of failure can be 10–15% of turnover, and in the service sector higher, at 35–40% of volume. In finding costs, one of the pitfalls is isolating only those things that can be easily measured, such as scrap, wasted materials, direct people costs, reworking, redoing, etc. The bulk of failure costs often lie in the non-producing sectors of an organization.

Successful quality costing involves working closely with accountants and supervisors. A pilot study should be used to establish preliminary figures from a small area of the organization to determine the scope of the work required. For many organizations, it may be sufficient to assess the proportion of time spent on errors and their appraisal, rather than becoming too concerned with financial accuracy.

The P–A–F model for quality costing has a number of drawbacks, mainly due to estimating the prevention costs, and its association with an 'optimized' or minimum total cost. An alternative – the process cost model – rationalizes costs of quality (COQ) into the cost of conformance (COC) and the cost of non-conformance (CONC) (COQ = COC + CONC) at each process stage.

Process cost modelling involves: choice of a process and its definition; construction of a process diagram; identification of outputs and customers, inputs and suppliers, controls and resources; flow-charting the process and identifying owners; allocating activities as COC or CONC, and calculating the costs. A process cost report with summaries and results is produced. The failure costs or CONC should be prioritized for improvements.

A working knowledge of an organization's processes and accounting system is essential for successful quality costing. A quality costing strategy should start with an assessment of the organization's quality management capability. Following this, the critical cost areas should be analysed using the right data, time scales, system, and reporting mechanisms.

## Tools and techniques for quality improvement

Numbers and information will form the basis for understanding, decisions, and actions in never-ending improvement. A set of simple tools is needed to interpret fully and derive maximum use of data. More sophisticated techniques may need to be employed occasionally. The effective use of the tools requires the commitment and involvement of the people who work on the processes. This in turn needs management support and the provision of training.

## Some basic tools and techniques

The basic tools and the questions answered are:

| | |
|---|---|
| Process flow-charting | What is done? |
| Check/tally charts | How often is it done? |
| Histograms | What do overall variations look like? |
| Scatter diagrams | What are the relationships between factors? |
| Stratification | How is the data made up? |
| Pareto analysis | Which are the big problems? |
| Cause-and-effect analysis and brainstorming (also cause-and-effect with the addition of cards (CEDAC), nominal group techniques (NGT) and the five whys) | What causes the problem? |
| Force-field analysis | What will obstruct or help the change or solution? |
| Emphasis curve | Which are the most important factors? |
| Control charts (including cusum) | Which variations are to be controlled and how? |

People operating a process must know whether it is capable of meeting the requirements, know whether it is actually doing so at any time, and make correct adjustments when it is not. Statistical process control (SPC) techniques will help here. Before using SPC, however, it is necessary to identify what the process is, what the inputs/outputs are, and define the suppliers and customers and their requirements.

All processes can be monitored and brought under control by gathering and using data. SPC methods, with management commitment, provide objective means of controlling quality in any transformation process. SPC is not only a tool kit, it is a strategy for reducing variability, part of never-ending improvement. This is achieved by answering the following questions:

- Are we capable of doing the job correctly?
- Do we continue to do the job correctly?

- Have we done the job correctly?
- Could we do the job more consistently and on target?

This provides knowledge of process capability and the impact of a quality system and SPC together is the gradual reduction of the variability in the ways things are done.

A second 'hard' management necessity – the tools – must be added, with the systems, to the TQM model to progress further round the never-ending improvement cycle.

# Part Four   The organization and teamwork requirements

## Organization for quality

The only point at which true responsibility for quality can lie is with the person or group actually doing the job. Separate, élite inspectors and checkers can cause abdication of this responsibility. The chief executive must take overall responsibility for quality. The quality function's role is the provider of systems and guidance.

Positive quality policy objectives must be accompanied by clear allocation of responsibilities within the management structure, particularly at the levels of senior executive and first-line supervision. Progress in quality improvement must then have the full cooperation and commitment of all employees. This means their involvement in process design, operation and control.

Managers are in control only when their subordinates can exercise self-control. The process of performance management then consists of clarifying responsibilities, developing performance indicators and objectives, and preparing action plans.

In devising and implementing TQM for an organization it may be useful to ask first if the managers have the necessary authority, capability and time to carry it through. A disciplined and systematic approach to continuous improvement may be established in a quality council (QC), the members of which are the senior management team. Reporting to the QC are the process quality teams (PQTs) or any site steering committees, which in turn control the quality improvement teams (QITs) and quality circles.

A QIT is a group brought together by management to tackle a particular problem on a project basis. The running of QITs involves several team factors: selection and leadership, objectives, meetings, assignments, dynamics, results and reviews. A Quality Circle is a group who do similar work who meet voluntarily, regularly, in normal working time, to identify, analyse and solve work-related problems, under the leadership of their supervisor. They make recommendations to management. Kaizen is a philosophy of small-step continuous improvement, involving all employees. In Kaizen teams, the suggestions and rewards are small but the implementation is rapid.

## Teamwork for quality improvement

The only efficient way to tackle process improvement or complex problems is through teamwork. The team approach allows individuals and organizations to grow. But employees will not engage continual improvement without commitment from the top, a quality climate and an effective mechanism for capturing individual contributions. Teamwork for quality improvement is driven by a strategy, needs a structure, and must be implemented thoughtfully and effectively.

John Adair's simple model of teamwork addresses the needs of the task, the team, and the individuals in the team, in the form of three overlapping circles. There are specific task, team and individual functions for the leader, but (s)he must concentrate on the small central overlap area of the three circles.

After initial problems are solved by teams, others should be tackled – successful solutions motivating new teams, but in all cases, teams should follow a disciplined approach to problem solving using proven techniques. Teamwork may mean a change in culture that must be supported by management through their activities and behaviour.

# Part Five   The implementation

## Communicating the quality message through training

People's attitudes and behaviour can be influenced by communication and the essence of changing attitudes is to gain acceptance through excellent communication processes. The strategy and changes to be brought about through TQM must be clearly and directly communicated from top management to all staff/employees. The first step is to issue a Total Quality Message. This should be followed by a signed TQM directive.

People must know when and how they will be involved in the TQ process, what the process is, and the successes and benefits achieved. The first-line supervision has an important role in communicating the key messages and overcoming resistance to change.

'Open' methods of communication and participation must be used at all levels. Barriers may need to be broken down by concentrating on process rather than departmental issues. There are four audience groups in most organizations: senior management, middle management, supervisors, and employees, each with different general attitudes towards TQM. The senior management must ensure that each group sees TQM as being beneficial. Good leadership is mostly about good communications, the skills of which can be learned through training, but must be acquired through practice.

All communication and training exercises must be planned and operated to leave nothing to chance. Managers will need training in communicating skills, particularly with respect to communicating in teams, talking to people, reporting and writing (including flowcharts), leading discussions and chairing meetings.

Training is the single most important factor in improving quality, once commitment is present. Quality training must be objectively, systematically and continuously performed. All training should occur in an improvement cycle as follows: ensure training is part of quality policy; allocate responsibilities; define objectives; establish training organization; specify needs; prepare programmes and materials; implement and monitor; assess results; review effectiveness.

Responsibility for quality training of employees rests with management at all levels. The main elements should include error/defect/problem prevention, reporting and analysis, investigation, and review. Needs for integrated quality training occur at four levels of the organization: very senior management, middle management, first-level supervision and quality team leaders, and all other employees.

Quality training programmes should centre round the basic principles of understanding processes and the seminars/workshops should be carried out in small groups. All quality training should be followed up with improvement projects and 'surgery' workshops. External help is often required to introduce TQM. Consultants should be selected carefully on the basis of qualifications, knowledge, experience, and demonstrated practical success in the industry.

## Integrating TQM into the business strategy

Senior managers in some organizations recognize the need for change to deal with increasing competitiveness, but lack an understanding of how to implement the changes. Successful change is effected not by focusing on formal structures and systems, but by aligning process management teams.

This starts with writing the mission statement, analysis of the critical success factors (CSFs) and understanding the critical or key processes.

Some of the obstacles to TQM implementation and resistance to change may be overcome through education, communication, participation, involvement, facilitation and support. The blitz or rapid-change approach should be rejected in favour of a slow, planned purposeful one, starting at the top.

Senior management may begin the task of process alignment through seven steps to a self-reinforcing cycle of commitment, communication and culture change. The first three steps are: gain commitment to change, develop a shared mission or vision of the business or desired change, and define the measurable objectives. The remaining four steps involve developing the mission into its CSFs, understanding the key or critical processes and gaining ownership, breaking down the critical processes into subprocesses, activities and tasks, and monitoring and adjusting the process alignment in response to difficulties in the change process. Goal translation then ensures that the 'whats' are converted into 'hows' using a quality function deployment matrix-based process.

Making quality happen requires not only commitment but a competence in the mechanics of TQM. Crucial early stages will involve establishment of the appropriate organization structure, collecting information, including quality costs, teamwork, quality systems and training.

Managers must understand and pursue never-ending improvement. This involves planning and operating processes, providing inputs, evaluating outputs, examining performance, and modifying processes and their inputs. There are three basic principles of continuous improvement: focus on the customer, understand the process, involve the people. In the model for TQM, the customer–supplier chains form the core that is surrounded by the 'hard' management necessities of a good quality system, tools and teamwork.

Successful organizations using TQM have learned that it is hard work, takes a long time, needs to be driven by the strategy through the whole business, relies on top and middle management commitment, and needs enthusiastic practical champions. The need for ongoing never-ending improvement must be emphasized throughout.

## Further reading

Adair, J., *Effective Teambuilding* (2nd edn), Pan Books, London, 1987.

# Reading, using, analysing the cases

The cases in this book provide a description of what occurred in 17 different companies, regarding various aspects of their quality improvement efforts. They may each be used as a learning vehicle as well as providing information and description which demonstrate the application of the concepts and techniques of TQM.

The objective of writing the cases has been to offer a resource through which the student of TQM (including many practising managers) understands how TQM companies operate. We hope that the book will provide a useful and distinct contribution to TQM education and training.

The case material is suitable for practising managers, students on undergraduate and postgraduate courses, and all teachers of the various aspects of business management and TQM. No real prior knowledge is assumed, but the selected highlights from John Oakland's book *Total Quality Management 2* have been drawn together in the previous section to provide a good platform from which to read the cases. Further study of that full text is recommended for those engaged in serious study of TQM or its implementation.

The cases have been written so that they may be used in three ways:

1 As orthodox cases for student preparation and discussion.
2 As illustrations, which teachers may also use as support for their other methods of training and education.
3 As supporting/background reading on TQM.

If used in the orthodox way, it is recommended that firstly the case is read to gain an understanding of the issues and to raise questions which may lead to a collective and more complete understanding of the company, TQM and the issues in the particular case. Secondly, case discussion or presentations in groups will give practice in putting forward thoughts and ideas persuasively.

The greater the effort put into case study, preparation, analysis and discussion in groups, the greater will be the individual benefit. There are, of course, no correct and tidy cases in any subject area. What the directors and managers of an organization actually did is not necessarily the best way forward. One object of the cases is to make the reader think about the situation, the problems and the progress made, and what improvements or developments are possible.

The writing of each case emphasizes particular problems or issues which were apparent for the organization. This may have obscured other more important ones. The diagnostic skill of the student will allow the symptoms to be separated from the disease. Imagination, innovation and intuition should be as much a part of the study of a case as observation and analysis of the facts and any data available.

TQM cases, by their nature, will be very complicated and, to render the cases in this book useful for study, some of the complexity has been omitted. This simplification is accompanied by the danger of making the implementation seem clear-cut and obvious. Believe us, that is never the case with TQM!


## TQM case analysis

The main objective of each description is to enable the reader to understand the situation and its implications, and to learn from the particular experiences. The cases are not, in the main, offering specific problems to be solved. In using the cases, the reader/student should try to:

- *Recognize or imagine* the situation in the organization.
- *Understand* the context and objectives of the process(es) described.
- *Analyse* the different parts of the case (including any data) and their interrelationships.
- *Determine* the overall structure of the situation/problem(s)/case.
- *Consider* the different options facing the organization.
- *Evaluate* the options and the course of action chosen, using any results stated.
- *Consider any recommendations* which should be made to the organization for further work, action, or implementation.

The set of cases has been chosen to provide a good coverage across different types of industry and organization, including those in the service, manufacturing and public sectors. The cases have been arranged in a sequence which follows the various parts of the Bradford Model of TQM:

- The foundations.
- The role of the quality systems.
- The role of tools, techniques and measurement.

- The organization, communication and teamwork aspects.
- The implementation and integration into strategy.

The value of illustrative cases in an area such as TQM is that they inject reality into the conceptual frameworks developed by authors in the subject. The cases are all based on real situations and are designed to illustrate certain aspects of managing change in organizations, rather than to reflect good or poor management practice. The cases may be used for analysis, discussion, evaluation, and even decision-making within groups without risk to the individuals, groups, or organization(s) involved. In this way students of TQM may become 'involved' in many different organizations and their approaches to TQM implementation, over a short period and in an efficient and effective way.

The organizations described here have faced translating TQM theory into practice, and the description of their experiences should provide an opportunity for the reader of TQM literature to test his/her own preconceptions and understanding of this topic. In some cases the name(s) of the organizations concerned have been changed to avoid embarrassment, but all the cases describe real TQM processes in real organizations.

## Further reading

Easton, G., *Learning from Case Studies* (2nd edn), Prentice-Hall, UK, 1992.

# Part One
# The Foundations for TQM

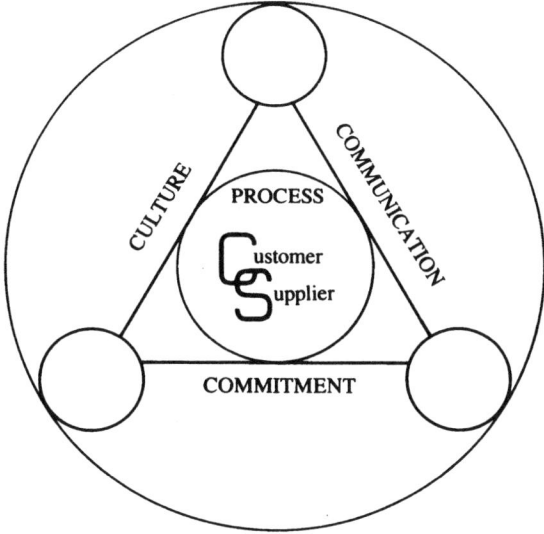

# 1 Culture change through total quality at Lynx

## Background

Lynx can trace its history over 150 years of transport and carrying in the UK, including about 35 years under public ownership. As a result, at the time Alan Soper joined the company as Managing Director in 1989, the company employed a long-serving, ageing but loyal workforce. They brought views and behaviour towards such '90s issues as quality customer service and continuous improvement from the experiences of past decades, often trapped in the time warp of those years and the fashion which they represented. The company dates from 1987, when NFC (National Freight Carriers) carrying companies were reorganized and rebranded as Lynx.

Briefly, the company turned over about £85m p.a., employed about 3500 people and was in the business of delivering small consignments and parcels to UK and European commercial addresses. As a result, it had a customer base across many different industrial and commercial sectors and, usually working to a distribution agreement, handled customers' regular distribution needs. Operationally much of the work was handled through a transport and sorting network which ensured that the movement of individual consignments – the production process – was cost-effective against other delivery methods, such as using a dedicated vehicle. All deliveries were made to time-sensitive commitments.

What Alan Soper found in 1989 was a highly departmentalized company, dominated by its network production process, in which selling was seen as a feeder process to keep the operation 'full'. The customer had no role in the company's thinking except as a provider of more parcels when they were needed. Being able to see the company like this on a first run round its establishments helped Alan see the earliest flickerings of a quality mission – observing what people actually do and wondering why they do it. He had read some stuff about quality and listened to some of the 'guru' thinking, so he was like many senior managers perhaps, a mixed bag of theory, ideas and half experiences, but he had drawn up an underlying personal belief from all this that the quality objective was almost entirely wrapped up with the behaviour of people at work. Perhaps this is obvious but, ironically, it is a massively important assumption to carry round a business.

In his first few months in the business, Alan spent a day with a delivery driver (he expected all the senior managers in the company to do this at least once a year). The driver went from customer to customer in the area of Nottingham, delivering and picking up parcels and driving the lorry. He was cheerful, friendly, and his main preoccupation was how many calls he made and how many parcels he delivered. Whether the parcels were the right ones at the right time and in the right place was clearly of secondary consideration. It was no surprise then for Alan to move from the 'production line' to the corporate office to find a survey of customers which said, in so many words, that the Lynx delivery service *did not* deliver the right parcels to the right place at the right time often enough, but emphasizing that their drivers were incredibly cheerful and friendly!

## Attitudes and behaviours

The important point for quality here was that the driver's behaviour was conditioned as much by the climate in which he worked as by his own attitude. Because the company was so network-dominated, the driver saw himself as a small-cog production worker in a vast machine process, driven by productivity targets, unaffected and unmeasured by errors and unable to influence the correction of errors.

This made for interesting musing for a new MD chewing over his future direction for the business. But it was actually much worse than this. Behind the driver lay a whole structure of operational organization, supervision and management who were also driven by productivity targets, also unaffected and unmeasured by errors and, most crucially of all, also unable to influence the correction of errors. It is only when the behaviour of managers is observed and considered that one gains some insight into what will happen to a company. The heart of a company usually lies with its front-line workers – its drivers in this case – but the destiny is to be found in the behaviour of its managers.

So when Alan observed the Lynx management population, he found a large quantity of 'parcel movers' with a very low proportion of managers with commercial abilities, an instinct for customer service and, most importantly, some power to change things so that errors could be eliminated and problems solved. Changing this state of affairs seemed to be an absolute necessity if any quality progress was to be made. He also realized that, because of this powerless structure, he was seen by the managers as the all-powerful one. Apparently he was expected to pull rabbits out of hats on a regular basis and thus drive the business forward, while everyone else in the company sat back and watched and, most significantly, expected their problems to be somehow solved for them. This seemed to be against the quality philosophy based on self-help and empowerment – ideally of *everyone*, but most certainly of managers.

## Beginning to change the culture

Alan Soper began with the management group and chose the 'onion skin' approach to change. That meant he would establish a powerful central belief system and method of working, share this with direct reports, move on through different levels establishing behaviour change at each pass – with casualties if necessary – until he was satisfied that managerial behaviour *would* act as though it could solve problems and overcome obstacles. In some ways the creation of a quality culture did not need problems to be solved; it merely needed a belief that it was worth having a go. Indeed one of the earliest requirements was to be able to support failed attempts. The old classical task-driven company would have rounded on all failure and actually suppressed initiative. Alan found he had to change these responses and applaud application and effort, sometimes in the face of glaring mistakes. So, into the central core of the onion were placed four simple concepts which seemed pretty obvious and yet had been lost sight of in the old company. They were:

1 Customers – what they want.
2 People – what they can do.
3 Progress – expecting it.
4 Profit – where it comes from.

The early statements probably did not count for much at the time because when a leader says 'I believe in people' or 'customers are jolly important', it carries no weight until he or she starts to behave accordingly. So, in the same way that Alan had observed the actual behaviour of managers as the key to future quality, he now gave notice to managers to observe him as the key to future quality.

The early sessions with the teams concentrated much more on style than substance. They used team games and non-work-setting exercises to let managers *experience* emerging values for themselves, so avoiding the trap of 'handing out' values cold. In this way, people at least had experienced what the senior management's objectives were, even if behaviour did not match up. The actual words used to describe the value system came directly from the top management team and were a direct reflection of their experiences of outdoor challenges. In fact they had them drawn up on a flipchart more or less as they were taking off their boots:

- Timeliness
- Quality
- Customer service
- Communication
- Profit hunger
- People development and accountability
- Loyalty

The top team were proud of these values which went into personal mission cards, meeting agendas, training programmes, project proposals and reports, and even into a series of concept paintings in the company's boardroom.

## The mission, measurement and costs

The Lynx mission was a vehicle to draw the company together. It required more formal preparation to give shape to the company's future, but once in place set a common framework for everyone's own objectives. The mission was:

> Lynx will become the best-loved company in the market.
> We will develop an obsession about meeting the expectations of our customers in time-sensitive transportation and information services, fulfilling the promises made to our customers' customers.
> We will do this by sticking to our principles and by stimulating our people to strive for high quality through the fostering of ideas and initiative.
> From this we will earn the right to thrive and grow.

The top team liked it because it had a sense of urgency and a memorable first line. They even found themselves the subject of a Letter-to-Editor column of a trade journal on that first line. This was seen to be a good thing, for the most important aspect of any mission is that someone remembers that there is one. The somewhat unexpected first line kept the mission in the forefront of people's minds. They happen to think *love* was exactly right – companies should be loved; if they are not, they will be neglected.

After that, it became OK to identify and measure failures, and the costs of non-conformance (CONC) for the whole business were established. The kinds of non-conformances identified included:

| *Company cost* | *Customer cost* |
|---|---|
| Lost consignments | Lost consignments |
| Damaged parcels | Damaged parcels |
| Misrouted parcels | Late deliveries |
| Damaged vehicles | Missed bookings |
| Late-entered data | |
| Lost customers | |

All company goals for service and product quality became zero failures or 100% achievement. In the past these had been set at 'tolerance' levels, implying that some failure was allowed – a kind of reject rate. But this was a service, not a product, and the customer experienced *every* item, including the rejects. So having *any* expectation of service failure builds in a permanent non-conformance cost – lost business.

All this energy directed towards the management processes and to behaviour change began to have an effect on individuals. Managers talked a lot about the 'core values' and these seemed to provide a common language across old departmental boundaries. Interestingly, the cynicism expected was almost non-existent, and this was put down to the introductory method of experiencing the values and not having them handed out.

There was much recognition of the maxim of making progress by improving lots of things in a small way, rather than by waiting for big events. Indeed, lots of things were improved and what *appeared* to be substantial progress achieved on many of the key non-conformance costs. This proved, however, to be a false dawn. After about a year of reasonable progress, the company seemed, for no apparent reasons, to go into reverse. Error costs rose and confidence was shaken. They learned the first rule of TQM implementation: that, although *measurement* is all-important, there is no final result, no ultimate measurement of success, in fact no achievement at all, just continuous improvement. For managers brought up on task and project work on clearly defined achievements, this was a hard lesson. It showed the Lynx management that TQM could not be treated as a project with a beginning, a middle and an end, but had to be part of the company furniture.

They next set about some practical steps to build the value system more firmly into the company's production system, through some rigorous process definition and an audit system, so that everyone could see how progress was being made, not just on non-conformance costs, but on the fundamental elements of how each job was done. This was more time-consuming, perhaps more boring, but certainly more powerful.

## The changing climate, communications and teamwork

As the climate began to change, it became equally evident that some managers simply would not make it. There was no choice here; managers who cannot respond or adapt must go. In some cases Lynx parted company with managers who may have met targets under older regimes, but who had become a positive constraint on the development of the values. This can seem harsh. The company gave a lot of power to the managers to change and influence their own ideas, but they were never allowed to work to different values.

It took Lynx about 2 years to get into reasonable shape, through the management layers of the onion. The next stage in tackling the blue-collar employees was both much harder and much easier. Harder, because the blue-collar people worked in a much more highly structured environment for payment systems, including union representation, and – perhaps most interesting of all – easier because, when a company gets through the restrictive practice of managers screwing up the final product, they find the front-line people always wanted to give customer service with a quality product and had it right all along!

This history with unions is a tricky one. People at work need representation to protect individuals from the excesses of powerful managers, but few unions approach this, other than through restrictions, having procedures only for pay and conditions and to regulate seniority. Yet real quality is always about change and continuous improvement, and Lynx found that their union had no procedure for dealing with change on a small-scale, day-to-day basis. It could handle big redundancy announcements but otherwise assumed that the company was a fixed and unchanging affair. The result of this was that the union could not perform an effective representation role and contributed to the considerable growth of fear among employees in the face of change.

The senior management decided to communicate the mission directly to the people, using training as the principal method. Large programmes followed as they covered large numbers of employees directly. Alan Soper warns, however, that training and communication are great initiatives, and you can have a lot of fun with both – but then, like any other piece of frippery, it can be ditched when a recession comes around and everyone has to be miserable again! When they looked at training and communication and similar classical human resource initiatives, again from the point of view of the employee, they realized that the emotions they were dealing with were some of the most powerful in corporate working life. They were:

- Belonging
- Recognition

For belonging, Lynx organized all their work into permanent work teams with an identified leader and a regular supply of team performance information. They organized training programmes on a modular basis to be personally driven by individuals with certificates for attainment of the skills needed by the company.

For recognition, they identified winners, from both individuals and teams. Tangible, but not monetary, rewards were made. They used house journals and noticeboards to highlight and celebrate winners and in this way events and changes were expected. These were often insignificant in themselves, but they gave huge messages to everyone about what the leader wanted and what happened when he/she got it.

These are some of the gains which the company can point to in the last 2 years:

*Non-conformance cost reductions*

| Lost consignments | *down* 40% |
|---|---|
| Damaged parcels | *down* 35% |
| Misrouted parcels | *down* 15% |
| Damaged vehicles | *down* 50% |
| Late-entered data | *down* 80% |
| Lost customers | *Record retention* |
| Customer satisfaction sampling | *up* 6% |

## The learning organization

The company had not yet achieved its mission. Alan Soper believed in fact that they had hardly started and that they made a mess of lots of things. But they had learned how to avoid TQM becoming just another fashionable idea for managers. For Lynx, it had not been primarily about process controls, or special-quality committees, or even about accreditation. It had been a way in which people worked together in a company, based on mutual respect and common goals, with little hierarchical structure, but not anarchic. It had been about the ability to value the contribution that a human being can make to an enterprise, so that (s)he is not seen merely as an inefficient machine, but treated in a way which gives him/her a sense of belonging and recognizes the contributions (s)he makes. 'Work needs to become disciplined fun.'

The mark of a quality company is not, Lynx management believed, one whose products are always perfect or which has lots of important-sounding committees, but one in which the desire for constant change and improvement towards increasing wealth is instinctively felt by all of its people. Lynx was a company striving for this aim, and they believed that the striving was probably enough.

# 2 Assessing TQM implementation in the Prudential Assurance Co Ltd, Life Administration Home Service Division

## Introduction

Prudential Corporation is one of the world's largest and strongest financial services groups. The Corporation's UK core business is conducted by the Home Service Division of the Prudential Assurance Co Ltd. Home Service's main businesses are life assurance, pensions, savings and general insurance. These products are serviced by some 9000 field staff working from nearly 180 branch offices.

The Life Administration group, with its offices in Reading and Belfast, supports this activity by providing essential administrative back-up for new business, servicing, accounts and claims for life and pensions business. An indication of the size and complexity of the operation is given by the following statistics:

Computer systems hold over 15 million contract records:

- 30 million direct debit transactions are processed each month.
- 100 000 proposals for new business are processed each month.
- 400 000 pieces of mail are sent to sales staff per month, as well as 500 000 letters to policy-holders.
- 120 000 telephone calls are received every month.

In May 1989 the Life Administration business plan defined key business targets and activities to be undertaken over a 3-year time frame (1990–1992). Extensive market research was undertaken as part of the planning process. Two main conclusions were drawn:

- Customers' requirements were defined but performance could be improved.

- Life Administration's productivity had to increase if its policy-holders were to receive first-class returns on their investments. Market trends indicated current staffing levels could not be supported.

The preferred way forward was to implement a TQM programme, which became known as the Way of Life. Targets were set for headcount, cost and productivity. Efficiency – doing things right first time – and effectiveness – doing the right things – became key drivers. A team of managers acted as facilitators to plan and support the quality initiative. These managers developed the Life Administration mission statement which was endorsed by the Life Administration Board. The company's TQM programme is detailed below.

# Leadership

## *Management involvement*

The Life Administration management have a style based on effective leadership and TQM. Management commitment, or rather the lack of it, is often cited as the reason why quality programmes fail. Within Life Administration there is no defined strategy for displaying management commitment, just a blend of management style which works. Some key management attributes which support quality improvement are listed below:

- they are champions of the cause.
- they participate.
- they listen.

The board of directors sponsored the TQM programme and senior experienced middle managers were assigned to the project team to facilitate the programme. The first stage was to develop an education package from which a TQM programme, called the Way of Life, was born.

The Life Administration Board was involved in establishing the mission statement, quality policy, and Principles and Values statements which describe the culture aspired to. They were also the first members of staff to be trained and the first to become involved with quality improvement activity. Such was the commitment from the senior management that the training alone represented an investment of over 4000 workdays across all of the group. This training was conducted by Life Administration line management rather than external consultants.

From the point when the decision was made to implement a TQM programme, the first 9 months were spent planning the first education

**Table 2.1** *Life Administration Home Service Division TQM programme*

---

*Way of Life TQM programme*

| | |
|---|---|
| May 1989 | Business plan approved |
| | Selection of consultants and facilitator team |
| Oct–Nov 1989 | Facilitator education |
| | Review of current position |
| Nov 1989–Jan 1990 | First phase of education prepared |
| Feb–July 1990 | First phase of education delivered |
| | Second phase of education prepared |
| Aug 1990–April 1991 | Second phase of education delivered |

*Business Awareness programme*

| | |
|---|---|
| Sep–Dec 1991 | Half-day Business Awareness sessions developed and delivered |

*Serving Customers – Our Way of Life programme*

| | |
|---|---|
| Sep–Dec 1991 | Two-day module Serving Customers – Our Way of Life designed and piloted |
| Jan–Dec 1992 | Serving Customers – Our Way of Life modules delivered to all staff |

---

programme before it was launched. The major milestones are summarized in Table 2.1.

Even though the original Way of Life programme was a major success, management were not complacent and were personally involved in the follow-up Business Awareness and Serving Customers – Our Way of Life programme.

Managers at board level actually taught the half-day business awareness modules which were given to all staff. They also always opened the 2-day residential customer-care programme, going back to stay overnight at the hotel used for the training, so that they could discuss quality with the staff in a relaxed atmosphere, and then returned again on the second day to close the session and to accept any actions which were beyond the scope of lower-grade staff. These actions became affectionately known as the 'live withs'. The programme was run over 50 times during 1992, and the senior management team were represented at every single event.

Senior management supported quality improvement in many other ways. For example, they delivered papers at international conferences on quality within Prudential. They promoted quality within Prudential itself, with Life Administration being viewed as a flagship. They also supported staff attending conferences and meetings on quality so that even junior members of staff had the experience of learning about quality from face-to-face contact with other companies.

In 1991, Life Administration was awarded the Northern Ireland Quality Award for service. The award was made after Life Administration submitted a written report on eight separate criteria. Of the eight criteria, they came top out of five and were short-listed alongside two other well-known leading organizations in quality. A site visit followed during which the senior management and staff were quizzed for several hours. They were delighted to receive the award, but the reason why they beat the opposition was more significant. In the words of the judges:

> The Award is granted for making rapid progress and achieving inspirational commitment from all managers and staff, so transforming an office working environment into a challenging and stimulating place to work.

### Way of Life review

The measurement of employees' perceptions was seen as an important element of the TQM programme. Consultants reviewed the attitudes and behaviour of Life Administration staff at the start of the quality initiative training. This was repeated a year later by the same consultants. Results are on a 1–10 scale.

|  | *Nov 1989* | *Nov 1990* |
| --- | --- | --- |
| How serious is management about quality? | 6 | 9 |
| How serious do you think your staff are about quality? | 5 | 8 |
| How well do individual managers work together? | 6 | 7 |
| How well do departments work together? | 5 | 8 |
| How does the company rate on employee communication? | 5 | 8 |
| How would your subordinate rate you in taking quality seriously? | 6 | 8 |

The results show significant improvement in all areas. The consultants concluded: 'The initiative has succeeded in bringing about substantial change in communications, behaviour and attitudes to quality throughout the organization. The process has been received with enthusiasm at all levels and as a result the environment for continuous improvement has been established'. Clearly, the training had established a climate for change and a desire to improve. There are now over 150 supervisor-led improvement teams which meet on a regular basis to work on quality improvement activities, working on over 1000 improvement ideas across Life Administration.

November 1991 saw the second review, which was conducted by different independent consultants. The review was conducted on a group interview basis, with a brainstorming session to list staff's views on the way the TQM programme could be improved. A total of 119 people took part in the review, which included the Life Administration Board itself. A total of 19 questions were addressed by the teams. The results of the review in ascending order are shown below.

*Scores are on a 1 (disagree) to 5 (agree) scale*

| | | |
|---|---|---|
| 1 | Everyone in the organization shares the same vision of quality | 2.38 |
| 2 | Systems and procedures are up-to-date and reflect best practice with today's technology | 2.50 |
| 3 | The management culture develops employee trust by personal involvement and viability | 2.63 |
| 4 | There are no barriers between internal departments | 2.67 |
| 5 | People are recognized for their contribution and work well done | 2.80 |
| 6 | We conduct regular surveys to determine customers' product and service expectations | 2.86 |
| 7 | Generally decisions here are made based on sound data with good input from my level | 2.87 |
| 8 | Customer satisfaction measures are set and published regularly | 2.93 |
| 9 | Employees feel confident that management will act upon employee initiatives | 3.00 |
| 10 | Management deal promptly with issues for improvement according to resources available | 3.01 |
| 11 | Management communication to all employees is regular and up-to-date | 3.33 |
| 12 | Teamwork is very good here | 3.50 |
| 13 | Training plans are prepared and implemented which are relevant to employee requirements | 3.68 |
| 14 | Throughout the organization there is a commitment to meet internal and external customer requirements | 3.69 |
| 15 | Target setting with measurement and publication of performance is normal practice | 3.90 |
| 16 | I know and understand the mission statement and quality policy | 4.11 |
| 17 | Employee participation in problem identification and solving is practised and encouraged | 4.16 |
| 18 | I believe in generating ideas for continuous improvement | 4.46 |
| 19 | I have personally participated in an improvement initiative in the past 12 months | 4.70 |

On the positive side, the review found that:

● Way of Life was highly visible and accepted by staff.
● Most people interviewed had personally taken part in quality improvement activity during 1991.
● There was no shortage of ideas.
● Commitment to provide customer satisfaction was high.

On the negative side, though:

● Management involvement needed to be more visible.
● The same vision was not shared.
● Computer systems and work procedures needed to be improved.

Action was quickly taken on the results of the review. For example, the Serving Customers – Our Way of Life Business Awareness programme addressed the concern over the shared vision.

### *Management quality action*

Measurement itself is useless unless it leads to action. The main process for review and action is through the contact process. Each 4-week period, a report is compiled listing all failures. This report includes corrective action plans.

The contact report is discussed at board level. It gives board members the opportunity to discuss issues in their area in an open team environment. This can lead to offers of help from other areas or ideas on the way to tackle specific issues.

The contact process doesn't only concern itself with performance-related measures. It also covers areas such as customer satisfaction results, employee survey results and customer complaints. To ensure staff are kept informed with both achievements and actions, the results of the contact process are cascaded through the team briefing network.

### *Management structure*

The organizational structure project is an excellent example of management commitment to quality improvement. Previously, departments were structured in a functional manner by product and transaction type. This proved to be a major barrier to customer service, since staff were transaction-focused. Often, several departments needed to contribute to a customer response which became delayed and uncoordinated.

The senior management team commissioned a complete review of the management and operational structure. A layer of management was eliminated, which improved the command and communication chain. Products and transactions are now combined into divisional groups which face a major customer, the field staff, with clear lines of access. Complex technical work is concentrated in specialist areas, which allows the divisional departments to focus on customer service.

Restructuring called for a complete redesign of the management roles and competencies, against which more than 150 staff were measured during a thorough and objective process.

With the new management structure in place, attention was turned to redesigning the clerical roles so that an even closer relationship would exist between multiskilled groups of staff providing a comprehensive service to specific district offices. One of the project objectives was to involve the staff directly in the design process. To support all this, the training and development programmes were completely rewritten.

Throughout restructuring, Life Administration have reviewed all the cultural influences, particularly the reward and recognition processes, to ensure that they fully and consistently support quality activities.

### Reward and recognition

As previously mentioned, the quality objectives and business objectives are indivisible, and so the focus on quality improvement is kept at all levels through the review of the operating plan and individual objectives. The results of the annual appraisal, which is based on the achievement of the objectives is a key determinant of an employee's remuneration. Every employee has customer satisfaction set as a key objective. But rewarding through the achievement of individual objectives once per year is thought to be too wide a time frame. To overcome this, there are three additional reward schemes which are designed to reward and recognize achievement.

#### Way of Life awards

First there is the Way of Life award scheme, which has a three-tiered bronze, silver and gold approach. The level of reward and recognition increases with the level of award. Bronze awards are considered by peers and are controlled by the area quality management teams. To obtain a higher value award, a presentation has to be given to the senior management team. This body either confirms the bronze, recommends a silver, or refers the achievement to the Life Administration Board. The Board then decides on the level of the award, gold or silver. Senior management's involvement in the award process is another visible sign of their commitment. Getting an award is not easy. To date, although there have been numerous bronze awards, there have only been five silver and two gold awards.

### Instant incentives

The Way of Life award process is quite lengthy due to its peer recognition element and is aimed mainly at team effort. Each manager has the authority to recommend an individual for an instant award when (s)he witnesses the individual giving exceptional customer service. The awards take the format of shopping vouchers.

### Challenge '92

As mentioned earlier, one of the management-led strategic projects looked at the structure of Life Administration. Challenge '92 was developed to support the changes.

The scheme is based on team performance, with teams being awarded points for meeting certain criteria. The criteria are not only volume-related but include accuracy and customer satisfaction measures.

### Review

Staff opinion was sought on these reward and recognition processes and there was a clear recommendation to combine all the schemes into one scheme which made no distinction between quality and business performance. Total quality had to be the way of doing business. The new integrated scheme retained many of the positive features of the earlier scheme, such as instant recognition and peer group recognition where appropriate, but offered more 'exciting' prizes. A tandem parachute jump with the Red Devils was one prize. This was not the 'failed' TQM facilitator's prize!

## Policy and strategy

The management team facilitating the quality initiative developed a mission statement which was endorsed by the board of directors.

The Life Administration mission statement affirms:

> We administer Prudential Assurance life business. Our purpose is to delight our customers by delivering a quality service, in a cost-effective manner, through the contribution of everyone.

Quite often, a company will have a top-level mission statement but nothing to support its implementation. In this case, they developed a set of 'principles and values' which translated the words contained in the mission statement into easy-to-understand bullet points which describe the culture they were trying to grow within Life Administration. These bullet points became known as the Way of Life statements.

### Our Way of Life

*We are committed to delivering a quality service to our customers*:

- The customer is the reason we exist and the key consideration in carrying out our day-to-day business.
- The customer is the person or area to whom we are providing a service.
- Everyone is a vital link in the service chain and the successful partnership between the suppliers of services and their customers is of primary importance.
- As individuals and teams we demonstrate our commitment to our customers by 'getting it right first time'.
- We will continually review, redefine and improve the quality of service we provide to meet the changing expectations of our customers.

*We recognize that our purpose can only be achieved through people*:

- We recognize that everyone wants to provide a quality service.
- Each individual has the right to know what is expected of him/her and the reasons why.
- We are committed to providing continuous education, training and development opportunities to enable everyone to realize their full potential.
- Each individual is responsible for providing a quality service.
- We encourage people throughout the organization to listen actively to each other and to voice their ideas and opinions.

*We are committed to creating a business-like and caring working environment*:

- We will communicate in an open manner, which mirrors and supports our Way of Life.
- Teamwork will play a vital part in achieving our purpose.
- Opportunity will be given to individuals and teams to make changes at the level where it is most practical.
- We actively support the local community and the wider environment in which we live and work.

The mission statement was not set in tablets of stone. In the later stages of the TQM programme the company used a copywriter to wordsmith the mission. This was then given to all the improvement teams for their comments. The feedback was invaluable and the whole process generated an improved mission with wider ownership.

The first step to implement the mission statement was to set business measures which focused on the key drivers. These were called the Key Business Indicators (KBIs), and these are related to key words in the mission, as shown below.

| *Mission* | *KBIs* |
|---|---|
| Quality service | Attitude |
| | Speed |
| | Accuracy |
| Cost-effective | Productivity |
| Contribution of everyone | Morale |

The current KBI targets are contained within the Life Administration business plan, which has Board-level approval. Sitting below the top-level plan are departmental operating plans which reflect the business plan targets on a department-by-department basis. The duration of these plans is 1 year. Although these are prepared by the departmental managers, there is a high level of involvement from the supervisors who contribute to these plans. Alongside the departmental operating plans sit individual objectives and accountabilities which detail the responsibilities of the senior managers, departmental managers and supervisors.

Although the planning process is labelled as a business planning process, Life Administration believe that business goals and quality goals are indivisible. For example, the business plan objectives talk of a 10% year-on-year reduction in the operating budget. This is being achieved through many actions which include ensuring processes are 'right first time' so that inspection can be dispensed with. Other objectives include a maximum 5-day turnaround time with zero non-conformances.

Implementing the TQM programme had two key parts. There were the 'hard' business measures based on the KBIs. But there was also the 'soft' cultural side, which is difficult to measure but easy to experience. Life Administration developed an organization which is best pictured in Figure 2.1. To help them achieve this cultural change, and to achieve their performance target, they developed a four-point quality strategy so that words could be turned into actions. The strategy was based on the following:

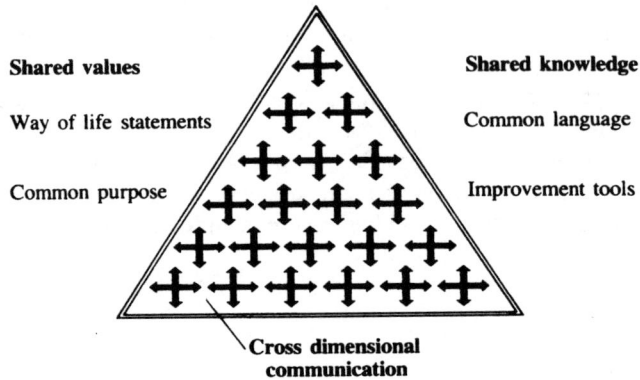

**Figure 2.1** *Awareness to action*

| Control of processes | Getting processes 'right first time' and having understanding of their interdependence. Service excellence can only be delivered through capable processes. |
|---|---|
| Customer-focused culture | Listening to customers and reacting quickly to their changing requirements. |
| Continuous improvement | Adopting continuous improvement as a strategic imperative and striving to exceed customers' expectations.<br><br>Within the continuous improvement segment of the quality strategy they consider six main areas. These are leadership, improvement activity, education, measurement and benchmarking, reward and recognition and continuance. |
| Communication | Keeping everyone in touch and promoting TQM within both Life Administration and Prudential in general. This involves upward, downward and horizontal communication. |

The main activity during the earlier years (1989–1990) was that of educating all staff. This education was so successful that it won a UK National Training Award in 1991. During 1991–1992 the emphasis on effective training continued and Life Administration was awarded another National Training Award in 1992 for its ISO9000/BS5750 programme.

## People management

Prudential had a very traditional culture. Before the TQM programme took hold, there was very little involvement from staff in any form of change. Middle managers spent most of their time protected by office walls, taking decisions in isolation. This was not an environment in which teamwork and employee participation could survive. The only quality improvement vehicle available was strategic projects, where middle managers appointed departmental managers on to project teams. They in turn appointed their first-line managers on to subproject teams, in some cases to do all the work.

Participative teamwork within Life Administration was launched through the Way of Life education programme. The programme made it clear why they had to change, gave the staff the tools so they could change, and empowered the staff to make changes.

There are four types of improvement activity within Life Administration:

1 *Strategic projects:* management-led and sponsored by a Life Administration Board member or other senior manager. These still play a key role.
2 *Cross-department improvement teams:* groups are formed voluntarily when a quality improvement opportunity is identified in one area and action has to be taken in another.
3 *Work groups:* work groups meet regularly to identify and implement quality improvement opportunities within their work area.
3 *Individual action:* individuals are encouraged to take action that will result in an improvement either in their personal performance or to their assigned processes.

The focus on quality improvement is kept by having quality improvement as a key objective written into everyone's objectives and accountabilities. This was necessary as it overcame what was the major obstacle to keeping quality improvement going – the conflict between improvement and work volumes. These problems have been minimized as the business measures are also the quality improvement measures, but it has still been a long education process to get people to understand that the way to achieve the business targets is by quality improvement action and not just by working harder. People had to learn to work smarter, and they did this by eliminating the many problems they faced day in, day out.

Figure 2.2 shows the progress made during 1991 in terms of the number of quality initiatives started and completed. However, it has not all been plain sailing. One of the drawbacks of the education process is that the training was given to teams by their first-line manager, and the effectiveness of the teams became a function of the competence of the first-line managers in training them. Getting the first-line manager to deliver the training ensured a high

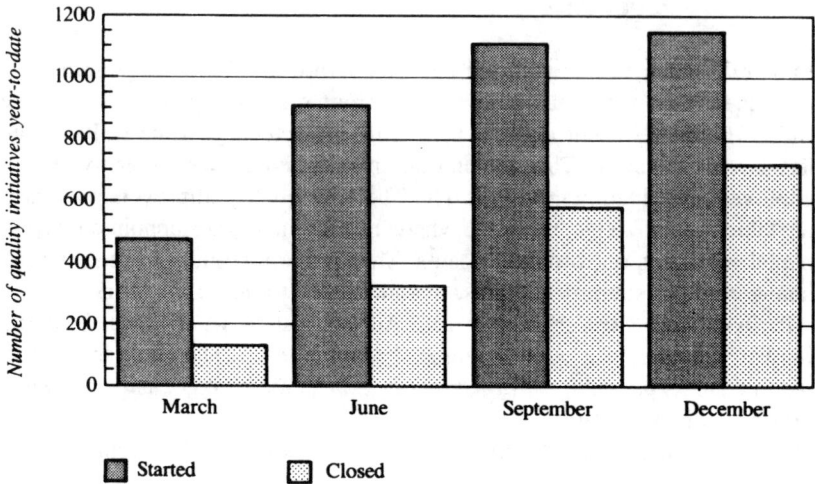

**Figure 2.2** *Way of life workgroup activity 1991*

degree of line ownership for the quality process, the training was made relevant on an area-by-area basis, and it gave the first-line managers some extra skills as part of the process. To support the first-line managers in their roles there was a support network put into place to control the process and give advice. This network was called the Quality Management Team (QMT) network. Each area has a QMT.

The QMT structure in itself is a good example of teamwork in action. As mentioned above, each area has a QMT, and each QMT has a representative on the Way of Life Forum (WOLF; Figure 2.3). The WOLF has a responsibility to the Life Administration senior management team, and WOLFs are always attended by at least one Life Administration Board member.

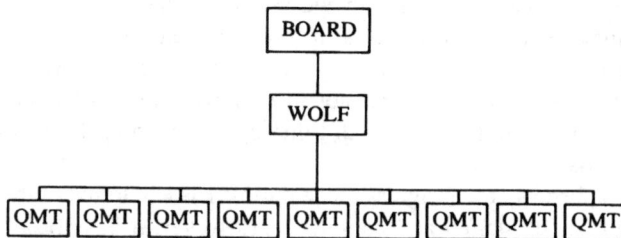

WOLF: Way of life forum
QMT: Quality management team

**Figure 2.3** *QMT structure*

When the QMTs were first established, they were chaired by the senior manager in the areas and consisted only of area management. As these groups evolved, a mixture of grades were introduced on to these teams and for the first time they had teams consisting of senior management, management and clerical-grade staff working together in order to achieve common objectives. This illustrates the major shift in culture that has taken place within Life Administration.

Although Life Administration has always had problem solving and on-the-job training, total quality management training did not start until February 1990. It would also be unfair to claim that the major improvements achieved resulted solely from quality training. Many other training initiatives have made a significant contribution, good examples being performance management and team briefing. Figure 2.4 shows the training plan for all quality improvement-related training, both planned and delivered. All training was delivered on schedule.

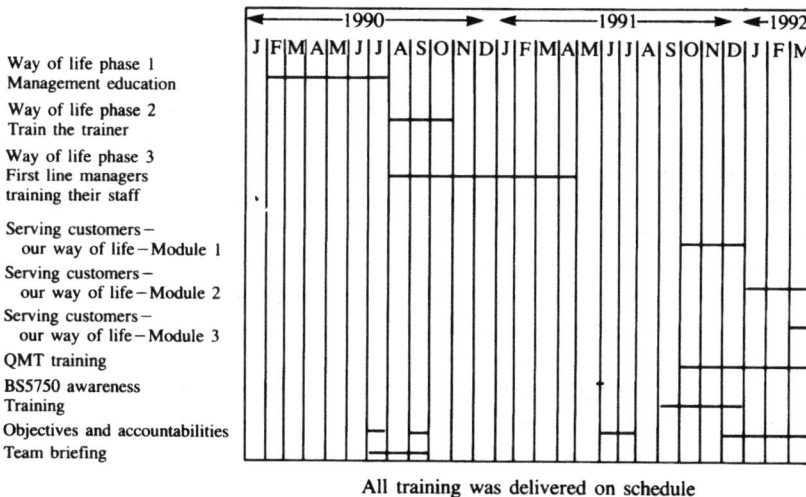

Figure 2.4 *TQM training schedule*

Attendance at conferences or quality events has not been included on the training plan, although these play an important role. This type of training is more on an individual basis, and is monitored like other individual training requirements, through the Life Administration Development Plan process. All the computer-based training packages that are available to staff have also been excluded. A hallmark of the training is that it is all very Life

Administration-specific. It addresses key business needs for Life Administration. The training programmes are designed to be interesting and even fun.

Each of the different training initiatives is discussed briefly below:

### Way of Life (TQM) training

The Life Administration TQM programme was launched by educating all staff. This training was so successful it has won a 1991 National Training Award.

As suitable off-the-shelf training material could not be found, it was written specifically to achieve the stated objectives and was Life Administration-branded. All training was conducted by Prudential staff and its effectiveness evaluated by independent consultants.

Training was in three stages. In the first stage, staff from board member to supervisor were trained over a 6-week period. The main objective of this training was to begin to change the culture and gain acceptance, at all levels of management, of the need to improve quality. Whilst this equipped supervisors with knowledge, stage 2 gave training skills, team leadership skills, preparation time and support.

The third stage was a living example of the quality initiative principles in practice, with teams working together to improve quality. The training was delivered to the clerical staff by their own supervisor. This enabled Life Administration to establish natural supervisor-led work groups with the objective of tackling quality improvements. The strategy adopted has successfully delivered a high level of employee involvement.

To achieve the main objective of sustained quality improvement activity, the training material was designed so that there was a 'seamless transition between learning and productive involvement'. It had to be flexible in physical design so that it could be used in the workplace, and had to allow for different learning speeds and styles of delivery. Work groups selected a problem which affected them and took a week-by-week structured approach to its elimination.

### Serving Customers – Our Way of Life

Written to the same exacting standards as the original Way of Life programme. Serving Customers – Our Way of Life took the organization a stage further forward. Whereas the focus during Way of Life was on the elimination of workplace problems, the focus of Serving Customers – Our Way of Life was a banner to achieving outstanding customer service. The programme was in two modules.

---

*Module 1 – Business awareness*

Half-day Business Awareness sessions were given to all staff. The first session was presented by the Head of Life Administration, Kippa Alliston, who discussed the 1991 business results plus the vision for 1992 and beyond.

The second session was delivered by Dr Westwood of Manchester Business School who gave his own personal view of the outlook for the financial services industry. This session was designed to make staff aware of the business imperative to improve both productivity and service. Finally, a serving Life Administration Board member presented a more local view to the staff in their area. The objective of these sessions was to share the vision for the future and prepare staff for module 2 of the programme.

---

*Module 2 – Barriers to customer service*

During 1992 all staff attended this 2-day module which gave them the opportunity to identify barriers to excellent customer service. The module started by discussing exactly what makes good customer service and what makes bad customer service. Examples were given of 'good companies' and 'bad companies'. Although the programme was given to all staff, the programme given to managers and supervisors had an additional section to enable them to lead customer care. One key learning point consistent with the Way of Life theory was that good customer service can only be delivered with capable processes.

At the end of the programme staff committed themselves to both group and individual improvement actions to remove the barriers to customer service. Barriers which were outside the group's control were accepted by senior management, and there is a process in place to feed back to the groups the management actions which have been taken.

---

## QMT training

One of the problems with many packaged training programmes is that they are very prescriptive. The view within Life Administration was that such prescription destroys innovation and personal ownership. Although this is true, a structured approach can have value in terms of direction. The QMT training package was developed to give QMT some gentle direction. It also provided refresher training in quality improvement tools, as one of the prime functions of the QMT is to provide support and consultancy.

### Objectives and accountabilities and team briefing

Although these are normally regarded as management processes, they are included here to reinforce the importance given to defining people's responsibilities and communication. Both were taught in a workshop environment.

With their Performance Management System (PMS), staff first draft their accountabilities and objectives themselves, before offering them to their manager for discussion. The objectives reflect the objectives in the area's operating plans. In this way, personal ownership of objectives are ensured.

In order to keep a focus on quality, quality objectives and accountabilities are incorporated into the PMS. For example, the actions which staff are committing to at the end of the Serving Customers – Our Way of Life programme are monitored through the PMS.

Life Administration always had a 'cascade' communication process, but a survey revealed that messages were not getting right the way down throughout the organization. A formal team briefing process with a supporting process to allow communication to pass up the chain as well as down it has subsequently been introduced. Weekly, bimonthly and, where appropriate, *ad hoc* newsletters are also used in the communication process.

### Team measures

A measurement system supports all improvement activities. The success of the quality improvement action is measured by a subset of the business success measures. A five-point measurement matrix is used:

1 *Customer impact*: evaluation of whether the quality improvement action has a major or minor positive impact on customers.
2 *Time*: Staff in the early stages of the TQM programme did not think that they had time to work on quality improvement activities. Time has therefore been made a measure of success, to reinforce to staff that time spent on quality improvement activity is a profitable investment.
3 *Money*: Direct cost savings in materials are evaluated.
4 *Service*: If a quality improvement has a positive effect on either the accuracy or speed of service, the improvement is classified in terms of major or minor effect.

5 *Morale*: One of the benefits to staff of quality improvement is that by removing quality problems, it makes their jobs 'hassle-free' and can remove some mundane tasks. Being listened to and having your idea implemented also gives greater job satisfaction.

Each team (or individual) evaluates the effectiveness of their improvement action against the above criteria when they close off their logged quality improvement initiative. The status of all the quality improvement initiatives, and benefits when closed, are recorded by the QMTs.

Each 4 week period the QMTs collate the data from the QMTs from all around their areas, and the total results across all Life Administration are issued back to QMTs in a summary report. The figures also go to senior management for review.

### Quality Week – 1993

The idea behind Quality Week came about following the attendance of some Life Administration staff at the National Society for Quality through Teamwork Conference in August 1991. A group of people decided to form a team to try to get more excitement into the quality programme. Several options were considered, but the idea of a Quality Week to celebrate the successes to date was chosen. This took place in January 1993.

The event was also an opportunity to involve everybody in the preparations for the move to new premises. New facilities and a brand new environment were seen to offer a tremendous opportunity. The acronym NBG (new ball game) was adopted for the week and various teamwork events took place throughout the week. The NBG theme manifested itself in teams within 10 leagues competing against each other. The leagues were just convenient groups of Life Administration staff. Will Carling, the England Rugby Team Captain, gave a talk on teamwork. A number of companies and organizations also held workshops and seminars for Life Administration staff. The workshops showed how other organizations were tackling TQM.

A review of the Quality Week found that it had rekindled enthusiasm for quality and proved it could be fun. Many staff benefited from seeing how other companies tackled quality and picked up lots of new ideas. The week certainly stimulated teamwork and the active participation in process improvement.

### General comments

The People Management area in Life Administration has seen major changes resulting from the TQM programme. The human resource planning process supports the company's policy and strategy in a dynamic way. Market research is carried out on employees to find out what their true needs are. Every employee has an individual training and development plan and all training is delivered on a project-by-project basis.

A management development section has been set up and this has produced a list of key management competences. In the reorganization accompanying the TQM programme, existing managers had to reapply for management positions to see if they met the new criteria. Those failing to meet the criteria were not appointed to managerial positions in the new structure.

The company runs various counselling processes, including a quarterly review of employee development plans and one-to-one training sessions. A mentoring system also operates. Employees are free to choose a mentor who is then used in the peer group recognition process. Health and Safety issues are managed in a progressive way. For example, the company provides excellent occupational health facilities, with centres staffed by nurses running well-women clinics, heart programmes, etc. A preventive approach is seen as vitally important for the well-being of all employees.

Commitment to people also involved the provision of the previously mentioned new office facilities. The old facilities did not encourage or promote quality. Employees could not be expected to do a good job in inadequate offices. The move to the new offices was also a good demonstration of teamwork in action. The move, involving over 1400 staff, was accomplished over two weekends with no operational disruption. The whole process was managed by a cross-functional team.

## Management of resources

The financial management at the Prudential works within the framework laid down by the company's policy and strategy. It is customer-driven and market-based. While the financial and accounting figures are used to track the business performance, the focus is on customer service and the market. Quality objectives are also the company's business objective and all financial decision making supports total quality.

The process of management of cash flow, working capital and costs is well-understood and fully documented. The process is subject to regular review as part of a strategy of never-ending improvement.

A Management Accounting Reporting System (MARS) was introduced during 1991 which gives ownership of budget down to department level, whereas before this was controlled at area level. Such ownership has allowed greater participation in the construction of the budget, with acceptance of budget restrictions imposed on Life Administration by the Prudential Board. Within each department, employees are informed about the overall and department budget, and are made aware of their responsibility to meet the targets.

The management of information resources is seen as a key to the success of the TQM programme. Computer systems play a vital role in the Prudential's operations and they are also one of the biggest barriers to quality improvement. Barriers may be the speed at which systems can be realistically changed, or the system designers' failure to meet the true needs of their customers, i.e. the system user within Prudential. A key customer–supplier team has been formed between Life Administration and the computer systems area to break down their barriers. The collaboration has resulted in the formation of a Life User Group, so that Life Administration has an influence on the way in which computer systems projects are resourced. Life Administration has a slice of the overall budget for Home Systems development and has a choice as to how that money is spent. It also reviews the value-for-money aspects, which has provided a key driver for Home Service systems in their own quality programme.

Computer system designers have introduced a process called Home Service Development Life Cycle for the development of new systems. The process, which is a form of phased project management with clearly defined checkpoints, requires a high degree of user involvement as the customer joins a user group to establish true business needs. The process also includes a System Implementation Review where the effectiveness of the development process is reviewed so that improvement action can be taken, if necessary. Three months after system implementation, there is a Post Development Review where the system itself is evaluated against the predefined business requirements. Life Administration takes part in both these reviews in the role of customer.

The involvement of the customer, i.e. Life Administration, will ensure that the systems effort is directed for the best effect. For example, the team has already decided to resource the clearance of the top 100 recorded system 'niggles' before moving on to any major changes. This will have a major impact on staff, who had previously perceived that they had to live with such minor problems. It is demonstrating that management want to 'get it right first time' for them and support their quality improvement activities with good information systems.

# Processes

Life Administration's philosophy is one of total continuous improvement. The effectiveness of all activities and processes is regularly reviewed. They learn from this experience and use this information in the planning process.

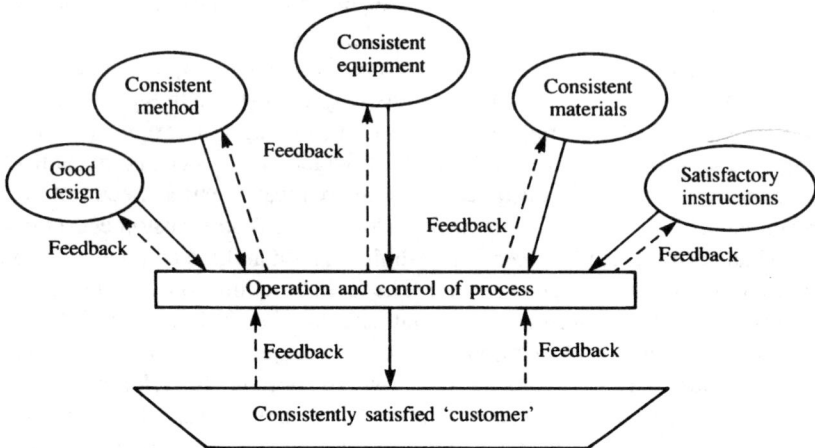

**Figure 2.5** *The process approach*

They have realized that 'doing things right' alone is not enough – they must also 'do the right things'. A tremendous amount of effort is going into reviewing exactly what they, as suppliers of a service, understand by 'the right things'. The way they examine the performance of their processes against targets also plays a key role in improvement activities. This is best summarized in Figure 2.5.

The importance of the ISO9000 Quality Management System was recognized at an early stage of the TQM programme. It was seen as a way of managing processes to deliver consistent outputs. There were no commercial pressures on Prudential to be registered to ISO9000. Registration would have only limited marketing benefit as the majority of the policy-holders would not have heard of ISO9000 unless they had come across it in their own business. However, the Industrial Branch area became the first area within an insurance company to become a registered firm following an assessment in December 1991.

There were many reasons why the decision was taken to register the Industrial Branch area of Life Administration. The administration of assurance business is by nature highly regulated by legislation. As a consequence, a quality assurance system of sorts had always been in existence. The benefit of extending this system to the ISO9000 standard was that the British Standard, with its focus on process control, contained some additional requirements that were perceived to improve the degree of control. Examples of these requirements are internal quality audits, control of non-conforming material and management review.

A second reason for seeking registration had more to do with the staff than quality assurance. Assurance administration is a complicated business. For some time there had been an interest among staff in reviewing all the existing procedures and documentation which controlled the processes. The ISO9000 registration project provided a necessary focus on procedures so that this desire could be realized. The unannounced surveillance visits would also keep people's attention on ensuring documentation is kept up-to-date, and the procedures are actually operated.

The company recognized the many benefits to ISO9000 registration, including:

- Demonstration of a company commitment to quality
- Improved consistency
- Reduction in waste and increased efficiency
- Management and process control
- A driver for continuous improvement

But the Prudential were looking for some additional benefit. For instance, they saw ISO9000 registration becoming an integral part of their TQM strategy. They believed that it would not be possible to deliver excellent customer service unless they had capable processes. They also saw registration as a useful lever in influencing the quality of service offered by some internal Prudential suppliers.

At the outset staff listed the requirements of the approach they could take. There are many ways of approaching registration. Some companies employ consultants to construct the quality system and others set up an internal project team to do it themselves. The company wanted to achieve registration with 100% staff involvement as it believed this was the only way to ensure total ownership of the quality system and that registration would lead to lasting benefit. Registration had to be more than a badge on the wall. They also wanted ownership of the goal, which was to be the first insurance company to have part of its administration organization registered to ISO9000. This also meant that they needed a fast-track approach.

ISO9000 is often introduced as a top-down initiative which can achieve the goal of registration, but fails to give lasting benefit due to a lack of ownership of procedures and disciplines. The Prudential sought help from consultants to develop a process which generated total involvement and commitment to achieving ISO9000 registration using the following principles:

1 *Humour*: Humour was used to break down barriers and inhibitions, creating a climate where people wanted to be part of the process.
2 *Recognition*: Individual contributions and achievements were rewarded with a variety of recognition awards which served both as a 'thank you' and as evidence that management cared.

3 *Teamwork*: Every employee, including senior management, was a member of a team, which created friendly competition as well as a sense of loyalty and commitment to one's peers.
4 *Deadlines*: By providing a clear timetable for each stage of the process, we ensured that systems, procedures and records were in place in time for assessment.

The awareness process included a wide range of visual materials based around a friendly beaver character by the name of Five-O-Go together with handouts, workbooks, recognition awards and control mechanisms. The principal elements of the process were as follows:

1 *Preparing the manual*: The first step was to write the quality manual, which was submitted to the British Standards Institution for their approval prior to the audit. A project team was given the responsibility of developing the manual, which was subsequently signed off by senior management.
2 *Teaser campaign*: An internal marketing campaign which used surprise, curiosity, humour and competition ensured all employees were aware of the goal – to be the first to achieve ISO9000 certification.
3 *Ready stage*: Commencing with a team briefing, all employees were involved in identifying, reviewing and improving procedures, using the 'beaver brainwave' process. It was important at this stage to identify and draft any missing procedures. All employees completed a checklist which ensured that they understood the process and were committed to the goal of registration.
4 *Steady stage*: Once all procedures had been drafted and agreed, the steady stage provided the opportunity to remove the bugs, establish accurate records and ensure consistency. Each team completed a time for reflection workbook which ensured their understanding of and adherence to the policy statements defined in the quality manual. Once steady stage had been achieved, a spring clean operation was carried out to ensure all out-of-date documentation was either archived or destroyed.
5 *Preassessment audit*: One month prior to assessment, a preassessment audit was carried out by independent auditors. The purpose of this was to expose all employees to the assessment procedure, and identify any major discrepancies. It also helped to eliminate complacency and apathy where necessary.
6 *Go stage*: This stage comprised a countdown to assessment, where employees were briefed on the assessment procedure, and what the auditors would require of them. It also ensured that the auditors received a warm welcome, and that employees responded positively to the assessment process.

7 *Celebration*: Registration was achieved in December 1991. Once registered, there was an opportunity to recognize the involvement and commitment of all employees and celebrate achievement of the goal by holding registration celebration parties.

In addition to gaining total employee commitment to the quality management system and subsequently gaining registration, the Five-O-Go! process was a major motivational and training success. The approach was perceived as radical but fun, and the staff were proud of their achievement, with significant improvement in morale and self-esteem.

The ISO9000 project was so successful that the company have already started to extend registration to other areas of the business. The benefits are due both to the fact that they achieved registration, plus the way they achieved it with 100% staff involvement. In the words of one of the BSI assessors: 'We have never seen such total enthusiasm and commitment from all staff to achieving the goal of registration'.

They have already begun to feel the benefit of the application of the ISO9000 standard within the Industrial Branch area. Most benefit is coming from the control of management processes, examples being internal audits (which are designed to be constructive and to improve processes), formal local management reviews and purchasing.

ISO9000 has been extended to other areas in a phased programme. Details of all the registrations are listed below:

- Industrial Branch Administration Offices in Belfast and Reading, December 1991.
- Life Administrations Technical Training and Management Training Departments, September 1992. (At the time, this was only the second company in the UK to achieve registration for its training department.)
- Life Administrations Business Systems Delivery Area to Tickit, December 1992.
- Life Administrations Life Claims Area, April 1993.

This ongoing registration programme improves process and management control and contributes to improved morale, communication and teamwork.

The tools of total quality have made a significant contribution to process improvement. They didn't want to make quality improvement 'tool-bound'. There were many examples where the only quality improvement action taken to solve a problem was people talking to each other to agree requirements. But, during the Way of Life awareness training, every member of staff was taught how to use various tools and techniques in their quality improvement activity. They were also given a simple four-stage problem-solving process to follow, which was designed to solve problems permanently. This four-stage process was called DICE. The process is:

1 *Define problem*: There are six questions to be answered, which include defining the problem in a non-judgemental way, assessing its impact on the business and setting a success measure.
2 *Immediate fix*: The message was: 'Do not pass on errors to your customer'. If some short-term action can be taken it should be, unless it tampers with the process.
3 *Corrective action on root cause*: Problem-solving tools are used to establish the root cause of problems and corrective action is taken to eliminate the root cause.
4 *Evaluation*: After the action has been taken, a period of evaluation follows to ensure that the root cause of the problems has been identified and eliminated. Benefit analysis also takes place within this stage.

This structured approach to problem-solving is the basis of a combined tool which they have called the QICPAC, which stands for Quality Improvement Cycle (Prudential Assurance Company).

Prudential fully understand that the control of processes is a key element in TQM. Service excellence can only be delivered through capable processes. A programme of work (project PRISM) to establish the best practice processes was started in 1991. A team of analysts worked with staff to chart all the existing procedures within Life Administration. Following initial charting, brainstorming and critical analysis sessions were held to agree best practices across all areas. These procedures were then implemented. Life Administration has estimated that project PRISM will deliver productivity improvements of up to £2m, and improve the speed and accuracy of many key processes.

## Customer satisfaction

As the quality objectives are also the business objectives, the measurement systems for quality improvement at a Life Administration-wide level are similar. There are some additional measurement systems which record quality improvement progress on a local scale and the effectiveness of the quality improvement process itself is evaluated annually by way of an independent review.

The three customer KBIs and the way they are measured are summarized below:

| *Customer KBIs:* | *Main Measurement* |
| --- | --- |
| *benefits to customers* | |
| | |
| 1 Attitude | Measured by quarterly customer satisfaction surveys. |
| | One-month service-level agreement reviews (SLA's) |
| 2 Speed | Measured by monthly sampling at departmental level |
| 3 Accuracy | Measured by monthly sampling at departmental level |

### Attitude

*Internal customers*

These customers are other departments within Life Administration. The main method used to monitor customer satisfaction is by reviewing the supplier's performance against established service-level agreements, or SLAs for short. Monthly reviews are conducted to discuss performance. Some areas also conduct internal customer satisfaction surveys.

The field staff also fall into this category. A comprehensive quarterly customer satisfaction survey is conducted to assess the level of service Life Administration is giving across various aspects of the business. There are three mainline administration areas: Industrial Branch area, which has offices in Reading and Belfast; Ordinary Branch area, and Personal Pensions area. Within these line areas, measurement is made against their performance on new business, servicing and claims. Performance is also monitored through SLAs. This is done in a similar way to that described above.

*External customers–policy-holders*

External customers are dealt with when servicing their contracts and paying their death claims or maturities. Most contact is by mail, although there is some telephone contact. Customer satisfaction is measured in three ways. All line departments keep a log of complaints. Great effort is put into resolving these complaints to the satisfaction of the policy-holder. Analysis is undertaken to look for trends so that preventive action can be taken.

A second way to monitor customer satisfaction is in the form of songs of praise. These are letters which record a customer's appreciation of the service they have provided, since they have taken the trouble to write and thank the company. The number of 'songs of praise' received is measured.

Benchmarks are also established for the industry by commissioning work through market research agencies.

### Speed and accuracy

Staff, independent of the areas being measured, select samples from the high business volumes to measure both speed and accuracy. Sampling techniques are used for the audits as they are the most effective given the volumes and current system technology. A significant achievement during 1991 was the introduction, in a pilot area, of a new system-based measurement system for speed. The system, based on a database called ACUMEN, counts all work that passes through the pensions new-business area. Both volume and elapsed time are measured and feedback is given to

**Table 2.2** *Life Administration speed and accuracy performance*

|                 | 1990 | 1991 | Mid 1992 | Dec 1992 |
|-----------------|------|------|----------|----------|
| Speed 5 days    | 92%  | 97%  | 95%      | 89%      |
| Speed 10/8 days | 93%  | 99%  | 99%      | 97%      |
| Accuracy        | 99%  | 99%  | 98%      | 98%      |

Speed: percentage claims processed within the specified time period.
Accuracy: percentage correct on completion of each stage of process.

the area the following day. This allows for immediate analysis and corrective action when failures occur.

An important aspect of this new system is the detail of the data. Whereas the current sampling systems record elapsed time from receipt of a proposal to the issue of a policy, the ACUMEN-based system breaks down the process and provides data at the various stages, i.e. proposal date to receipt in Reading, proposal receipt to acceptance and proposal acceptance to issue of policy. Such detail reduces the process scope in the case of failure and makes for more effective corrective action.

The 1990, 1991 and 1992 results for speed and accuracy are shown in Table 2.2. Customer satisfaction results are shown in Figure 2.6. In the case of the speed figures, in 1990 the secondary target was 10 days and in 1991 it was 8 days.

The slight deterioration in the speed measures was due to two main reasons:

Field satisfaction survey

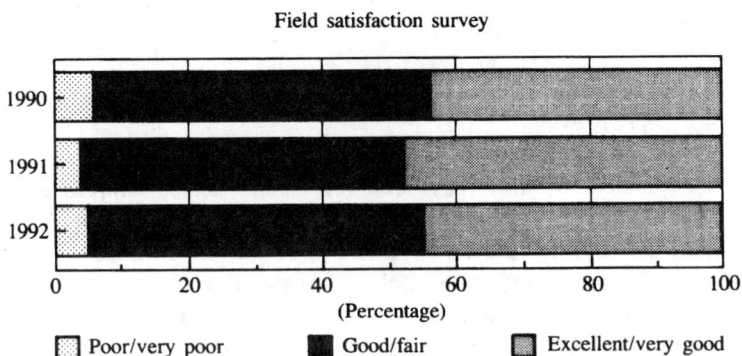

**Figure 2.6** *Life administration customer satisfaction results*

1 The volume of work exceeded the forecast volume.
2 A major internal customer, the field staff, went through a restructuring exercise to improve service and productivity during the last quarter of 1992. This had a major knock-on effect on Life Administration in that there was a major increase in enquiries from the field staff during this period of uncertainty and a resulting decrease in the quality of the inputs supplied to Life Administration.

The field satisfaction survey shows a tightening of customer expectations due to improved service.

## Recent developments

The performance measures described above were part of a philosophy that attempted to achieve the best possible performance. The word 'possible' was open to interpretation and Life Administration have now realized that they need to strive for superior performance in all their business areas. They also questioned whether they measure the right thing and a Quality Initiative Team reviewed the whole measurement question as part of the Customer Experience Measures project. This project was set up under the direction of the Head of Life Administration to provide more meaningful and reliable customer-focused management information.

The first phase of the project identified the key business transactions, then key activities and recommended a system of core measurements to be applied to each of the key transactions. The three core measurements are detailed below:

| *Core measurement* | *Measure* |
|---|---|
| 1 Speed | Average speed of each response time to perform complete transaction |
| 2 Accuracy | Correctness on despatch of each stage of process |
| 3 Interaction | Attitude |
| | Helpfulness |
| | Respect to the customer |
| | Politeness |
| | Keeping promises |
| | Telephone technique/manner |
| | Care and sincerity |
| | Ownership |
| | Contactability |
| | Ability to contact right person at first attempt |

> Telephone answered promptly
> One reply to customer's enquiry
> Documentation
> Easy to understand
> Well-presented

The above measurement system represents a mix of 'hard' and 'soft' measures. Market research highlighted the need to develop a set of 'soft' measures to complement the traditional harder measures. Handling a death claim requires sensitivity and this should be measured. Many of the new measures (e.g. speed), represent true end-to-end measurement. Previously, in measuring the time to get a policy to the customer, work that couldn't be processed for any reason was excluded for measurement purposes (e.g. forms incorrectly completed by customer). This has changed under the new system and 'time to perform complete transaction' represents a true end-to-end measure of the process cycle time.

The second phase of the Customer Experience Measures project took the analysis of the measures and key transactions a step further to identify what customer measures could be put in place, and the techniques that could be used to provide the measurements. Four measurement techniques were proposed:

1 Speed audits for the speed measures.
2 Accuracy audits for the accuracy measures and the interaction (documentation) measures.
3 Telephone audits for the interaction (attitude, contractability and documentation)
4 Customer surveys for the interaction (attitude) measures.

The objective of the phase 2 report was to gain approval to pilot the proposed measures for partial implementation in January 1993. A time-scaled action plan was developed to implement the new system during the first half of 1993.

## People satisfaction

The 'people' KBI is morale and this is monitored by surveys. An annual attitude survey is conducted across all Life Administration. The results are analysed in terms of a communication index, morale index, training index and service index. The results of the last survey are shown below:

| Index | May 1991 | Target |
|---|---|---|
| Communication | 54 | 50 |
| Morale | 56 | 50 |
| Training | 55 | 50 |
| Service | 66 | 50 |

The Way of Life reviews, considered in the leadership section, also provide extensive information about aspects of people satisfaction.

## Impact on society

As a provider of a service, the Prudential is not directly involved in activities impacting upon the environment and ecology as is, say, a chemical company. However, the company's management is conscious of the 'green' movement and its obligations to play an active role in this area. There is no written environmental policy; however, Life Administration actively promotes certain environmentally friendly practices. For example, all suppliers are made aware of the company's preference to use recycled or environmentally friendly products. 'Green' products are always chosen for stationery, etc. The company also operates comprehensive systems to promote recycling of paper and some plastic products.

The company works with local councils to promote environmental issues. This involves setting targets for space, heating and lighting consumption; general and proper waste reduction, reuse and recycling; incentives for reduced vehicle use through car sharing, etc. The move to new office premises in Reading resulted in considerable energy savings.

The Prudential is actively involved in many community activities at both a national and local level. These activities include support to charities and the involvement in education and training activities in the community. A recent innovation has been the launch of the Prudential community investment programme, outline details of which are given in Appendix B. Prudential employees are actively involved in the organization and running of many activities in the community.

Some examples of this activity are listed below:

● During 1992, £20 000 was donated to local hospitals, schools and the community of Reading in general.
● A large donation of £10 000 was made to the Delwood Cancer Unit in Reading.
● Many members of staff also engage in other activities to support the local community. These include:

(a) Young Enterprise Scheme, where employees give up their own time to go and help schoolchildren develop business acumen.
(b) Various sponsored charity events.
(c) Several employees are members of the BBONT club, which stands for Berkshire, Buckinghamshire, Oxfordshire National Trust Club, where volunteers go out to help the environment.

## Business results

The business results for 1990, 1991 and 1992 are shown in Appendix A. Non-financial measures include the KBI productivity. This is measured by 4-weekly productivity measurement and budget monitoring.

During 1991 productivity was measured in most operation areas using the British Standards (BS) method. Areas counted work volumes, which were scaled by unit times to give a theoretical workload. This workload was compared with the actual utilization time, which led to the calculation of the BS figure. Work in 1991 on productivity has allowed them to put more accurate productivity measures in place across all operation areas. Calculations of accurate standard times for all processes now allows pinpointing of problem areas.

Significant productivity gains were made in 1991. For example, the median productivity for the Ordinary Branch area improved from 76.8 to 99.6% during the period January 1991 to December 1991.

**Table 2.3** *Life Administration cycle time comparisons 1991–1992*

(a) Productivity – new business: average time per case

|          | *Life Assurance* | *Pension* |
|----------|------------------|-----------|
| May 1991 | 40 min           | 56 min    |
| Aug 1991 | 43 min           | 52 min    |
| Jan 1992 | 37 min           | 48 min    |
| May 1992 | 30 min           | 38 min    |
| Jan 1991 | 58 min           | 57 min    |
| Aug 1992 | 28 min           | 37 min    |

(b) Productivity – claims: average time per case

|          |        |
|----------|--------|
| Aug 1991 | 19 min |
| Aug 1992 | 16 min |

Productivity improvements are also reflected in the dramatic reduction in cycle times for many key business activities (Table 2.3).

In addition to these productivity improvements, there have also been savings of £5m in operation costs.

## Conclusion

The Prudential Life Administration Group's approach to TQM is a comprehensive example of the involvement of people in process improvement in a service environment. The programme is actively led by management and has delivered significant improvement to customer service in many areas of the business. This in turn has improved the overall effectiveness and efficiency of the business. Maintaining this momentum and quality focus is a challenge but events such as quality weeks help everyone celebrate their successes and stimulate the search for new improvement opportunities.

Although this case has only looked at a small part of the Prudential Group, it is typical of the TQM approach across the whole company. The Prudential Board is committed to customer service and adding customer value.

## Acknowledgements

The authors would like to acknowledge the invaluable help of the following people in the preparation of this case:

Mr K. Alliston, Prudential Assurance Company Ltd.
Dr S. Tanner, Prudential Assurance Company Ltd.
Mr R. Walker, Industry Motivation Ltd.
Ms S. Dawson, John McDonald Associates.
Mr J. McDonald, John McDonald Associates.
Mr R. Jones, Universal Sound Principles.
Mr G. Binney, Ashridge Management College.

# Appendix A   Business results

**PRUDENTIAL**

## Home Service Division

## 1992 Results

### Getting Fit for the Future

Yesterday Prudential Corporation announced its 1992 results. This report deals with Home Service's contribution to those results. A report on the overall results will be issued later.

1992 was a difficult year. The recession continued and consumer confidence remained low. At the same time competition became more intense, both within the Direct Sales sector and outside. Despite this, we achieved a creditable sales performance and have made a good start on further restructuring our business to achieve our twin aims of increasing sales and reducing costs.

At the half year I reported on the start of Field Management Restructuring, the reorganization of our sales management into five teams of Regional Managers and 180 Branch Managers. The programme has now been successfully rolled out and we have moved to the next stage, the reorganization of the support structure for Branches.

The Divisional Office restructuring was announced in November. The plans involve replacing the 12 Divisional Offices with a Branch Service Centre at Bristol and the establishment of five Regional Business Development Units.

The next stage is the introduction of changes to the way we operate in the Field. Consultation with staff on "Fit for the Future" outline proposals continued throughout the latter half of 1992 and we have used this feedback to shape our proposals. In February 1993 we began negotiations with the NUIW on the overall structure and the likely changes to terms and conditions.

While the salesforce has been going through these changes, Head Office has also been undergoing reorganization. The majority of Head Office functions announced their headcount reduction targets during November and these plans have been implemented in early 1993. The most significant of these is within Home Service Systems, where staff numbers have been reduced from 660 to 450.

In December we announced our decision to transfer our Commercial business to Provincial. Specialist Commercial staff transferred to Provincial in January, but we will continue to accept renewal business until 1 May.

I am grateful to staff for their commitment and hard work at a time of considerable change. Without your support, the achievements of 1992 would not have been possible. I cannot promise that 1993 will be any easier, but with your continued help I know that we can achieve our vision of delivering best customer value and becoming the biggest and the best in the business.

Managing Director
24 March, 1993

Home service premiums and profit (£m)

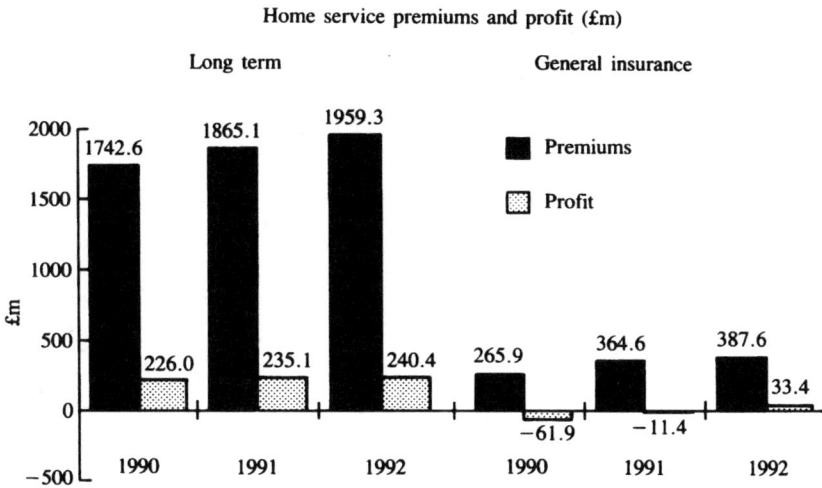

- Total Home Service profits of £273.8 m were 22.4% up on 1991.
- The increase is principally due to the very welcome turnaround in the General Business result.

- Long-term premiums were 5% above 1991 levels, helped by a 10% increase in sales of Home Service single premium products.
- The rise in General Insurance premiums is a result of increases in premium rates.
- The policy-holders' share of total profits distributed for 1992 was £1400 m. A man aged 30 paying £30 per month into a 10-year savings with-profit plan started 10 years ago will receive £6296 on 1 May 1993 – an equivalent rate of return of 10.8%.

# Home Service Division

# Life New Business Sales

**Annual premiums**

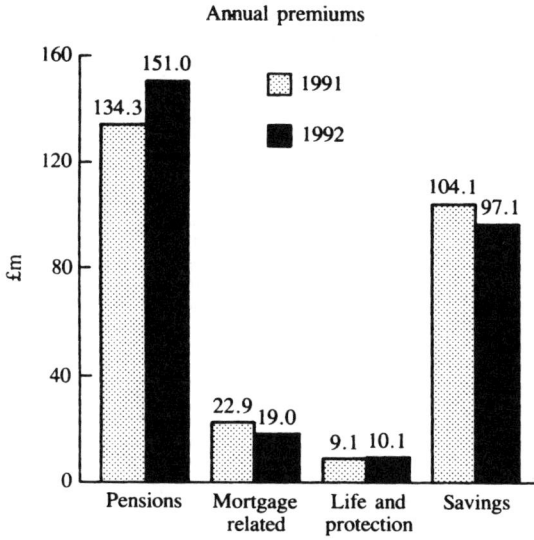

**Single premiums**

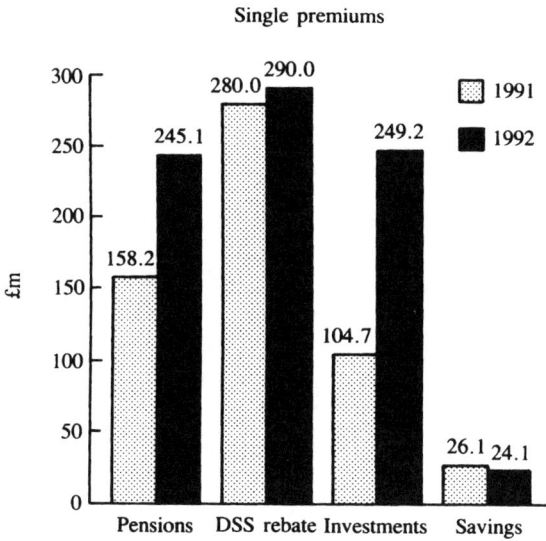

- The highlight of the year was the strong sales of single-premium products. Single premiums, excluding DSS rebate, were 79.4% above 1991, supported by high sales of Prudence Bond and Pension Transfer business. Launched late in 1991, Prudence Bond sales in 1992 totalled £181 m.
- The DSS rebate figure is the amount of premiums receivable for the 1991/92 tax year, and largely relates to business sold in previous years. New DSS business sold in 1992 totalled £11 m.
- Annual premium sales have improved by 2.6% from the low level of 1991, with pensions sales making the strongest contribution.
- Our sales target is an increase in Ordinary Branch product sales (measured as annual premium+1/10 single premium) of 50% over the 1991 level. We achieved a 16% increase in 1992.

# Home Service Division

## General Insurance 1992 Results

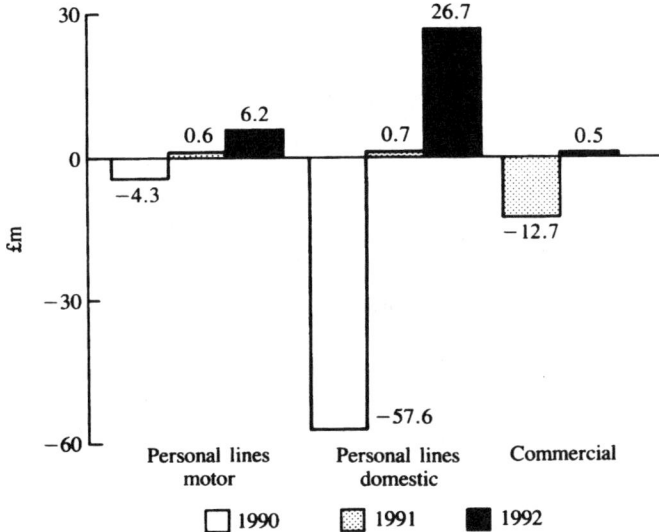

**Personal lines**

● The significant improvement in Personal Lines profit results from better claims experience and premium rate increases. This has reduced the claims ratio from 73.3 to 63.3%.

● Weather-related claims were 14.2% down on 1991. However, domestic theft claims increased by 8.9%.

● The decline of our in-force policy base has continued, with year-end-in-force policies for both motor and domestic lower than in 1991. The overall fall in our policy base by 9.8% has been offset by the increase in average premiums, so that gross written premiums were 7.1% higher than in 1991.

**Commercial**

● The Commercial account benefited slightly from the consequences of the sale to Provincial; however, the improvement over 1991 is very welcome. The result would have been seen as marginal had we been continuing in this business.

# Home Service Division

## Expenses

Gross expenses

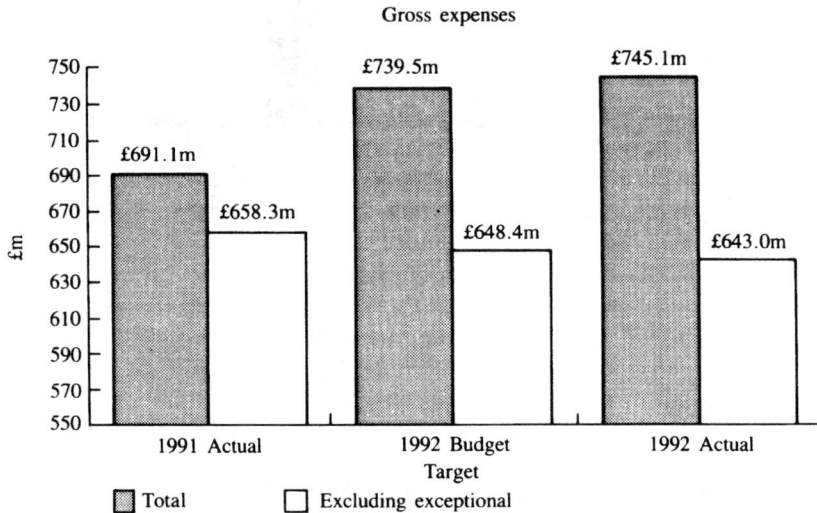

- 1991 Actual
- 1992 Budget Target
- 1992 Actual

■ Total     □ Excluding exceptional

- Gross expenses are calculated before deducting Systems income from other divisions, service charges, costs allocated to claims and deferral of acquisition expenses on general business. They also include Group overheads. So gross expenses are greater than those reported in Team Brief, which are net of these amounts.
- Exceptional items include expenditure on Field Management Restructuring, the Divisional Office Review, Scenario 3, the relocation of the Data Centre, the redundancy programmes, Genesis and Commercial disposal costs.
- Of the target expense reduction of £100 m, the major Key Action Plans implemented by the end of 1992 will contribute £36 m per annum (Field Management Restructuring – £16 m; Genesis – £10 m; Divisional Office Review – £7 m; Data Centre Relocation – £3 m).
- The restructuring of Home Service Systems implemented in early 1993 will contribute a further £4 m savings per annum.
- Our expense levels are also benefiting from lower interest rates, which have reduced the cost of the staff mortgage subsidy by £11 m.

# Appendix B: Prudential community investment programme

## Management Briefing

### Information for senior management of Prudential Corporation

Prudential will announce the first details of its community investment programme on May 28 1993. Over the next five years, the Corporation will be supporting those in the UK who care for sick, elderly or disabled dependants in their own home, through a national programme known as the Prudential Carers' Initiative.

Prudential will work in partnership with two voluntary organizations in the development of its Carers' Initiative: The Princess Royal Trust for Carers and Crossroads, the UK's leading voluntary agency in the provision of respite care in the home.

The project will be run by Corporate Communications, which in the past has responded to appeals from various charities and community organizations in the UK.

Following a review of the role of its community support, the Prudential board approved a programme for the next five years which will focus on two issues only – carers and safer communities.

The overall objective has been set:

*To establish Prudential as an innovative and effective participant in addressing the key social issues affecting the community. This will be achieved through long-term and dedicated support for research, prevention, education and community care programmes directed towards specific target areas.*

The first step in the programme, to be announced by Mick Newmarch on May 28, is the Prudential Carers' Initiative.

Mick Newmarch, who is a trustee of the Princess Royal Trust, is keen that Prudential takes the lead in raising public awareness of carers' needs and of the contribution they make to society.

In particular, he hopes that other companies will be persuaded to look at how they too can help to improve community care.

A strategy to promote the Initiative and involve business areas is now being devised.

Carers are those who, in their own home, look after a parent, child or family friend, dependent on the carer because of age, health or disability.

The partnership between Prudential and the two voluntary organizations has two main objectives:

- To further develop the network of carer centres in the UK through The Princess Royal Trust for Carers.
- To enhance the quality of respite care schemes through Crossroads in the same locations.

## The Princess Royal Trust for Carers

The Trust is a fund-raising charity, established by HRH The Princess Royal, specifically to benefit carers.

It has a vision of society in which carers are properly valued and supported by government and community, so enabling them to share and fulfil their caring role as effectively and as happily as possible.

The mission of the Trust is to:

- Raise public awareness of carers' needs and of the contribution they make to society
- Provide information counselling and support to carers.

Key objectives of the Trust are also to identify hidden carers in the community and address the problems of carers in employment.

The Trust aims to establish carer centres in every local authority area throughout the UK, and is able to lever funds from local authorities to do so. Since the first centre was opened by HRH The Princess Royal in January 1993, another nine have been established.

## Crossroads

Crossroads is the UK's leading voluntary agency in the provision of respite care in the home.

It offers help for carers who need a regular dependable break from their task, in order to have some time of their own.

Since it was established in 1974, Crossroads has set up more than 200 schemes located within Social Service local authority districts, funded by local statutory services.

Crossroads has four main objectives:

- To relieve stress in families or people responsible for caring
- To avoid admission to hospital or residential care of people in care, should the household be unable to look after them
- To supplement and complement existing statutory services
- To maintain a high standard of care.

## The Prudential carers' initiative

This newly formed partnership will establish new carer centres and develop respite care services in the same locations.

The carer centres will meet many of the needs already identified by carers themselves: particularly respite care, access to information, and the opportunity to meet with others in similar situations and overcome feelings of isolation.

They will provide a service to all carers, regardless of the condition of the dependant – such as physical disability, mental handicap or illness, terminal illness or senility.

They will also provide support, advice and guidance from easily accessible town centre sites, staffed by a manager and a small team of volunteers.

Preliminary discussions are taking place in Sutton, Mid Glamorgan, Newry and Mourne, North Tyneside, Lincs, Essex, Sefton, Sheffield, Hammersmith and Fulham, Bristol and Reading.

*The aim of Management Briefing is to inform managers in advance of public announcements, allowing them to plan further communication to their own staff at their discretion.*

# 3 TQM in the research and development environment – a balanced approach between 'hard' and 'soft' quality: Esso Research Centre

## Background

The Esso Research Centre is part of Exxon Corporation, the worldwide multinational petrochemical company; the two largest Exxon businesses are petroleum and chemicals, both of which are represented at the Esso Research Centre. The worldwide petroleum business involves the discovery, production, transportation and marketing of petroleum products. The chemicals business manufactures, distributes and markets chemical products ranging from commodities such as ethylene to specialty chemicals used in a wide variety of applications. Research in Exxon is carried out in a number of laboratories specializing in different business aspects, ranging from crude oil production to the quality of the finished petroleum and chemicals used by consumers. The Research Centre, just south of Oxford, UK, has two separate functions, the Petroleum Product Quality Research and Development (R&D) activity, and the Performance Chemicals Technology activity.

The Petroleum R&D is aimed at development of petroleum fuels and lubricant products principally for European use, although some products are developed for worldwide application. The Performance Chemicals Technology Centre focuses on the development of specialty chemicals manufactured worldwide for inclusion in finished fuels and lubricants. In addition to new product development, both organizations provide technical services to assist product manufacture and marketing. A third function of the site is to provide service facilities and resources which support both of the petroleum and chemicals research groups. These range from a common restaurant to the evaluation of the performance of fuels and lubricants, physical and chemical techniques for analysis of products produced, and other operational functions which both groups need in order to operate.

# The TQM beginnings

The petroleum research function's history in the total quality process goes back to the mid 1980s, when a mixture of external and internal factors began to affect the site. Externally, the business importance of being certified to the BS5750 (ISO9000) and Ford Q101 standards was increasing in the UK, and needed to be reflected in the technical service role. The chemicals businesses were also beginning to recognize the value of TQM in their operations, and were interested in encouraging the use of quality concepts by their suppliers within the Research Centre. Also at this time, a decision was taken by the Analytical Section to apply for certification to the National Measurement Accreditation Service (NAMAS), in response to some of their customers' interests and an internally driven process called Changing Gear, aimed at increasing employee motivation and self-esteem. Probably the most influential factor at this stage, however, was the appointment of a management team, which was convinced of the need to develop and encourage the people on the site to be more responsive, effective and efficient, in the eyes of the Exxon business groups which fund the petroleum research function. The team believed that the application of some form of TQM was the correct approach to the achievement of this end, so the issue was not whether to, but how to, apply the TQM philosophies.

In the exploratory phase of the site's experience in TQM, virtually no published methodology was available for a research organization to select the right approach. Indeed, some of the language used by some of the quality 'gurus', e.g. 'get it right first time' and 'zero defects', was definitely off-putting to people involved in research. In the latter case, the end-result is not always as predictable as in a manufacturing operation, where much of the available TQM experience had been gained.

Searching for some relevant expertise, the management group selected a management consultant, an occupational psychologist, who introduced a model of quality (Figure 3.1), which consisted of two dimensions: the operational and expressive dimensions of quality, both of which must be at a high level for total customer satisfaction to be generated. It emphasized an important feature which needed to be recognized in a research function, that *cooperative relationships* between individuals and teams of people (e.g. R&D, and business groups) are as important as the actual research carried out by R&D groups.

The model was introduced to the whole petroleum site management group, which was then encouraged to develop it. This resulted in several new initiatives with on- and off-site groups, including attempts to measure customer satisfaction in both the operational and expressive dimensions. This model had a significant influence on the future development of the site's quality process, because it emphasized the importance of the 'people'

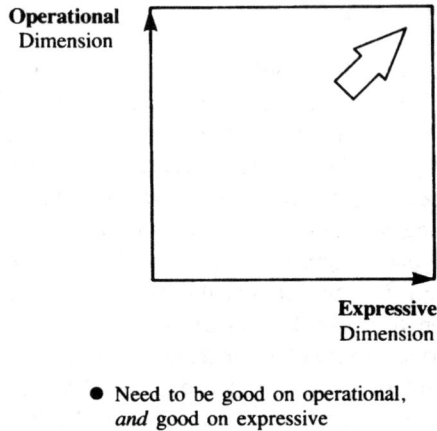

● Need to be good on operational,
   *and* good on expressive

**Figure 3.1** *Two-dimensional model*

dimension of quality. However, it lacked an important feature, the 'how to' dimension which is needed to achieve good operational and expressive results.

As this exploratory phase progressed, further external developments were occurring. The use of the ISO9002 standard was spreading throughout Europe, including Exxon's lubricant plants and business lines, and the concepts of TQM were becoming more widespread in application in Exxon, particularly in the chemical and petroleum business lines serving the automotive industries.

## Consolidating and managing the process

At this stage, the site management group decided to consolidate the site's quality process and appointed a full-time quality manager. Further examination of approaches offered by consultants were made, and one was selected. Although the approach adopted was originally developed by a manufacturing industry leader in quality (Rank Xerox), it was felt to be adaptable to the research process. There were several elements in the approach, including the 'process' dimension – the 'how to' which was lacking in the earlier experimental phase. The two-dimensional model (Figure 3.1) was, therefore, modified to the three-dimensional model shown in Figure 3.2, the three dimensions being product or service (equivalent to the operational dimension in the earlier model), people (equivalent to the expressive dimension) and process (how the product and relationships were produced). The training also

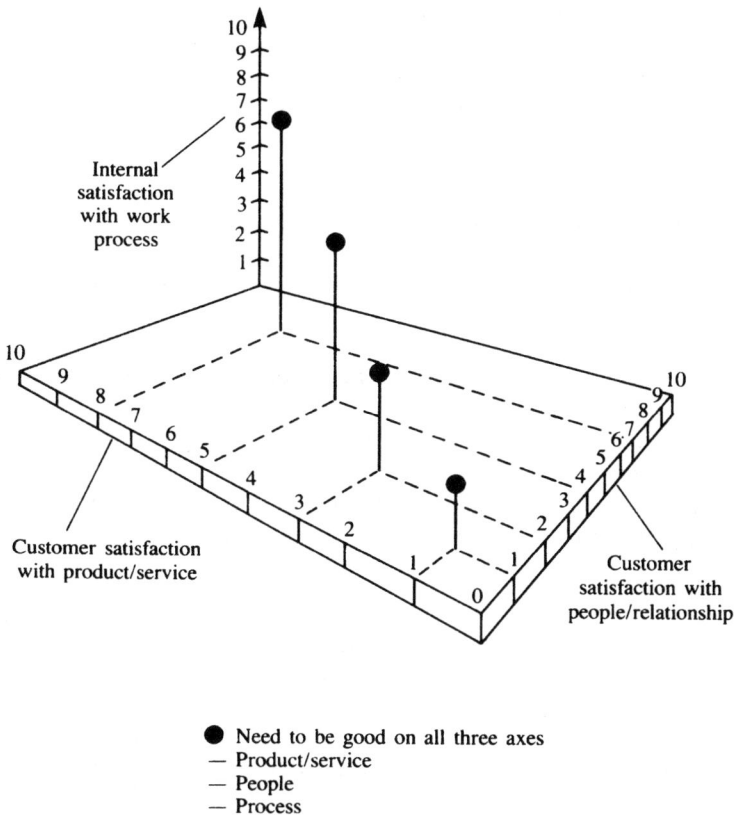

**Figure 3.2** *Three-dimensional quality model*

included a nine-step quality delivery process which covered work group missions, outputs, customers and processes, and a six-step problem-solving process. Tools such as flow-charting, fishbone diagrams, team work and brainstorming were also included.

This training package was given to the whole site over a period of about 12 months and resulted in many quality improvement projects, encompassing how new products were developed, new facilities were installed and scheduled, hazardous waste disposed of, contractor support planned, suppliers paid, and so on.

Although it was also recommended that the site adopt a formal cost of quality measurement system, this recommendation was not adopted. It was felt that it would be difficult to apply the concepts in detail to an R&D operation, where 'failure' can be turned into an important learning point, or where the 'lost opportunities' of a project not taken up at the time of its completion may turn into a positive benefit in later years, when the results and information used in the project may be used in further research work. The principle of a prevention-based approach to maximize research effectiveness was adopted, however.

## Benefits derived – so soon?

This phase of the development of the Research Centre quality process resulted in many benefits:

● Many of the improvement projects were aimed at site problems which had hindered site effectiveness.
● The importance of the internal customer and quality chain concepts were recognized.
● The process management model (Figure 3.3) was shown to be useful in identifying the process flow, and measurement opportunities.

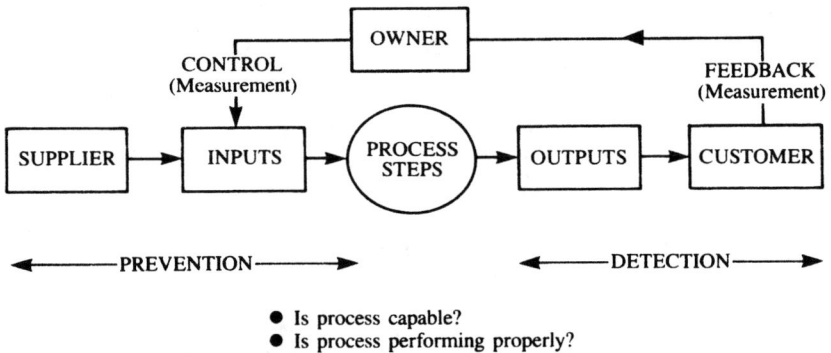

Figure 3.3 *Process management control*

● An improved image with business groups resulted, which later was seen as vital in obtaining their agreement to future development of the site role.
● The value was demonstrated of the flow-charting and brainstorming quality tools to aid process definition and problem-solving.

## Integrating TQM into the strategy

The next development in the process stemmed from a desire to improve the connection between business priorities and some of the improvements generated by staff. In some parts of the site, quality was seen as a separate activity to the normal job, quality behaviour being exhibited during quality improvements projects, which were not translated into equivalent behaviour on the normal, day-to-day job. The measurement of process effectiveness and efficiency also needed building. It was felt that the quality process development so far had been focused more on 'the here-and-now', rather than on 'the future'. Fortunately, through contacts that the management group developed with other Exxon groups, and expertise available through the Exxon Chemical chair in TQM at Bradford, an extension to the approach was developed based on an IBM methodology which focused more on the future direction of the site, and led to prioritization of the improvement effort through definition of longer-term goals, critical success factors and key processes. This methodology was supplemented by two other tools, one a method for development of strategic goals, and the other a model of organizational effectiveness which couples work objectives/tasks with values and behaviours. A summary of the final model the site now uses as a framework is shown in Figure 3.4.

The site now discusses its quality process as a mixture of 'hard' quality – business goals, driving process control and improvement – and 'soft' quality – values, driving people's behaviour. Both 'hard' and 'soft' quality have to be addressed in a balanced approach. The 'hard' quality track relates to the original operational dimension, the 'soft' quality track to the expressive dimension, in the original two-dimensional model of quality introduced in the

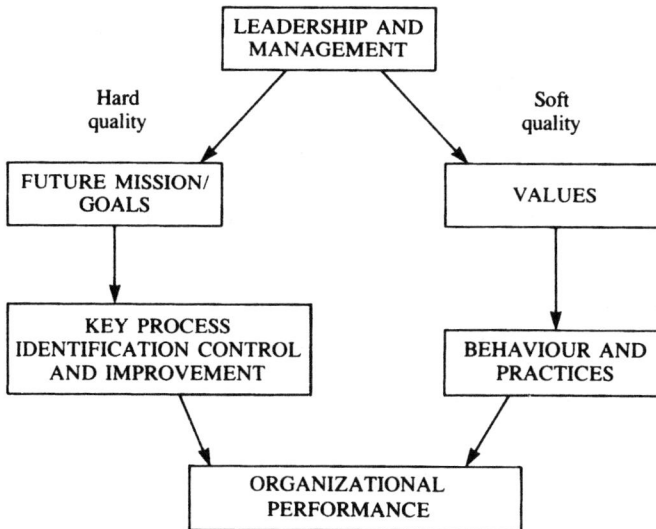

**Figure 3.4** *'Hard' and 'soft' quality aspects of the framework*

early phase. Management workshops have been held on leadership and management style, and values and preferred behaviours defined. Having emphasized that both 'hard' and 'soft' quality tracks need working, it has to be said that the site feels more comfortable dealing with 'hard' quality issues than 'soft' quality issues, as one might expect in the scientific and engineering culture of a research organization.

Further extension of the use of the ISO9000 standards has been made on the site, to support the increased use of this standard by the Exxon business groups customers. This use of quality assurance standards is also seen as a method of providing control for processes such as product development, where control through the conventional use of data and statistical process control (SPC) techniques is slow or inapplicable. Effectively, 80% of the site activity is now included in some form of external quality assurance. This produces the following benefits:

- improved clarity of roles and responsibilities;
- definition of best practices, and written procedures to follow, built on these practices;
- improved communications with business colleagues;
- better documentation of research processes.

## The key learning points

So what are the learning points from this experience? The site believes:

- The quality process can be applied to an R&D environment, and can produce useful business benefits.
- The concept of the internal customer and the customer–supplier chain has now become well-ingrained in the site culture, with all of the resulting benefits.
- The ISO9000 and NAMAS standards, applied carefully in a 'minimum bureaucracy' style, has added value to key processes, such as product development.
- The process takes much longer than expected to become embedded in the culture of the organization – patience is needed.
- Constancy of purpose is needed to maintain momentum; it is sometimes difficult to concentrate on quality principles when there are pressing and changing business priorities.
- Measurement of the value of the quality process in a research environment is a continuing challenge.
- Achieving the right balance between process discipline, and creativity, which was a concern with adoption of the ISO standards, has not

materialized to any great extent; perhaps this is due to the predominance of development versus pure scientific research at the Research Centre and the 'minimize bureaucracy' approach used in writing the quality system.

- There is no 'off-the-shelf' methodology which immediately can be applied to the R&D environment, and one had to be developed in-house. Although this *may* have slowed the process, it is believed that a home-grown methodology is more likely to gain ownership and be sustainable at the Esso Research Centre. This is an important conclusion, judging from other experiences with TQM, in which 'package' approaches have been shown to fail in a research environment.
- The integration of new management group members with different backgrounds has increased in difficulty as quality has increasingly been integrated into the Research Centre culture, rather than being seen as a separate entity.

In the future, the site anticipate continued application of the balanced 'hard' and 'soft' quality approaches using the framework described in Figure 3.4. Continued attention will be given to the collection of data, and use of standards such as the ISO9000 and NAMAS series to support process control and improvement, and the development of cooperative partnerships between the on-site divisions and external business groups.

## Acknowledgement

This is from a case study by Dr Roger C. Price, Quality Manager at Esso Research Centre, Abingdon, UK.

# Part Two
# The Role of Quality Systems

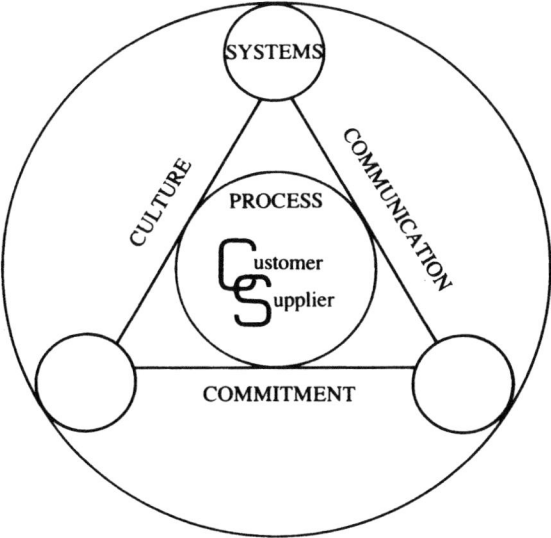

# 4 Quality systems and TQM in the Tioxide Group Ltd

## Introduction

The Tioxide Group Ltd, part of the ICI group of companies, is the second largest producer of titanium dioxide pigments in the world. With nine factories on five continents, it is the only truly international producer of titanium dioxide pigments. Tioxide pigments are used in applications where high opacity and whiteness are required. These include paints, plastics, paper, textiles, printing inks and a wide range of other special applications. The company also manufactures a wide range of titanium-based chemicals; in fact, the world is surrounded by examples of the use of Tioxide products.

Tioxide has been at the forefront of the quality movement for many years. Over the last decade it has been involved in quality circles and teamwork, Statistical Process Control (SPC), quality systems and quality costing. All these quality initiatives have converged to give an effective ongoing TQM programme.

## The commitment to quality systems

The Directors of the Tioxide Group started to become aware of the importance of quality systems such as BS5750 and ISO9000 in the mid 1980s. Customers in the plastics industry were experiencing the quality pressures from the automotive industry and they had no hesitation in passing on some of this pressure. By the mid 1980s they started to receive questionnaires asking about their plans for implementing BS5750/ISO9000. At about the same time, Tioxide became aware of the marketing implications of BS5750/ISO9000. The marketing strategy was one of differentiation based on the level of technical support and the services provided for customers. Tioxide have the largest technical support group for customers in the industry. The implementation of BS5750/ISO9000 across the Tioxide Group would provide a further opportunity for differentiation.

The strategic importance of BS5750/ISO9000 was discussed at board level during the latter half of 1986. In January 1987 the main board made a decision that all the manufacturing sites in Tioxide should prepare for registration to BS5750: Part 2/ISO 9002. The board's commitment to this was communicated in a Vision Statement (Appendix A) which addressed several areas, including quality and a statement by the Chief Executive (Appendix B).

## The quality systems programme

A Group Quality Manager was appointed to facilitate the implementation process across all manufacturing sites. The appointee was from a technical services background and had a good knowledge of the plastics industry, and the quality pressures that this industry was experiencing. The role of the Group Quality Manager was essentially that of an internal consultant to the manufacturing sites. He was responsible for overseeing the Tioxide Group plan and reported directly to the executive director responsible for quality. The Group initiative ensured that a harmonized approach to ISO9002 was adopted across all the sites.

The Tioxide Greatham site was chosen to pilot the European registration programme. There were several reasons for this. Greatham was a very quality-aware site and had several quality initiatives in the early and mid-1980s. A site reorganization had resulted in the appointment of a new Quality Manager. Greatham's products were also unique within the Tioxide Group and it was located close to the group purchasing department, research and development (R&D), and UK sales office. Government funding was also available for this registration, through the Department of Trade and Industry.

The total quality message implicit in the Vision Statement was expressed in a simpler total quality Policy at site level. The Greatham Total Quality Policy is outlined below.

- Fulfilling our customers' needs is second only to the safety of people.
- Our business success is based on supplying customers with a high-quality product and service.
- Quality is the responsibility of all our employees.
- Quality demands investment in people which is made through education, training and development.
- Our continuous programme of quality improvement is maintained through teamwork and structured problem-solving.

At about the same time, a massive training programme for BS5750/ISO 9000 was initiated throughout the group. Special auditing courses for the chemical industry were developed in association with leading consultants, and these produced a team of professional auditors. The course was recognized by the Institute of Quality Assurance. Tioxide place great emphasis on training and many managers and supervisors were trained as auditors. This training programme was complemented by on-site training for operators and supervisors. At the Greatham site a series of 1-day awareness courses, called Quality Days, took place.

The road to registration was a little bumpy at times, but the learning curve was extremely steep. It became apparent at an early stage that the standard was not written in the language of the chemical industry. However, the company overcame this, and as a result then had a major influence in drafting guidelines for the chemical industry via the Chemical Industry Association. There was also something called the quality perception gap or, to put it bluntly, the company's systems proved not to be as good as they thought they were. The first audit by external consultants was a salutary experience. It was a rude awakening for several of Tioxide's managers, who thought that registration would be a formality for a quality-aware and technically oriented company. The operations relied heavily on informal procedures and an overreliance on 'experts'.

After approximately 18 months' hard work, Tioxide submitted its first site application to the British Standards Institution. The assessment of the Greatham site was carried out in January 1989 and this led to a formal registration on 1st May 1989. Greatham was the first chloride titanium dioxide plant in the world to be registered to BS5750: Part 2/ISO9002. The experience gained with the Greatham registration was used to good effect at other sites in the UK and Europe. A series of other site registrations quickly followed. By the middle of 1990 all European pigment manufacturing sites, together with Tioxide Australia and Tioxide Chemicals, were registered to ISO9002, and there were several firsts amongst these registrations (Table 4.1.) Tioxide Australia was the first sulphate titanium dioxide pigment factory in the world to be registered to ISO9002.

**Table 4.1** *Tioxide Group Ltd site registrations*

| Date | Site | Registration |
|------|------|-------------|
| August 1988 | Tioxide Australia | First titanium pigment plant in the world |
| May 1989 | Greatham | First titanium pigment plant in Europe |
| May 1989 | Chemicals Division | |
| December 1989 | Tioxide France | First joint BSI/AFNOR assessment |
| January 1990 | Grimsby | |
| March 1990 | Tioxide Italy | First BS5750/ISO9002 registration in Italy |
| April 1990 | Tioxide Spain | |

BSI = British Standards Institution; AFNOR = French standards authority equivalent to BSI.

## The benefits of quality systems

A documented quality management system is a major step forward in achieving quality. Today, all Tioxide's European sites have effective quality systems, enabling the rapid and accurate transfer of information for reference, measurement, corrective action, training and continuous improvement. The critical procedures have been written by the people who use them – the process owners. Procedures and work instructions have been reviewed, improved and updated. The operational efficiency and key quality indicators, such as process capability indices, have shown significant improvement.

The registration programme has given quality a much higher profile within the company. People at all levels and in all departments have been actively involved in the programme. Everyone has received training in quality and nearly 400 people have been trained to undertake quality audits throughout the group. Tioxide staff use auditing in a positive and constructive way. The internal audit systems are designed to drive the process of continuous improvement.

The Tioxide Directors' initial expectations of further differentiations by service quality have been realized. As a result of the registration programme, the Tioxide Group is now in a better position to meet the specific requirements of customers rather than sell them a standard product. In the absence of a quality system, it would be impossible to control the large number of customer specifications that they now deal with. Tioxide have also been able to improve their strategic relationships with customers. With their experience of quality systems, they have been able to help many customers with their quality programmes. As a result of this, Tioxide have retained and developed these key accounts in an increasingly competitive environment.

## Quality management developments

During the early phases of the programme, the Tioxide directors and senior management realized that a purely system-type approach would not by itself create a total quality company. Tioxide already had a successful Quality Circles Programme in place. This had started in the early 1980s and their commitment to Quality Circles was recognized in 1988 when Tioxide won the Perkins Award, the UK national award for Quality Circles. The need to empower people to participate in continuous improvement activities and the use of tools such as SPC were seen as key elements in the development of Tioxide's total quality strategy.

# Empowering people

Empowering people to participate actively in Tioxide's quality initiative was mainly achieved through a programme entitled Lodestar.

The Lodestar programme was a major Tioxide TQM initiative from 1988 to 1990. It emphasized customer satisfaction, the role of innovation throughout the organization and the crucial role of all people in achieving business success. The message of Lodestar and its clear demonstration of management commitment were propagated throughout the organization by means of a series of residential workshops. A workshop lasted for approximately 1 week and encouraged participants to address themselves constructively to improvement in its widest sense. All participants drew up action plans aimed at contributing to the overall improvement of Tioxide's operations. Every employee attended a Lodestar workshop and these were followed up by shorter workshops and meetings to review the programme of improvement activities. The Lodestar workshops created tremendous enthusiasm but unfortunately not all the improvement activities were focused on the strategic needs of the business.

# Teamwork and a participative environment

The need for active participation and a team approach was recognized at an early stage by Tioxide. As early as mid 1986 a completely team-oriented operation was in place at the Tioxide Greatham site. This is illustrated in Figure 4.1. Teams operate in two modes – a control mode concerned with day-to-day operations and an improvement mode concerned with quality and overall improvement. The teams are multifunctional in nature and job rotation is an integral part of many teams. For example, in the shift teams, shift workers take turns at controlling the process. Section teams are responsible for running the plant and a typical section team would include a manager, a supervisor, an engineer and technical assistants. Barriers between functional departments are further broken down by the different departments chairing each team in succession. Section teams meet monthly in the improvement mode and, assisted by a coach, usually a senior manager, they address issues relating to safety, quality, quantity and cost.

The management operations team is concerned with budgetary control in all areas in its control mode. In its improvement mode it is concerned with all aspects of business improvement, including quality improvement. It also provides the necessary quality leadership to achieve the goal of total quality.

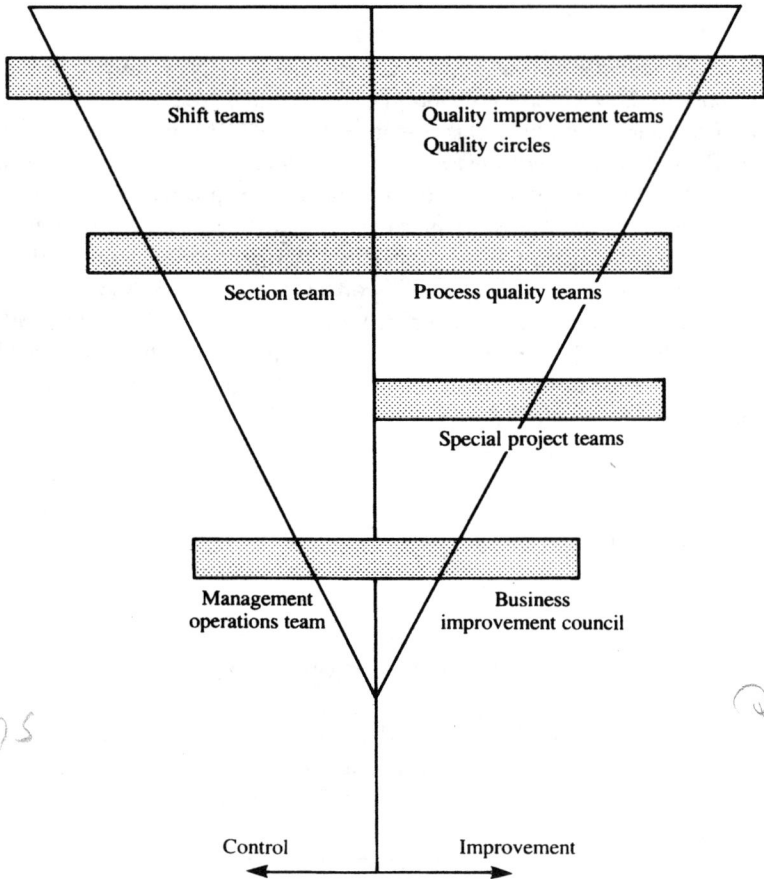

**Figure 4.1** *Tioxide team structure for TQM*

## The tools of TQM

SPC techniques have been used for many years in some factories. SPC has made much slower progress in the chemical industry than in the engineering industry. Many factors have contributed to this, including sampling difficulties, the inherent nature of the process control and measurement delay problems.

In 1989 a major new SPC initiative was launched with the formation of the Tioxide Group SPC Forum. A major systematic SPC training programme was launched with a view to widening the use of SPC across the whole Tioxide Group. Training of managers and supervisors was carried out at the group level, using specially developed training material. Operator training was carried out at site level. Process capability studies, covering the whole product range, are an ongoing feature of this SPC initiative. At many sites, process quality improvement teams. (PQITs) have been formed to look at key areas of the process. These teams are multidisciplinary in nature and have been trained in advanced SPC techniques, including Taguchi methods.

The SPC Forum enables the various sites to exchange ideas on SPC and process improvement. Each site is represented by an SPC coordinator. The Forum meets on a regular basis to consider the latest developments in SPC and to monitor progress across the group.

Customers are taking an increasing interest in SPC and many major customers require SPC data as part of the contractual requirement. SPC training has also been provided for some customers as part of a wider strategy of developing customer relationships.

Tioxide has developed its own computer-based SPC system, called ACQUAINT. This incorporates the latest developments in SPC for process industries. The system allows the rapid electronic transfer of SPC data between sites and to certain customers, if required. The system is in its second stage of development, with the provision of foreign language menus and a simpler and easier to use version for process operators.

The SPC initiative was subjected to a major review in the first quarter of 1993, with a view to adopting a harmonized approach across the European sites, based on best practice in the chemical industry. The resulting harmonization programme will focus on:

1 The adoption of standardized computer systems for capturing process data.
2 The deployment of the ACQUAINT SPC system to all the manufacturing sites.
3 The adoption of common procedures for the review of process stability and capability.
4 The integration of SPC with automatic process control (APC) systems.
5 The development of expert systems to facilitate operators on the process.

# Recent developments

The registration programme focused mainly on the process and customer interface areas. The principles of BS5750/ISO9000, however, can be extended across the whole of the organization's operational areas to give a total quality system. This process is currently taking place in Tioxide. Environmental issues and safety and health are being integrated into the system at the manufacturing sites. An internal audit of a section now covers quality, safety and health and the environment. In many cases the safety requirements and the quality requirements have been built into the same procedure.

The company is also considering the registration of areas not covered in the scope of the original site registrations, such as the Group Marketing and Sales operation. The Marketing Quality Assurance (MQA), Specification for Marketing, Sales and Customer Assurance, which relates in part to BS5750: Part 1/ISO9001, is being actively examined. Areas such as R&D and central laboratories should similarly benefit from the introduction of quality systems.

The key business areas/processes are shown in Figure 4.2. Areas currently covered by the site ISO9002 registrations are shown together with those areas that would be addressed by an ISO9001 registration and MQA registration for the European operations. In general, ISO9001 addresses the functions of design/developments, production and, to some extent, installation and servicing, in relation to conformance to specification. The MQA specification addresses the functions of management, marketing, sales and customer assurance in relation to conformance to a specification which meets customer needs, preferences and expectations.

In mid 1992, the Tioxide Europe senior management decided that the TQM programme required a new focus. The new TQM initiative should not be just an extension of the current site-based quality programmes. The focus should be on improving the European business in a planned, purposeful way making even wider use of the principles of TQM. This will be achieved by concentrating on process alignment and recognizing that people's roles and responsibilities must be related to the processes in which they work. The new emphasis is on business improvement in key strategic areas. Techniques such as Process Quality Management (PQM) and self-appraisal using the European Quality Award criteria will play an important role in this phase of the programme.

## Summary

Tioxide is an example of an organization using a management-led evolutionary approach to TQM. Initiatives in seemingly quite different areas have converged to give an effective TQM structure. People have been recognized to be the most valuable resource an organization has and extensive programmes aimed at achieving effective participation have been successful. However, the importance of systems and techniques has also been fully recognized and major initiatives in the areas of quality systems and SPC have shown equal success. In particular, the Group Quality Systems Programme has been a major driving force in Tioxide's TQM initiative.

$S \rho$

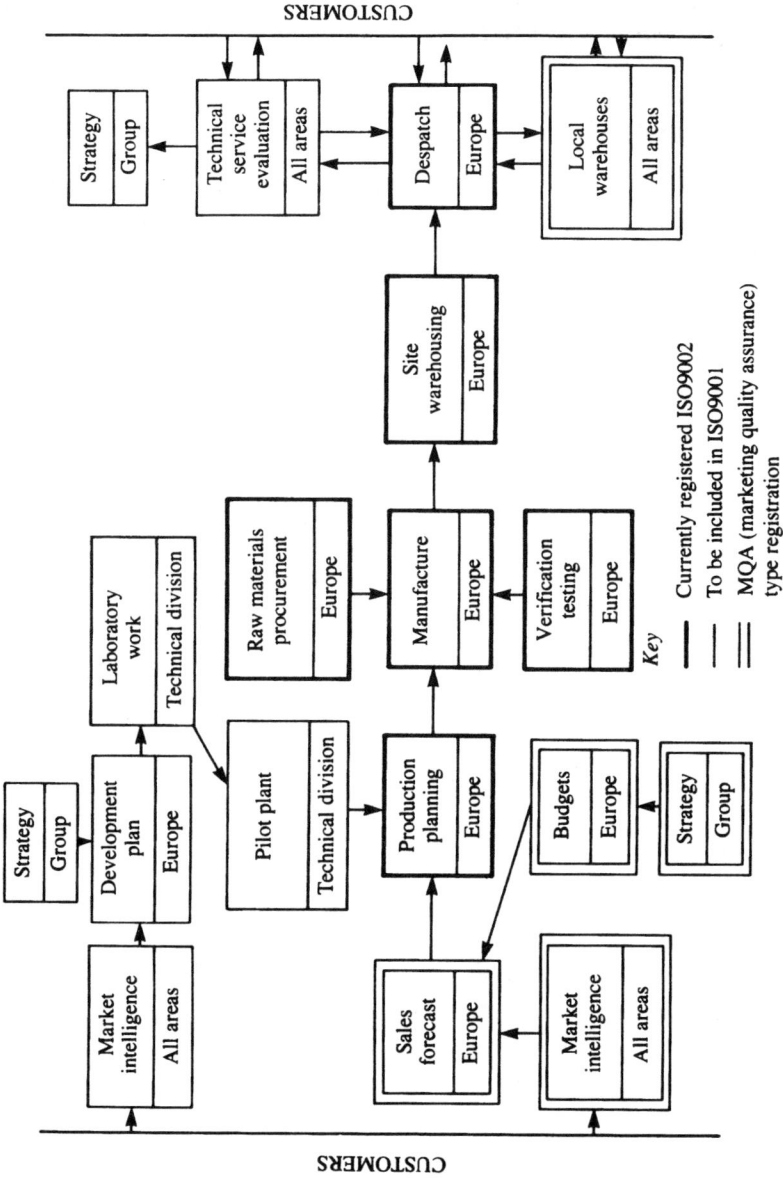

**Figure 4.2** *Key business areas and quality management systems*

The Tioxide approach to excellence is a good example for others about to embark on the TQM journey. For many organizations, this will seem a less daunting challenge when viewed in the context of building upon a range of more easily understood initiatives.

## Acknowledgement

The authors would like to acknowledge the invaluable help of Dr Mike Hird, Tioxide Europe and Mr J. Collingwood, Tioxide Group Ltd, in the preparation of this case.

# Appendix A: The Tioxide Vision Statement

Tioxide Group is a worldwide leader in titanium pigments and related chemical products. Our mission is to be the best in everything we do and to provide a satisfactory return on our assets to sustain profitable growth. We will achieve our aim by placing the highest value on being a customer-driven organization, by improving continually the quality of our processes, products and services, and by developing the potential of our people to the greatest extent.

Our strength as a Group is based on a shared view of the following important values and responsibilities and our determination and ability to fulfil these commitments in all our operations around the world.

## Customers

Customers are our first priority. We are committed to identifying and satisfying our customers' needs by means of close cooperation across a broad front, and through joint innovation and the supply of high-quality products and services to our mutual benefit.

## People

People are our greatest strength. We are committed to providing a working environment in which open discussion and mutual respect will be encouraged, permitting everyone to realize their full potential through participation, communication and the delegation of authority with accountability. Our selection, training, education and development programmes will be designed to encourage leadership qualities and provide opportunities for advancement.

## Quality

Quality is vital to our business. To meet our customers' needs we are committed to product and service excellence through Total Quality Management. Our Group-wide Quality Assurance Programme will conform to internationally recognized and independently audited standards. We shall seek similar quality performance standards from our suppliers, developing with them mutually beneficial partnerships.

## Innovation

Continuous improvement by innovation in our technology, marketing and supporting services is essential to our success. We will foster creativity and teamwork and freedom to act in all aspects of our business and will recognize, reward and celebrate our achievements.

## Environment

We wish to be welcomed and respected members of our communities. We are committed to providing a safe and healthy environment and working conditions of the highest quality by undertaking a programme of continuous improvement in the methods of operating our factories and in the disposal of effluents.

# Appendix B: Statement by the Chief Executive

## Introduction

*In 1987 Tioxide's Chief Executive announced the Group's commitment to quality by making the following statement:*

## Tioxide – Chief Executive's statement

Running our business today is a team activity which includes every single person in our organization. We are all working together with a shared vision and shared commitment which provide the foundation and building blocks for our future success.

Our mission is to be the best in everything we do and to provide a satisfactory return on our assets to sustain profitable growth. We are committed to identifying and satisfying our customers' needs by the supply of high-quality products and services.

Quality is important to every one of us in Tioxide. We should be aware of the benefits to our customers and to ourselves in getting it right first time. Quality applies to all aspects of our business – not only to the products, their packaging and delivery, but also to all of the supporting activities essential to our success.

Our approach to quality throughout the Group is to obtain and maintain registration to the International Quality Systems Standard ISO9002. This will provide the formal framework for quality assurance on which we will build and innovate.

I am confident that, by following the guiding principles for our Group *Vision Statement*, we shall succeed in satisfying our customers' needs to our mutual benefit, while gaining satisfaction from a job well-done.

# 5 Quality systems in CarnaudMetalbox PLC, Foodcan UK, Perry Wood Factory

## Introduction

The CarnaudMetalbox Perry Wood Factory in Worcester is part of the Foodcan UK business, a major manufacturer of cans and components in the UK. The Perry Wood factory produces three-piece cans for the food industry. The company's customers cover a wide range of well-known brand names, in both human and pet foods.

In 1987, following some very tough problems in the market place, CarnaudMetalbox Foodcan (then Metalbox Food Packaging), decided to look at its business strategy very closely. While it had established itself as a leading manufacturer of packaging (particularly in metals), customers were demanding a more responsive and cost effective service. They started to look at alternative sources of supply and CarnaudMetalbox began to lose market share.

In analysing why this had come about, managers recognized that prices needed to be more competitive and they had to address costs and organizational issues. However, they also knew that their competitive advantage was based on quality and customer service and they needed to strengthen this advantage. The senior management set about examining how they could sharpen that edge whilst at the same time reducing operating costs.

## Quality management at Perry Wood

Various senior managers at Perry Wood were aware of the ideas of the quality gurus, but it all seemed rather remote and theoretical to these hard-nosed can makers at the time. However, they became convinced that TQM was the right route for the business to succeed. A practical route forward was required and quality systems such as BS5750/ISO9000 seemed to be an appropriate vehicle.

Some managers were certainly attracted to the idea that you could apply for and get a certificate which implied that your quality was better than those who did not have such a certificate. For most managers this was their first impression of BS5750/ISO9000. They were later to discover that these initial impressions were ill-founded. Furthermore, they also discovered that the use of a sound quality management system was far more important to them than outside certification. However, these first impressions did help to build up in managers at the time a blind faith in the cause of quality without which they would probably not have achieved their mission in the planned timescale.

Towards the end of 1987, the company decided that all Metalbox Food Packaging sites would be registered to BS5750 Part 2/ISO9002 by the end of 1988.

The senior management team at Perry Wood quickly recognized two things:

1 Pulling together a quality management system would require a full-time input from at least one of the management team if they were to succeed in the timescale (approximately nine months).
2 A quality management system was only a starting point as far as TQM was concerned.

They responded by appointing a full-time total quality manager, a role that now exists at all Foodcan UK plants.

# The initial review

The initial task was first of all to establish what BS5750 required them to do. For this they assembled a multi-disciplined team of people from all levels within the factory – shift managers, supervisors, line engineers, QA inspectors, operators, etc. to review the situation.

Within 6 weeks, the following had been established:

1 They did not have a comprehensive quality management system that would meet the requirements of the standard.
2 What they already had documented was either out of date because of changes that had occurred, or was not complied with for various reasons.
3 They had no formal managed calibration system, something very important to BS5750/ISO9000 certification.

4 Their system for traceability was not good enough to prompt effective corrective action.
5 No-one knew of, or understood, the quality policy.
6 The sixty-year-old factory did not exude a quality image.
7 The system for quarantine of sub-standard product was not consistent.
8 People did not understand all the quality jargon being bandied about.
9 If a quality management system was to be successfully created, it would need to be created by the workforce and not for the workforce.

## The implementation process

In order to enhance the management involvement and commitment, Perry Wood soon disbanded the original full-time task force and created eight major projects geared to completing the work needed for a successful audit and certification. The objectives of these projects were allocated to departmental managers and they were encouraged to set up teams to include relevant supervisors and shop floor personnel. These were Perry Wood's first embryonic TQM teams. Networking with other plants also contributed to the development of TQM across the company.

Each project team uncovered previously unrecognized staff who would later form the foundations upon which they could start to build a TQM culture. An additional asset, built in at this stage, which was also unrecognized as such at the time, was the time-scale for the process. From conception to delivery of a healthy quality system took nine months. According to the total quality manager, this is as near to the experience of pregnancy as any man is likely to get! Such a tight time-scale is generally not to be recommended but many companies fail to achieve the necessary momentum to get their system running because they fail to target a date for audit, or make the date far too remote. In this respect the external audit is a useful spur rather than an end in itself. Nerves before the full audit were quite natural - no-one, however, was prepared to let the workforce down and put off the audit. Despite the doubters, all tasks were completed with enthusiasm and determination. In September 1988, the Perry Wood site gained registration to BS5750: Part 2.

Elements of their implementation approach fitted well into Perry Wood's evolving TQM Strategy, and they have since built upon these early foundations. The experience showed that a documented quality management system that establishes where you are now is not a bad place to start for any company uncertain of where to start their TQM journey. For Perry Wood, formal review of quality started to change the emphasis for measuring business performance; traceability helped problem identification and problem solving and corrective action laid a foundation for continuous improvement.

# Recommendations for successful implementation of a quality management system

Looking back on their BS5750 programme, the Perry Wood team have drawn up the following advice for other organizations about to embark on the registration journey.

1  Do it because you believe it can help you improve, not because everyone else is doing it.
2  Find someone in the organization who will passionately believe in it. There will be days when everyone else will want to ditch it.
3  Set up a team of multi-disciplined people to determine what you specifically will need to do. This should consist of staff at all levels. This gives the task a higher profile and also creates some grass roots enthusiasts for later on.
4  Disband the team as soon as they have accomplished the task, otherwise ownership of the system will never develop.
5  Set up teams led by managers to carry out the work needed. Make sure as many people as is practically possible get involved.
6  Keep your workforce informed and interested. Perry Wood gave every employee a three hour quality induction to explain what the audits would entail, what the jargon meant, why they were doing it, etc.
7  Set yourself a challenging time-scale. However, keep your eye on the ball. No customer will thank you for letting them down whilst you put together your system. Key resources need to be dedicated to putting the system together so you need to plan availability as well as maintenance of existing control systems.
8  Believe in your people. The experts for writing your quality procedures are not the QA manager or an outside consultant, but the people actually carrying out the tasks concerned. Ask yourself this question: 'If your employees are not capable of documenting, or telling you what they do, what likelihood is there that they will consistently comply with an imposed procedure, written by someone who, at best, could not perform the task as well or, at worst, could not perform the task at all.'
9  Be prepared for continuous change. Most companies find that the major difference between a successful system and an unsuccessful one is the extent to which it allows for and encourages change. In today's climate a quality management system that you start to put together today will be going out of date by the time it is implemented.
10  Talk to other companies who have been through the process. Much time can be saved avoiding common problems already faced and solved.

## Developing the TQM programme

In early 1990 statistical process control (SPC) became a key issue for CarnaudMetalbox and was seen as the next step on from quality systems. Leading experts in the field of SPC made presentations to the company and one of its leading customers. The increasing interest of customers in SPC generated renewed commitment at many of the CarnaudMetalbox factories.

The Perry Wood Factory started their SPC initiative in April 1990. There had been an earlier attempt to introduce SPC but this had failed due to an over-emphasis on statistics rather than the practicalities of process control. The project started in a similar way to their ISO9002 project with a review of current practices.

## The SPC review

An initial review by consultants working with staff from the quality department quickly established that:

1  A comprehensive set of log sheets and, in some cases charts, was used to monitor the process.
2  Existing mean charts used internal manufacturing specification limits instead of statistically based action and warning lines.
3  There was a general reluctance to take corrective action based on action signals from these charts. Supervisors were responsible for corrective actions, but more accountable for production targets.
4  Line operators generally found the tolerance based charts to be useful, whereas supervisors considered the charts a hindrance to production. Line operators could only take corrective actions when authorized by supervisors.
5  There was a lot of data collection at various stages of the production process, but little use was made of this other than simply to classify it as OK/not OK.
6  Many processes offered improvement opportunities using SPC techniques.
7  The seven basic tools of TQM could be used in an effective way to identify and solve problems. Many production problems were of a recurring nature.

## The SPC programme

The Perry Wood Management Team demonstrated their commitment to SPC by attending a one-day SPC awareness seminar in July 1990, and subsequently sponsoring a series of three-day SPC workshops for middle managers and supervisors. An SPC co-ordinator, reporting to the total quality manager was appointed at an early stage of the programme. In-house SPC training materials were developed by the SPC co-ordinator and during the first year of the programme, the majority of operators received some SPC training.

A series of SPC projects was set up and many teams were involved in the successful solution of critical quality problems. This project work was complemented by development work in the field of SPC systems and techniques appropriate to Perry Wood's production processes.

Since introducing SPC, Perry Wood has improved the stability and capability of many of its production processes. There has also been a considerable drop in the level of defects and waste. People are also playing an increasingly active role in continuous improvement activities using SPC techniques. The SPC initiative encouraged a wider participation in teamwork and gave the TQM programme a new boost. The earlier ISO9002 programme provided an ideal foundation for the SPC initiative.

## The next steps

The quality management system at Perry Wood is a framework on which a quality culture has been built. Since establishing their quality management system, Perry Wood has moved on to develop their TQM process further. A clear focus on continuous improvement, closer relationships with customers and suppliers, and the measurement and improvement of processes using tools and techniques like SPC, are part of this ongoing process.

Perry Wood has tackled the issue of team organization of work into customer-driven cell manufacturing where the workforce are organized into self-managing groups with clear goals and authority to run their own processes and solve their own problems. Other techniques such as failure mode and effect analysis (FMEA), have been used to improve key areas of the process.

Building on information they now have on process capability, Carnaud-Metalbox world-wide have embarked upon a major commitment to total productive maintenance which will help improve overall equipment effectiveness and continue to harness the efforts and ideas of all the people in the organization. Already, building on its TQM foundations, Perry Wood is a committed factory to this process.

Perry Wood is a good example of a learning organization that is constantly harnessing the ideas of TQM to improve its business.

## Acknowledgement

The authors would like to acknowledge the invaluable contribution of Mr Jerry O'Brien, CarnaudMetalbox, in the preparation of this case.

# Part Three
# The Tools and the
# Improvement Cycle

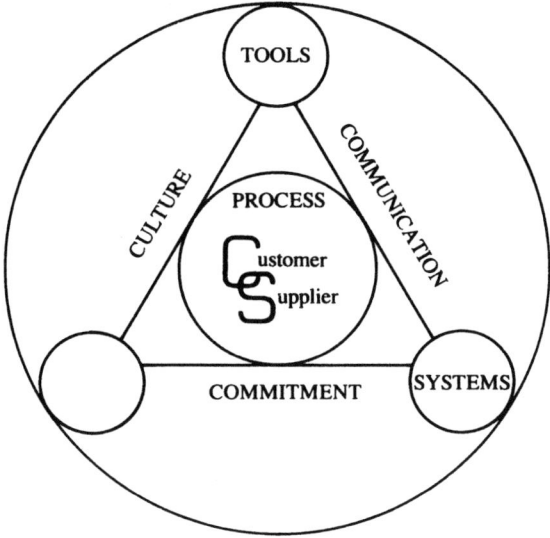

# 6 Problem-solving and the use of improvement tools and techniques at Hills Industries

## Introduction

Hills Industries is a wholly owned subsidiary of a South Australian public listed company, has a turnover of £5m and 110 employees. It has been based in Caerphilly (10–15 miles north of Cardiff) for about 20 years. Hills manufacture rotary clothes dryers, various outdoor and indoor drying devices and a range of garden and industrial sprayers.

When Managing Director Mark Canny arrived from Australia a few years ago to head the British subsidiary, he found its management hierarchical in style, with senior managers involved in decisions which should be delegated to subordinates. As a young Australian brought up in the automotive component industry, and exposed to Japanese quality demands and management philosophy, he wanted to change to a more informal, team-based approach.

At the same time Mark was required to introduce the parent company's system of material requirements planning (MRP) and saw the quality assurance standard BS5750 (ISO9000 series) as a market necessity for the future.

This case study concentrates, however, on the manufacture of sprayers and the use of tools/techniques for quality improvement. At Hills, the manufacturing process for sprayers commences with the production of a bottle which is blow-moulded from high-density polyethylene. The bottle is then printed and placed on to a conveyor belt where various components and subassemblies are added to the bottle. The subassemblies are produced on the side of the flow line; the components come partly from in-house manufacture in other sections (for example, injection mouldings) and also come from outside suppliers.

## Quality problems

There is a very great sensitivity within Hills to the quality of the sprayers produced. This sensitivity originates mainly from the very adverse results of the production of poor-quality sprayers 7–8 years ago. At that time Hills developed a new range of products which they released on to the market before a satisfactory testing programme had been completed. The products were visually very appealing and sold very well. Unfortunately, the customer dissatisfaction with poorly performing products was so bad that the products returned in great quantity. The upshot of this was that Hills suffered a significant loss of market share. That market share has never been completely regained and the story remains a part of the company folklore.

Last year, Hills decided that certification to BS5750 would become a market-place necessity for them within the next 2 years. Certification was already a precondition for trade in a number of other industries. After vigorous management debate, Hills decided to embark on a TQM programme, with BS5750 certification being simply a milestone in that process. Some 6–8 months after commencing the programme, Hills suffered a burst of sprayer returns. Although they did not yet have a system for recording returns, their sensitivity to sprayer quality meant that they picked up the problem very early. At this time, the engineering team and a number of senior management were heavily occupied in a major capital-spend programme in another part of the business. Accordingly, it was an ideal opportunity to make use of the philosophies of TQM, whereby the problem was given to a multidisciplinary team rather than to a group of engineers and/or a group of management.

## The problem-solving approach

The team was assembled with great care and, of the five members of the team, three had day-to-day involvement with the manufacturing process; the other two members were from engineering and sales management.

The first step was to take the team through a training programme on scientific problem-solving. The original training of the sprayer team was conducted by an outside consultant who was helping Hills with its TQM
... It is very common for a group of people to see a problem and, clearly defining what the problem is, jump to conclusions as to
n should be. To avoid this happening the training focused on
olving problems which was a step-by-step process. This
he problem-solvers carefully researched the problem and
beginning the process of devising various possible
ocused on brainstorming, fishbone diagrams, Pareto
agrams, histograms and tally sheets, amongst other

techniques. The team was then given a clear definition of the problem which the management wanted solved and they then set about the task.

After collecting an amount of information, the team decided that the production process should be stopped completely and that all line operators should be involved in a thorough analysis of the products in the finished goods store. The team made this proposal to management, the management accepted the proposal and the line stoppage was put into effect. The line was stopped for a total of 20 days. This was a very important sign to the workforce that the company was serious about quality.

The team was now working hand-in-hand with all of the members of the production unit. They produced a process flow diagram and made judgements about those parts of the process which were under control and those parts which needed further investigation. They also carefully examined every sprayer in the finished goods stock and kept tally charts of the faults which they found. These results were then put on to a Pareto chart so that the actions could be prioritized. The charts were produced by hand and were very simple. Their view was that there was no need for computer-aided devices in this area.

The operators were given the authority to stop the line when they found a problem of any sort with the process. This authority has not been abused. When it has been used, the reasons have always been justified and very sensible. The company management felt that the front-line operators must have greater involvement in finding solutions to day-to-day problems and then, of course, implementing those agreed solutions.

## Tackling major issues

The largest problem by far was the apparent random occurrence of an overly long internal dip tube (this tube carries the fluid from inside the sprayer to the delivery lance in the spraying process and excessively long tubes caused blocking at the base of the sprayer). The team visited the supplier of the tube. Working with the supplier they discovered that the supplier did not recognize that the length of the tube would have a material effect on the performance of the sprayer. Hills had not previously recognized this either and had never discussed it with their supplier. Accordingly, the supplier had always treated the length definition as a minimum requirement and, accordingly, supplied the off-cut lengths as a longer piece. Once Hills had discussed this problem with the supplier, they were very willing and able to comply with Hills' real needs of the component.

The second problem on the Pareto chart related to snapping pump handles. These handles were made of an ABS compound and the finished component needed to have a compromise of strength and flexibility. Following what they had learned from their dip tube experience, Hills contacted the supplier of the pump handles. It transpired that the supplier of the pump handles had been unable to obtain the normal grade of ABS used in the process. The supplier instead purchased a more expensive grade of ABS compound assuming that if it was more expensive, it must be better. As it transpired, the more expensive grade of ABS had superior strength characteristics but less flexibility. Hence this new grade of ABS produced a component which failed under various conditions. The corrective action in this case was of course very straightforward.

Buoyed by these two successes, the team moved on to look at the ongoing process of sprayer production. They grouped their findings and recommendations into three categories:

1 Process control
2 Incoming supplies
3 Operator training

The team made a presentation to management and requested help in resolving the issues they had highlighted.

In terms of operator training, there were two issues that could be very easily addressed. Firstly, the supervisor constructed a simple chart showing which operators had been trained to work on which sections of the assembly process. This chart highlighted the need for further training to fill the gaps. Once this training was complete, the operators were more easily able to move from one position to another, therefore increasing their interest and enthusiasm in the job which, of course, translates into better-quality performance.

Secondly, the operators recommended that there should be simple diagrammatic work instructions at each workstation. These work instructions would mean that an operator moving to a new workstation would be able to have an instant refresher course on the job which was to be done at that station. The team co-opted a member of the engineering staff to produce these diagrams and asked the maintenance section to install large boards at each workstation in order to display the diagrams. When the boards were installed (as per the team's design) it was suddenly realized that the effect was to leave operators feeling quite isolated. They were now unable to see the majority of the flow line and were unable to see their fellow workers. If these boards had been installed as a management idea, the effect would have been to create a confrontation. Because the boards were installed to operator specification, however, ownership of the mistake was accepted and the boards were modified to enable them to display the work instructions while also allowing good visibility for the operators.

Since this early work, the improvement process has continued in the sprayer section. It must be noted, however, that sometimes the process does not flow smoothly and early gains are sometimes partially lost. The improvement process requires constant reinforcing, work and input from all those involved. Some of the reversals suffered have been quite large and have led to periods of low morale but, because there are memories of the success achieved, this situation has always been able to be turned around.

## The use of Statistical Process Control (SPC) at Hills Industries

There were two different examples of SPC at Hills Industries which are worthy of consideration:

1 *Where they did not use SPC*: As a step in the manufacture of pressure sprayers, a unit called a pressure relief valve (PRV) is assembled. This valve works by releasing air from the sprayer if the pressure within the vessel becomes too high. The PRV consists of a rod which moves inside a cylinder with an 'O' ring around the rod to produce the seal. At the upper end of the cylinder there is a step. If the 'O' ring passes the step, the gas is released.

Given the safety-critical nature of the PRV, the subassembly was 100% tested on the production line, using a 'go/no-go' gauge. The company did not, however, keep any data on either percentage rates of failure or, more specifically, measures of the pressure at which individual batches of PRVs released.

Fortunately, the workforce had become quite aware of sprayer quality and were committed to improvement and a member of the workforce noticed that the number of reject PRVs was very high in a particular batch. The operator informed her supervisor and an investigation was undertaken.

The investigation showed that, when a rod was at the lower size limit, the 'O' ring at the lower size limit, and the cylinder inside diameter at the upper size limit, the subassembly had minimal interference and effectively did not work. The major saving grace was that the fault was fail-safe – the PRV would release pressure far too early.

Given this discovery, the company was able to change its specifications and tolerances for the components involved. Unfortunately, the company had gone through a number of years of producing faulty subassemblies, which were discarded, without learning that, although the individual parts were to specification, the specifications were inappropriate.

2 *Where they did begin rudimentary charting of a process*: Absenteeism amongst the direct workforce had always been the 'stock/standard' reason (or excuse) for any failure to meet the production plans at Hills. The

management believed that the company had high levels of absenteeism but were unwilling to take on extra staff to cover this because, if all direct workers arrived at work on a given day, then labour utilization would be low, i.e. there would not be enough work for them all.

The Personnel Manager began to tackle this problem. Among her first activities was the keeping of a run-chart of the number of people absent each morning. After collecting the data for a short time, she saw a pattern and accordingly searched back through the records to examine a longer period of data. The run-chart showed that the absenteeism was in fact fairly stable – the fluctuations from the mean were not very large. Accordingly the company could quite confidently take on extra staff to cover expected, ongoing absenteeism without any real risk of being overstaffed on particular days. Additionally the management were able to compare themselves with other companies in the area. They discovered that their absenteeism rates were, in fact, very modest when compared to other factories nearby.

The information which Hills Industries gleaned from the simple run-chart enabled the management team to make some fundamental decisions about staffing levels and meaningful judgements about performance relative to local conditions.

## The broad issues

The broad issues highlighted by the case are:

1 The tools and techniques are just that – they do not provide quality in themselves, and they rely on the environment in which they are used.
2 Tools and techniques fit into two broad categories:
   (a) Waste – problem-solving (to eliminate waste)
   (b) Random variation – SPC (to measure and control the variation).
   N.B.: 'Waste' and 'problem' have broad definitions and refer to any process which can be improved.
3 Achieving quality is an ongoing process which will never be complete – a journey, not a destination.

## Being more specific

The specific reasons/lessons regarding problem-solving of the case are:

1 Hills Industries regarded themselves as lucky to notice the increase in product returns of sprayers – they did not (at that time) have a rigorous

returned goods/customer complaints system in place, and the increase in returns was not so dramatic that it was noticed easily.

The lesson the company learned was that it might not continue with this luck – a system/feedback mechanism was needed to tell the managers how customers felt about the products.

2 The time-honoured method for dealing with problems, such as product returns, was to call in the 'experts' (engineers and senior manager) – Hills were lucky that they were all too busy at the time!

3 The critical steps in the new approach were:
   (a) All of the people involved were given training in problem-solving.
   (b) The direct operators were very involved in the investigation progress.
   (c) The team was given a clear, unambiguous brief of what was required of them.
   (d) The management decision to accept the stopping of production sent a strong, clear message that solving this problem was being taken seriously.

4 The root causes of the problems turned out to be deceptively simple – moreover they were the result of good intentions and lack of communication.

5 As a result of being involved in the investigations and recommendations for improvement, the direct operators have a greater understanding of the process and a greater commitment to ongoing improvement.

The specific features/lessons of the Hills case, regarding the tools of quality improvement including SPC, are:

1 The use of a go/no-go test had hidden the real *cause* of problems for a long time.

2 Simply rejecting the rejects had meant that they had passed up an opportunity for improvement.

3 Hills' first steps with SPC have shown that they can become *proactive* rather than *reactive* with regard to quality in all areas of business activity.

# 7   Customer satisfaction, quality improvement and the use of SPC tools at Charter Chemicals

## The company

Charter Chemicals is a relatively small subsidiary of the better-known Charter Oil Company. Using naphtha purchased from the parent company, Charter Chemicals manufactures polyethylene, polypropylene and polyvinyl chloride. These three products are sold to hundreds of companies in western Europe and are the basic raw material for a host of plastic products, including bags, bottles, pipes, cables, kitchen accessories and motor vehicle components.

The present structure of Charter Chemicals evolved during the restructuring of the chemical industry in the early 1980s. The success of this painful rationalization could be seen in the second half of the decade when Charter and its competitors produced record profits, year after year. Such a boom could not last for ever, of course, and in the early 1990s there were clear indications of a declining market for many plastic products. The problem was further exacerbated by new competition from the Middle East and the Pacific basin. It was very clear that the high plant utilization of the late 1980s would no longer be the norm, and that profits would fall rapidly.

Such a decline would be very disturbing even if it occurred gradually and were spread equally across the petrochemicals industry. For Charter Chemicals the impact of recession was magnified by the growing popularity of 'single sourcing'. Many of Charter's customers were suppliers to the large motor manufacturers who had, since the early 1980s, been actively reducing their supplier base. The purpose of this movement was to reduce variability in raw materials and to improve customer–supplier relationships. For those companies removed from the list of approved suppliers, the effect was traumatic. Even for the retained companies, close scrutiny by important customers often acted as a catalyst for cultural change and often raised questions such as: 'Why don't we subject our suppliers to a similar process?'

Thus it was that Charter Chemicals was asked by its customers to provide evidence of ability to meet agreed specifications. Such requests were directed to the Technical Services Manager, Ron Howard, who found that more and more of his time was being taken up drawing together the required information or explaining why it was not available.

Without doubt the most difficult requests for Ron to deal with were the ones he did not fully understand. At one stage he was wrestling with a carefully worded letter from the Quality Manager of an important customer, Porritt Pipes (see Appendix A).

## Customer communication

Ron Howard suspected that the letter from Porritt Pipes was written by someone who understood the questions he or she was asking. This was not always the case. One or two other requests had been so badly worded that Ron was not sure precisely what information was required, nor how it would be used, nor even if the recipient would be able to understand the data that was sent. With the Porritt letter, however, he felt sure that the writer was eminently capable of comparing suppliers and would not look favourably on any supplier which tendered incomplete or 'laundered' data. He convened a meeting with the Production Manager (Polyethylene) and the Quality Manager to discuss the information requirements of Porritt Pipes and the ability of Charter Chemicals to supply what was needed.

The first to arrive was Bill Johnson, the Quality Manager. Bill left university in 1965 with a degree in chemical engineering to join Astrochem, which was absorbed into Charter in 1985. He had been a very loyal servant of both companies and had no desire to work elsewhere, but he would have been a contender for early retirement, if customers like Porritt Pipes were to take their business elsewhere.

'I sent you a copy of the Porritt letter, Bill, what do you make of it?' asked Ron as he poured the coffee. 'Well, I've brought along some data on process capability which will help us to answer questions 4, 5 and 6. I believe Didier is bringing some control charts. They will be relevant to questions 1, 2 and 3, but question 7 on long-term improvement is the tricky one. We should have tackled this problem of reducing variability a few years ago when the profits were good. I warned you at the time.' Bill Johnson spoke the words as if rehearsed many times.

## Process control charts

Ron was about to reply that predictions made during the good years are not very relevant to current problems, when the door opened and in breezed

Didier Grave, the Production Manager, and greeted them with, 'Hi, you guys'. Didier spoke English with the cultured American accent that results from watching movies on television in his mother country, Belgium. 'What the hell are we going to tell Porritt about our long-term plans for reducing variability? Seems to me that Joe Porritt has been reading Deming. I've been saying for years that those guys in Research and Development should be doing Taguchi experiments to help us achieve more consistency. But it's too late now. Half of them have been made redundant.'

'Everyone seems to know what should have been done', agreed Ron. 'Let's focus on what needs to be done now. Let's go through the Porritt letter item by item. Are we or are we not using control charts to monitor the polyethylene process?'

'Well, yes and no', Bill admitted. 'We aren't using SPC charts on the reactor yet but we are using them on the extruder.'

'But the reactor precedes the extruder. Surely it would make sense to apply SPC at the reactor,' Ron exclaimed. 'You mean that the polymer leaving the reactor could be off spec and we wouldn't know this until after it had been extruded. A bit late then, isn't it?'

'Better late than never', Bill retorted. 'I'm only the Quality Manager. I can't make anyone on the plant use SPC charts. I've publicized the benefits of SPC and tried to persuade each of the plant managers to implement it. Some have, some haven't. Didier is the only person who can make it happen'.

It was true that the reactor manager and the extruder manager did report to Didier Grave, but he did not accept that he could make either of them use SPC charts. 'None of my guys have had the SPC training. How can they ask process operators to plot control charts if they themselves don't understand them? Apart from which, they could never find the time for introducing any new initiatives. Since the cutback, everyone's working flat out'.

'We put 68 people through the 3-day SPC course last year. Where the hell are they all?' Ron asked. 'Well, they are not in my department', Didier snapped. 'My lads don't have time to go on courses. I think you'll find that all this SPC expertise is in three locations: Quality Department, which doesn't seem to be responsible for quality any longer; Research and Development, which isn't interested in current production; and the local Job Centre. Those lads who were put on the severance list snapped up every course available, to enhance their CVs'.

Ron was appalled. The situation was worse than he imagined. 'Well, who fills in the charts on the extruder?' he asked. 'The process operators', Bill replied. 'I released one of my laboratory staff to go down there and train them. You remember Arthur Ball – he used to work on extruders before he joined my group. Yes, Arthur set up individual charts for melt index and density then he taught the operators how to fill them in. He tells me they accepted the charts without any problems. Are these the ones you've brought with you, Didier?'

'They are indeed, but I don't think you could send these to Porritt,' Didier explained as he lay the control charts on the table (Figures 7.1 and 7.2). 'They are in a hell of a state. The lads have scribbled all over them'.

Ron pored over the melt index charts whilst Bill examined the other sheet containing the control charts for density. 'There isn't much written on this sheet. We could easily clean it up with Snopake', Bill suggested.

'Perhaps I could get my guys to redraw the charts', Didier offered. 'If other customers are going to ask for control charts we need to produce something more presentable. Better still, could one of your quality lads knock something off on a computer, then my operators needn't be involved with these SPC charts at all?'

Ron Howard had been struggling to decipher the comments written on the melt index charts, whilst at the same time trying to listen to Bill and Didier. He was now thoroughly confused. Didier Grave, the Production Manager, seemed to be saying that his staff did not want to know about SPC charts. On the other hand, Bill Johnson, the Quality Manager, claimed that his responsibility ended when the charts had been set up. 'What's the purpose of these control charts?' Ron asked. 'Who benefits from them? Who really wants them, apart from Joe Porritt?'

'Remember the TQM model from our training?' Bill reminded them. 'The essential components of TQM are management commitment; a good-quality system – we have BS5750, teamwork and SPC tools. Responsibility for quality *must* rest with the process operators, their supervisors and their managers. They need to pull together as a team, using whatever tools are appropriate, to build quality into the product and get it right first time'.

This well-rehearsed monologue from the Quality Manager seemed to make good sense to Ron but did not find favour with Didier. 'We sweated blood producing that Quality Manual and all those damn procedures', he snapped. 'It got us the 5750 registration and I suppose it was worth it in the end, but the Quality Manual says nothing about SPC charts, so why should we let Porritt's letter disrupt our agreed procedures? You know damn well we are sending them good polymer because every laboratory result is in specification. Show Ron those capability graphs, Bill'.

## Process capability

Bill had used a computer package to perform what he called a capability analysis. This had produced histograms for the density and the melt index from 50 samples of polymer taken at 4-hourly intervals from the extruder. Printed under each histogram were the capability indices (Figures 7.3 and

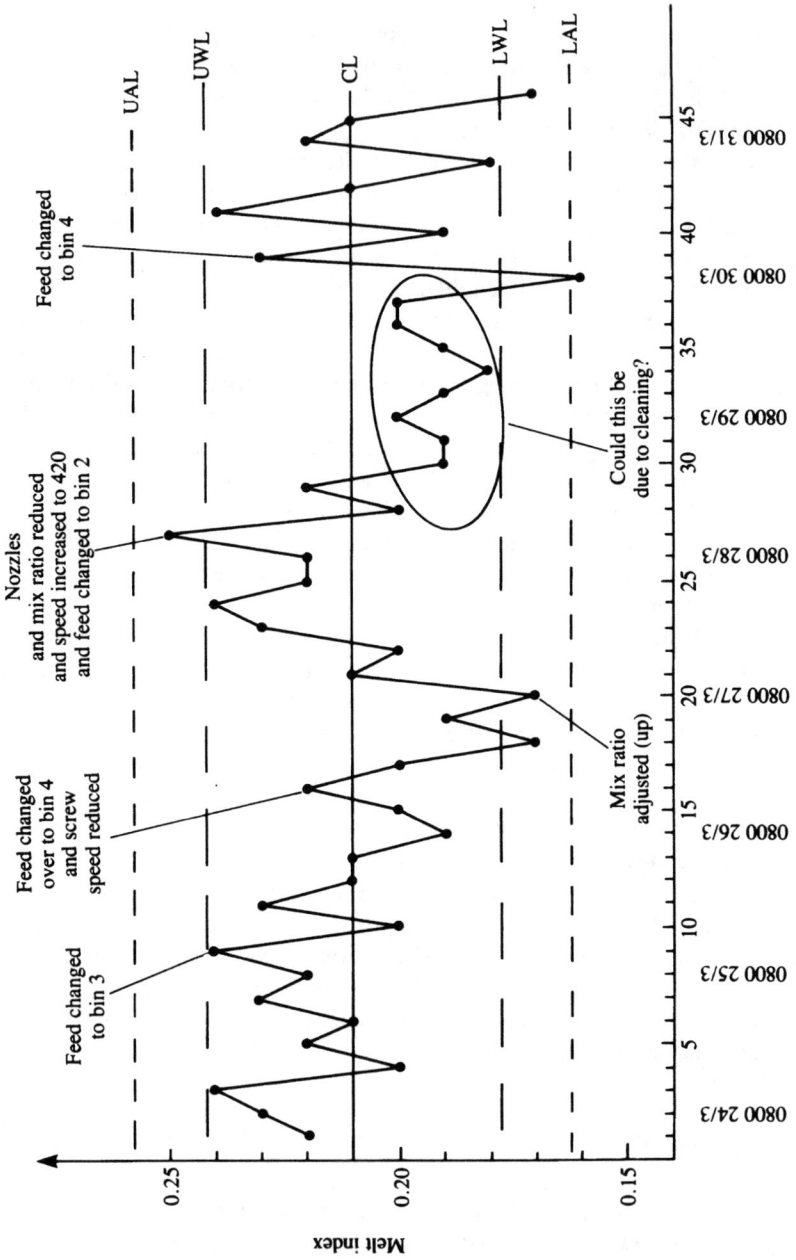

**Figure 7.1**

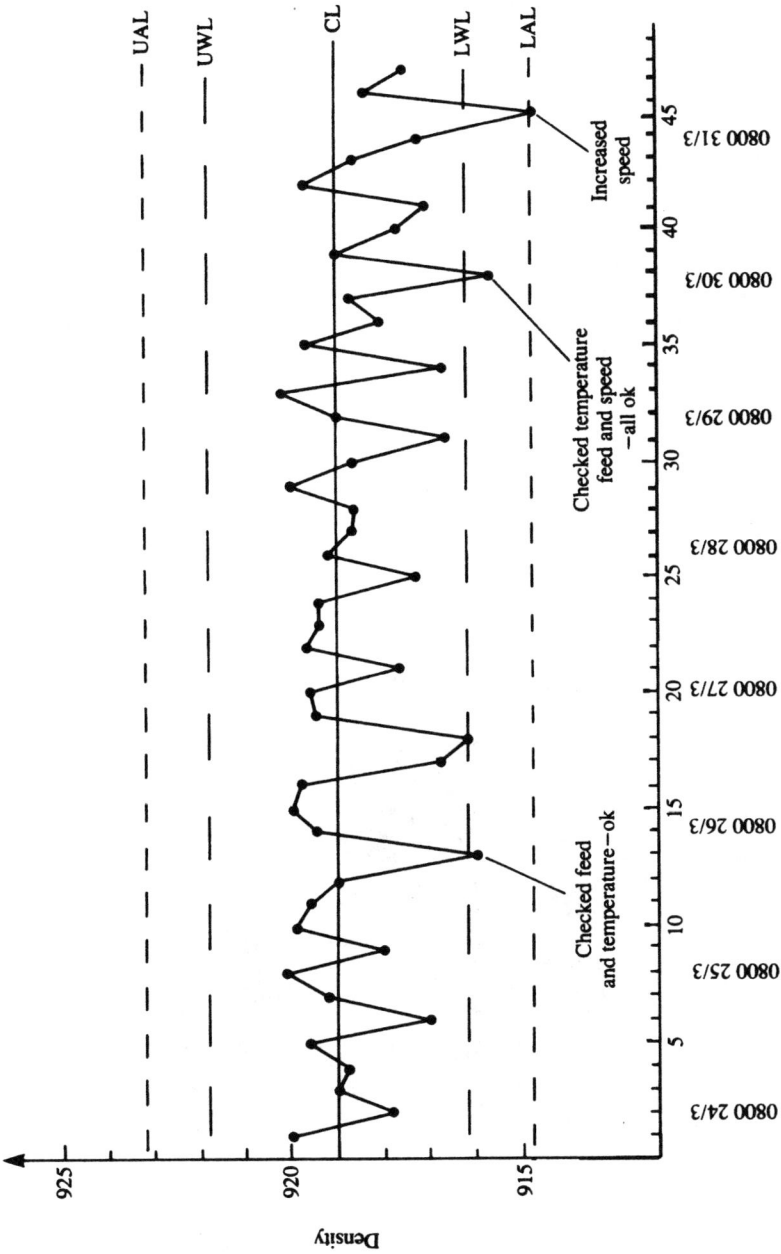

**Figure 7.2**

7.4). Suspecting that Ron and Didier might not be familiar with these indices, Bill Johnson explained: 'Cp and Cpk are process capability indices. An index less than 1 implies that we are producing polymer which is outside the specification'.

'Good heavens', Ron gasped, 'This index is only 0.7188. That must be terrible'. He was looking at the capability analysis for melt index. Below the histogram he had noticed; 'Cp = 0.7188'. 'Well, it's certainly not good', Bill agreed. 'But the Cpk is slightly worse, at 0.6793'.

Didier had been scrutinizing the density analysis, but he now turned his attention to melt index. 'Just a minute, Bill, these capability indices are crazy. You said that a Cp or Cpk less than 1 indicated out-of-spec polymer, but you can see in the histogram that every melt index result was within the specification'. 'You're right', Bill acknowledged, 'they are all in spec.

File: A: \CASE.DAT
Melt index

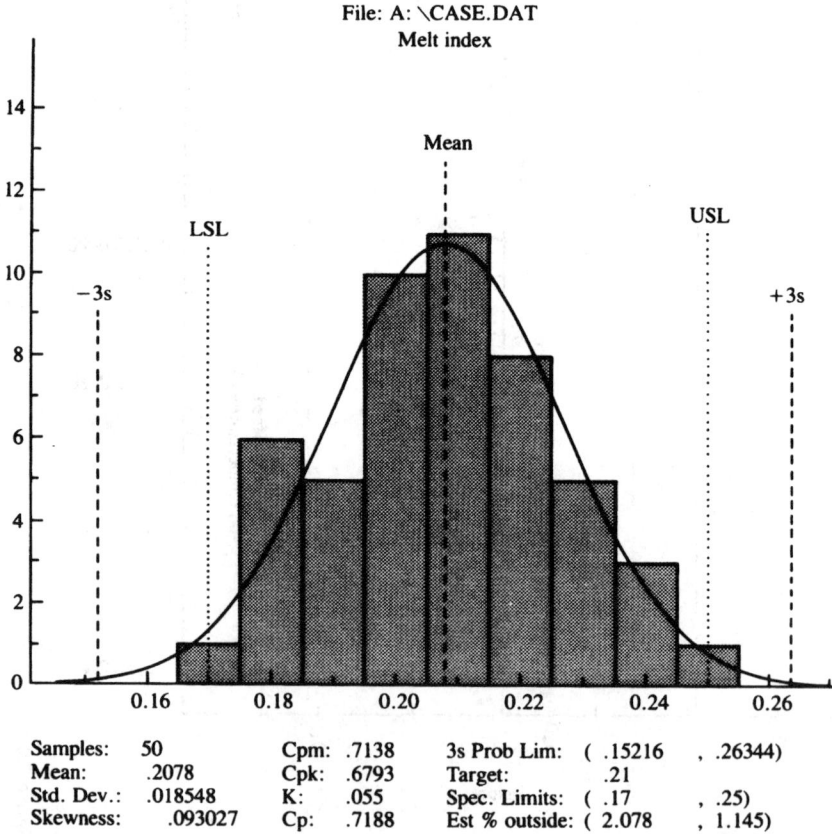

| Samples: | 50 | Cpm: | .7138 | 3s Prob Lim: | ( .15216 | , .26344) |
| Mean: | .2078 | Cpk: | .6793 | Target: | .21 | |
| Std. Dev.: | .018548 | K: | .055 | Spec. Limits: | ( .17 | , .25) |
| Skewness: | .093027 | Cp: | .7188 | Est % outside: | ( 2.078 | , 1.145) |

**Figure 7.3**

File: A: \CASE.DAT
Density

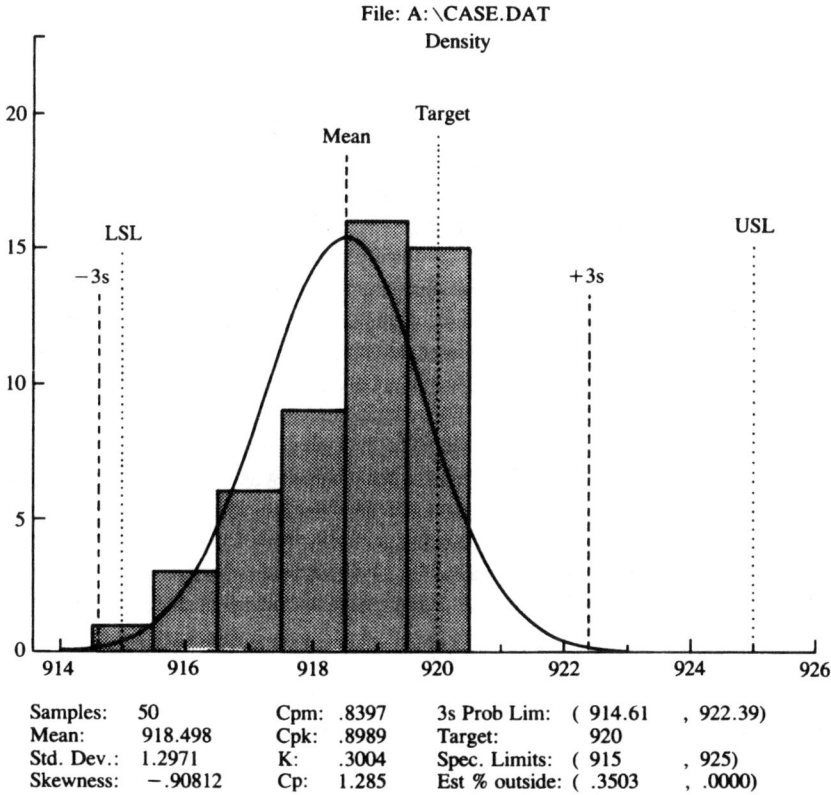

| Samples: | 50 | Cpm: | .8397 | 3s Prob Lim: | ( 914.61 | , 922.39) |
|---|---|---|---|---|---|---|
| Mean: | 918.498 | Cpk: | .8989 | Target: | 920 | |
| Std. Dev.: | 1.2971 | K: | .3004 | Spec. Limits: | ( 915 | , 925) |
| Skewness: | −.90812 | Cp: | 1.285 | Est % outside: | ( .3503 | , .0000) |

**Figure 7.4**

Capability indices can be very misleading. I think the picture is more informative but Porritt are asking for calculated indices'.

'They are asking for capability indices and I've got to provide them,' Ron Howard asserted, and continued, 'How do we know that this is the best we can do? This data only covers about 8 days, I guess. If we use more results we might get bigger capability indices. Have you tried any other data, Bill?' 'Yes, I have. The more data I use, the lower the capability·indices I seem to get. I suppose this is to be expected. It's quite easy to produce consistent results over a very short period, but much more difficult to achieve this over a long period'. At this point Didier exploded. 'The other analysis is even more crazy. It gives a Cp of 1.285, even though one of the results is out of spec. How do you explain that, Bill?' 'Well, the Cp index doesn't take account of whether we are on target or not. So it's only an indication of what we could achieve if we were on target. On the other hand, the Cpk does take account of the setting of the process, which is why the Cpk is usually lower. It is 0.8989 in this case'. 'You're right, Bill, the mean process density is only 918.5 but the centre of the specification is 920', Ron confirmed. Turning to the Production Manager, he asked; 'Could you not get closer than that?'

Didier was slow to respond. He could not explain why the mean density should be so low during this period, but he noticed that the centre line on the control chart was set at 919 rather than 920, which he would have expected. He wondered if the extruder manager had changed the chart recently or if the centre line had always been at 919, since the chart was set up. 'Perhaps it's got something to do with the peculiar shape of the density histogram,' he suggested. 'I'll tell you what, you guys, we are not going to sort this out today. I need to know exactly what is going on down at the extruders and how they are using these SPC charts'.

Ron was reasonably happy to postpone decisions until Bill and Didier could speak with more authority. On the other hand, he was extremely unhappy to be saddled with the burden of responding to customer requests of this nature. 'This is only the tip of the iceberg', he groaned. 'We haven't yet touched on question 7, about reduction of variation, and I haven't shown you the letter I received today from Jacksons. That could prove to be even more difficult' (see Appendix B).

## Broad issues from Charter Chemicals

Variation in product and process quality results from either random (common) causes or assignable (special) causes. When random causes only exist, they are likely to be elusive, and the process is described as being 'in statistical control' or stable. The capability of a process may be judged by checking that it is in control and assessing the degree of random variation. There must, however, be a distinction between process accuracy (centring or setting) and precision (spread). Accuracy is usually easier to change than improving precision. Processes distributions reflecting stability show evidence of only random causes of variability, and this output is predictable. A failure to understand and manage variation often leads to unjustified changes to the centring of the process, which can result in an unnecessary increase in the amount of variation.

Process capability is assessed generally by comparing the width of the tolerance or specification band with the overall spread of the process. This can be assessed by a comparison of the process standard deviation and the specification width, which gives the process capability indices. The Cp index is the ratio of the spec width to 6 standard deviations; the Cpk index is the ratio of the width between process mean and the closest tolerance limit, to

3 standard deviations. Hence, Cp measures the potential capability of the process, if centred; Cpk measures the process capability, including its centring. Values of the standard deviation, and hence Cp and Cpk, depend on the origin of the data used, as well as the method of calculation. Unless the origin of the data is known, the interpretation of the results will be confused.

The capability of a process, and the Cp or Cpk values are a function of the specification, the total random variations and the techniques for control. The process precision results from the sum of multiple sources of random variation, and can only be reduced by identifying and addressing these sources. 'Blending', of any sort, including extrusion, is an operation which can disguise the real causes of process variability. Failure to recognize, investigate and eliminate assignable causes of variation means that they can go on needlessly adding to the total variation. Evaluating process capability from data should lead to the identification of major problem areas. The actual behaviour of processes is never totally known; the constant presence of random variations always masks the absolute truth. The interpretation of the control charts in this case can be assisted by examining their likely behaviour for assumed changes to a process. Variability must be managed. Assignable causes must be recognized and *their* causes investigated – no compromise is sensible.

For successful use of SPC, there must be management commitment to quality, a quality policy, and a documented quality system. The main objective of the system should be to cause improvements through reduction in variation in processes. Teamwork plays a vital role in continuous improvement and good communication mechanisms are essential for successful SPC. Improvements based on teamwork around the processes and the techniques of SPC should lead to quality products, lower costs, better communications and job satisfaction, increased productivity market share and profits and higher employment.

Implementing SPC is not an easy process, but the requirement to adopt SPC techniques is growing rapidly in all industries. The simple recording and charting of process data and information can have a significant impact on understanding, enthusiasm for quality and subsequent performance. Customers are increasingly pressing for knowledge of process capability and this external 'threat' can be a very effective source of motivation to do something. However, the implementation of SPC techniques, without a proper understanding of their meaning, can be disastrous. Understanding includes the following:

- All work is carried out by processes.
- The responsibility for managing processes and product quality needs to be shared.

- There is always process variation present.
- 'Failure' requires investigation and remedial action, not apportionment of blame.
- Common training is a route to common understanding.

Without understanding, commitment and support from senior management, no management system, including SPC, can succeed. A major barrier to the effective introduction of SPC is often an unwillingness to devote adequate resources to proper training at all levels of the organization.

## Acknowledgement

This is from a case study by Roland Caulcutt, BP Chemicals Lecturer in SPC, University of Bradford.

# Appendix A

**PORRITT PIPES**

Gas Kiln Street
Brudford
Darkshire
BD81 3LT

Mr R Howard
Technical Services Manager,
Charter Chemicals
Northend Road
Barfield
Midshire

Dear Mr Howard,

*Material Quality – Supplier Capability*

Now that our major suppliers have achieved registration to BS5750 (ISO9000, EN2900), the next stage in our Total Quality Management initiative requires that we review the capability of all suppliers. We believe that our ability to meet the increasing demands of our customers is dependent upon our receiving raw materials of consistent quality.

Thus we need suppliers who can demonstrate their ability to produce to the target value with minimum variation. Mere conformance to specification can no longer be regarded as a guarantee of contract renewal.

You supply us with the following:

1 High-density polyethylene – Grade CC20
2 High-density polyethylene – Grade CC21
3 High-density polyethylene – Grade CC22

For each of the items listed would you please supply the following information:

1 Are you using statistical process control charts to monitor the manufacturing process?
2 If the answer to question 1 is 'No', what plans do you have for the introduction of SPC charts?
3 If the answer to question 1 is 'Yes', please provide copies of charts recently completed.

4 Can you quote values of appropriate process capability indices for each of the parameters in the agreed specification?

5 If the answer to question 4 is 'No', what plans do you have for the determination of capability indices in the future?

6 If the answer to question 4 is 'Yes', please supply appropriate indices and supporting diagrams based on the data from which the indices were calculated.

7 What procedures and techniques are you using to achieve long-term reduction in variation from delivery to delivery?

We appreciate that you may not be able to supply all of this information immediately, but we hope that you will endeavour to provide as much as possible and to establish procedures whereby you can quickly respond to further requests of this nature.


Yours sincerely,




P Johnson
Quality Manager

# Appendix B

**JACKSON PLASTICS**
**Industry Road**
**Hallfield**
**Gloomshire**
**HD13 4LX**


Mr R. Howard
Technical Services Manager
Charter Chemicals
Northend Road
Barfield
Midshire


Dear Mr Howard,

Further to our letter 31st March and your reply of 16th April, we agree with your conclusion that you are 'very close to the target on average'. Furthermore, we accept that the melt index of your polyethylene is as consistent, from delivery to delivery, as that we receive from other suppliers. *None the less, we find that your polymer does not perform well in our injection moulders.*

When using your polymer we get more void and weak spots in our moulded components. Clearly, one single defective granule of polyethylene can cause a defect in a component. We do not ask you to guarantee every granule, of course; we simply require you to furnish evidence of variation from granule to granule within each 5 tonne delivery.


Yours sincerely,



John Blackburn
Quality Manager

# 8 Quality costing at Zentech Computer Services Ltd

## Introduction

Zentech Computer Services Ltd was originally part of a larger conglomerate, the Lennox Group PLC. Lennox developed over the last 20 years through a series of mergers and take-overs. Late ventures into the computer industry proved to be unsuccessful and seriously damaged the group's financial performance. Two years ago, Lennox was forced into a major rationalization process. The computer services division was the subject of a management buy-out just under a year ago and Zentech Computer Services Ltd was formed. Alan Brooke, the present Managing Director, was the driving force behind this buy-out.

## Background

Zentech provides a number of computer bureau services, including payroll and accounting services. It employs 40 full-time staff and is located in Bradford. The company operates a large mainframe computer from its Bradford office. This is used to process clients' data. A small team of computer programmers and analysts is based in Reading. The programmers, and some of the users, are linked to the computer by a communications network. Also linked into the network is a computer in Manchester, which is owned by another organization; this latter machine provides back-up in the event of a failure of the Bradford machine. A diagram of the network is shown in Figure 8.1.

During the current trading year, the company expects sales of approximately £3.6m. As a result of the buy-out and the recent sale of a 'non-core' business, there are no meaningful comparative accounts for previous years. The Finance Director is currently designing a system of management

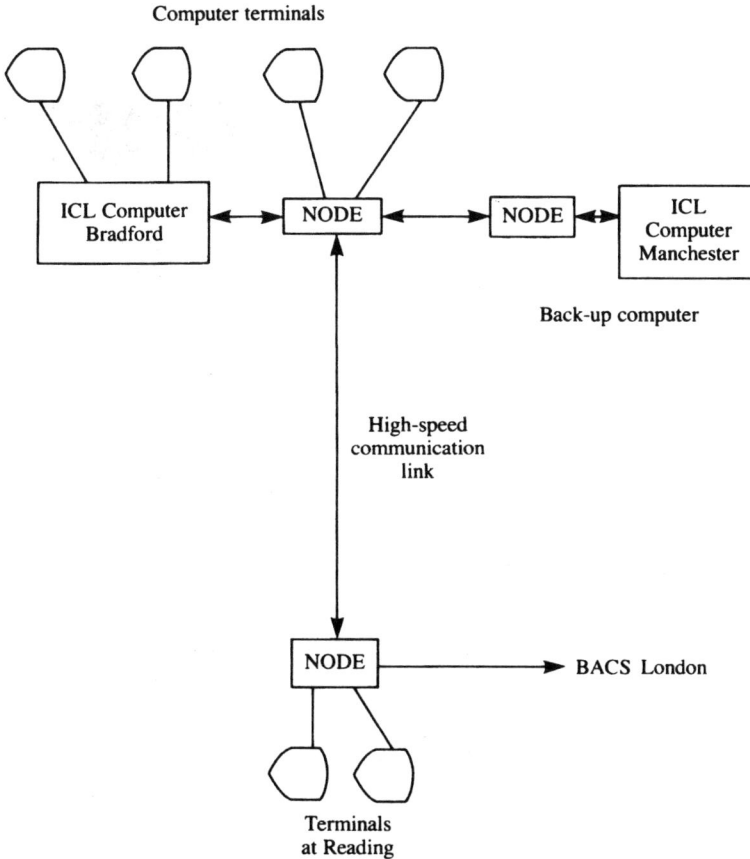

**Figure 8.1** *Communication network*

accounts. Appendix A gives a projected trading profit-and-loss account for the current financial year. A summary balance sheet at the time of the buy-out is shown in Appendix B.

## Company Services

The company operates a range of services (i.e. separate software suites), mostly in the field of payroll, sales ledger and purchase ledger. Some of these services are 20 years old, whilst new systems are currently being developed. Depending upon the services, customers may submit data to the company for processing in the form of paper documents (by post or fax), by telephone, or

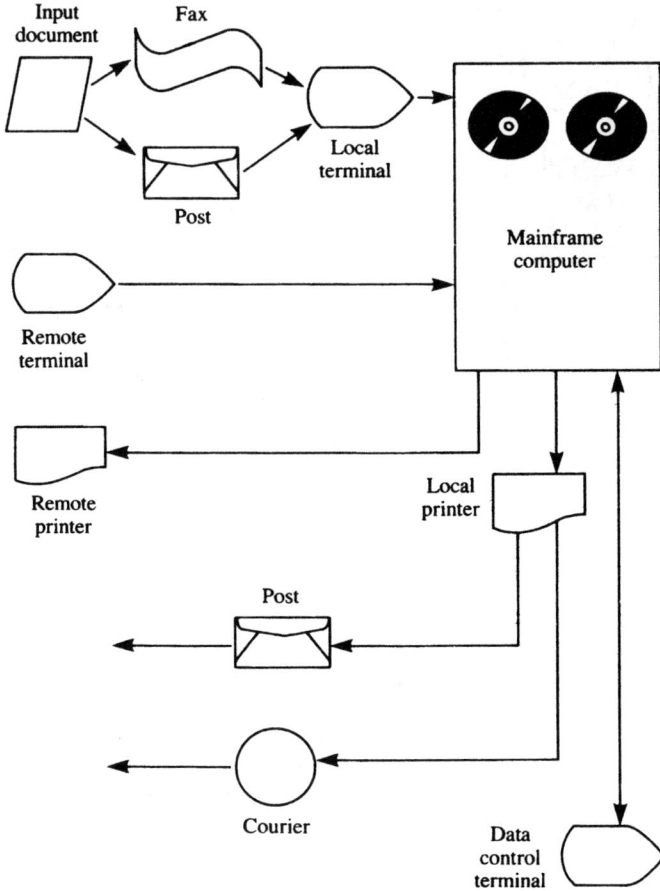

**Figure 8.2** *Key elements of service*

by computer terminal. Output may be returned to customers as printed documents (by post or courier) or may be printed out on a remote printer in the client's own premises. The key elements of the services offered are shown in Figure 8.2.

Many of the company's services were originally developed by third-party organizations, such as major accounting firms or banks. An example of this is the WIZZ-PAY service. Further details of this service can be found in Appendix C. Other services are the traditional direct services, where the company processes data directly on behalf of the client company. Many of the company's direct customers are small businesses employing 20–50 people. However, a number of large organizations, such as municipal councils and

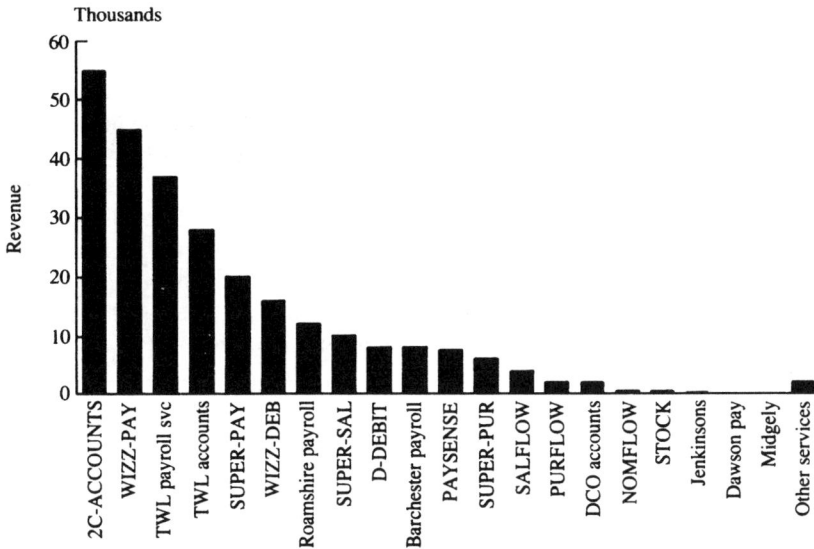

**Figure 8.3** *Zentech Computer Services Ltd: profile of services as at March*

health authorities, directly use the company's services. All third-party services are exclusive to a particular customer, although they often use similar computer programs. Some of the direct services are exclusive to a single direct client; others are generalized and are used by a variety of clients. A key feature of most services is the ability to transfer funds directly to recipients' accounts by means of direct transfer to the Bankers' Automated Clearance System (BACS).

Zentech's revenue depends heavily upon a handful of services. A diagram showing how revenue varies between services can be found in Figure 8.3. Further details are shown in Appendix D.

## Company organization

The day-to-day management of the various services is controlled by the four Product Managers, each of whom has a number of data control staff to check input, set up appropriate controls to ensure that the data is correctly processed, and check that output is correct.

The four product groups are:

1 Third-party services – Payroll.
2 Third-party services – Accounts.

3 Direct services – Payroll and Accounts.
4 Other services.

To provide immediate help to any user experiencing difficulties, the company operates a Help Desk, which is staffed throughout office hours. This acts as a first point of contact for all users, irrespective of service. The operation of the company's computers is in the hands of the Operations Department. This department also ensures that the communications network operates correctly.

The company employs approximately 40 full-time employees and between 10 and 30 part-time data preparation staff. Data preparation is undertaken at Bradford. The organization chart of the company is shown in Figure 8.4.

## Assignment

You have been asked by the Managing Director of Zentech Computer Services Ltd (Mr Alan Brooke) to prepare an estimate of the company's quality costs. This is required before the next Board Meeting. Because of the short time available, you only have time to make five interviews before preparing your draft report. Mr Brooke has arranged for all directors to be available tomorrow.

On your previous visit to the company you have established the information contained in the attached Zentech Computer Services Case Study. Your task is to review the Case Study material and then plan out your interviews.

The assignment can be handled as a group or individual exercise.

### Group exercise

Team members role-play the five directors who are interviewed by the remaining team members. Interview Briefs are provided for this role-playing. The whole team discuss their experiences in gathering and providing information, which is a central part of quality costing.

### Individual exercise

When you have decided what questions to ask the directors, you should proceed to the next part of the case, Interview Briefs. This details the information that was available. Compare this with the information that you would have obtained. You may have learnt something about the difficulties of estimating quality costs.

After conducting the interviews and gathering the available information, the team or individual should prepare a quality cost report.

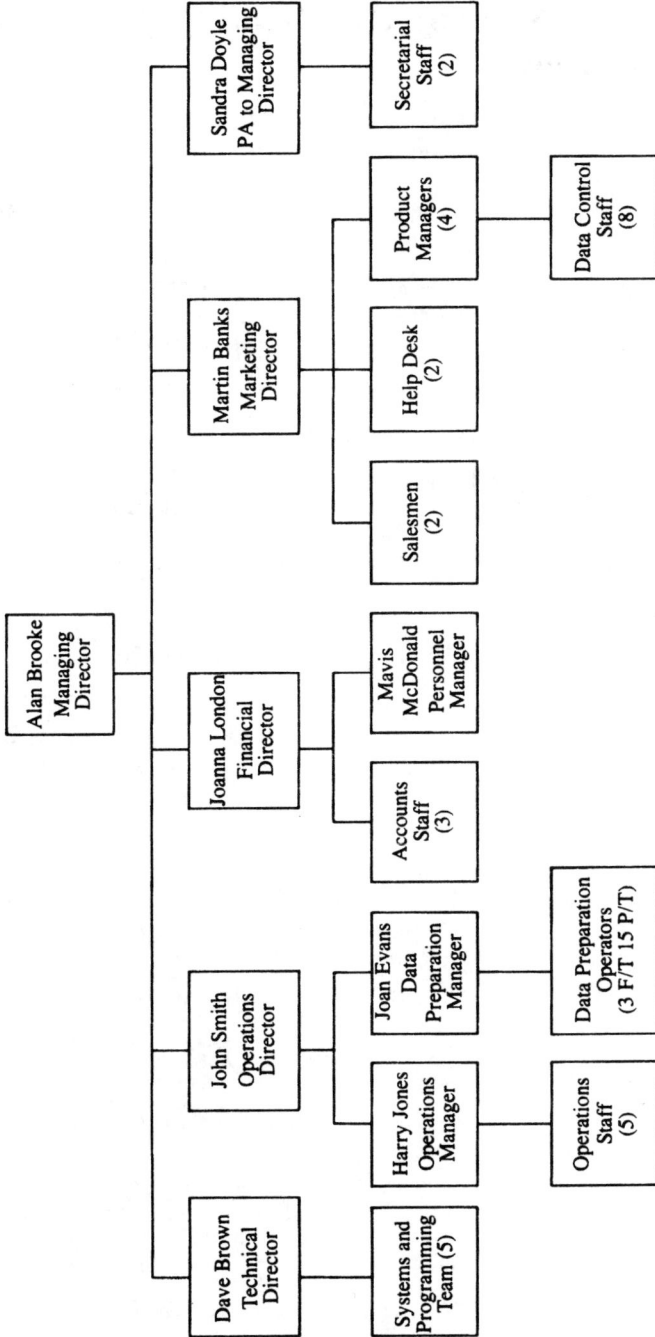

**Figure 8.4** *Zentech Computer Services: organization chart*

# Appendix A: Projected trading profit and loss for year

|  | £ | £ |
|---|---:|---:|
| Revenue |  | 3,550,000 |
| *Costs* |  |  |
| Payroll and salaries | 1,550,000 |  |
| Purchases and supplies | 150,000 |  |
| Premises – rent, rates, etc. | 150,000 |  |
| Computer costs (maintenance and rental) | 50,000 |  |
| Communications network costs (maintenance and rental) | 100,000 |  |
| Back-up computer costs | 75,000 |  |
| Depreciation | 550,000 |  |
| Other costs | 350,000 |  |
| Total costs |  | 2,975,000 |
| Trading profit |  | 575,000 |

# Appendix B: Summary balance sheet

*Fixed assets*

| | | |
|---|---|---|
| Computers | 3,985,00 | |
| Cars | 195,000 | |
| Other assets | 190,000 | |
| Less depreciation | 1,635,000 | |
| | | 2,735,000 |

*Current assets*

| | | |
|---|---|---|
| Cash at bank | 45,000 | |
| Debtors | 505,000 | |
| Stocks | 325,000 | |
| | 875,000 | |

*Current liabilities*

| | | |
|---|---|---|
| Creditors | 210,000 | |
| | 210,000 | |
| Net current assets | | 665,000 |
| Total assets | | 3,400,000 |

*Financed by*

| | | |
|---|---|---|
| Paid-up share capital | 300,000 | |
| Loans | 3,100,000 | |
| | | 3,400,000 |

# Appendix C: Press release

Chartered Accountants Store and Co are transferring the operation of the computer-based payroll service that they operate on behalf of their clients to Zentech Computer Services Ltd.

The service, to be known as WIZZ-PAY, will be transferred from the computer currently operated by Store to Zentech's powerful ICL computer located at Bradford.

The transfer will provide Store's clients with many benefits:

- Eliminate the need for a cost increase that would otherwise have been inevitable.
- More flexible data entry, allowing clients to submit data through on-line terminals or via telephone as well as by hand-written documents.
- More comprehensive assistance through use of Zentech's Help Desk.

Responsibility for the system will remain with Store, says Partner Clive Parker. 'By transferring the operation of our service to the specialists, we can provide our many small-business clients with a better deal at a lower cost. It leaves us free to concentrate on giving our clients financial advice'.

Zentech Managing Director Alan Brooke claims that the deal is a part of Zentech's strategy of concentrating on the areas where it has a clear competitive advantage – the provision of third-party computer bureau services.

# Appendix D: Zentech Computer Services Ltd: profile of services – as at March

| Service | Application | Type | Customer | Date commenced | Monthly revenue (£) |
|---|---|---|---|---|---|
| 2C-ACCOUNTS | Accounting | Third-party | 2c Investors | 1984 | 54,567 |
| WIZZ-PAY | Payroll | Third-party | Wizzo & Co | 1991 | 44,298 |
| TWL Payroll Svc | Payroll | Third-party | TWL | 1987 | 36,450 |
| TWL Accounts | Accounting | Third-party | TWL | 1985 | 24,534 |
| SUPER-PAY | Payroll | Third-party | Bank of Heligoland | 1990 | 19,425 |
| WIZZ-DEB | Purchase ledger | Third-party | Wizzo & Co | 1991 | 14,550 |
| Roamshire Payroll | Payroll | Direct | Roamshire Health | 1986 | 11,523 |
| SUPER-SAL | Sales ledger | Third-party | Bank of Heligoland | 1989 | 9,678 |
| D-DEBIT | Direct debit | Third-party | 2c Investors | 1982 | 8,130 |
| Barchester Payroll | Payroll | Direct | Barchester CC | 1984 | 7,910 |
| PAYSENSE | Payroll | Direct | Various | 1978 | 6,844 |
| SUPER-PUR | Purchase ledger | Third-party | Bank of Heligoland | 1989 | 5,407 |
| SALFLOW | Sales ledger | Direct | Various | 1983 | 3,180 |
| PURFLOW | Purchase ledger | Direct | Various | 1981 | 2,004 |
| DCO Accounts | Accounts | Direct | Various | 1971 | 1,936 |
| NOMFLOW | Nominal ledger | Direct | Various | 1982 | 1,077 |
| STOCK | Stock control | Direct | Various | 1973 | 993 |
| Jenkinsons | Stock control | Direct | Jenkinsons | 1977 | 375 |
| Dawson Pay | Payroll | Direct | Dawson Fibres | 1986 | 295 |
| Midgely | Payroll | Direct | Midgely M/c Co | 1983 | 250 |
| Other services | Various | Direct | Various | 1971 | 1,875 |
| Total | | | | | 255,301 |

# Zentech Computer Services Ltd interview briefs

## Managing Director's brief

### *Alan Brooke*

### *1. Information to volunteer*

1.1   You were instrumental in organizing the buy-out. You felt that the previous owners didn't understand the business and neglected it. They didn't invest. You intend to rectify their mistakes.

1.2   You are concerned about quality, especially since a mistake in processing a customer's data could result in the company having to pay compensation.

1.3   You think that the company is wasting money through not getting quality right.

1.4   You need an estimate of quality costs to convince the rest of the Board that it is worth spending money on a TQM programme.

1.5   Your aim is for the company to be a major force in the third-party processing of data. You would like to be the largest company in this marketplace. You believe that working according to high standards will be essential to achieve this.

1.6   You are the Board Member most concerned to get the company's quality right.

### *2. Information to give if asked*

2.1   You currently spend about 10% of your time on activities related to investigating the causes of quality problems and the organization of actions to prevent their recurrence.

2.2   Under the previous management there was no attempt to capitalize on the company's strengths – especially its ability to run profitably other systems that third parties could only provide at a loss. You are now making this a major feature of your marketing plans.

2.3 The company recently had to pay compensation for lost interest to users of the SUPER-SAL service because of a failure to transfer funds into their bank accounts. The incident cost the company £1,250. It also damaged the firm's credibility with certain people within the client organization.

2.4 You now insure against compensation claims. The Financial Director knows the details.

2.5 You often have to use couriers to get output to customers within agreed time limits. Better organization would have meant that you could use the post. You don't know what sums are involved.

2.6 The operations department frequently has to rerun jobs. You don't know exactly how frequently.

2.7 You were recently informed that the operations department has overordered preprinted stationery and it had to scrap several years' supply of a certain type of pay-slip.

2.8 You believe that data control staff are underused and poorly managed. They often seem to have nothing to do and spend much time chatting amongst themselves; at the same time they appear to work a lot of overtime.

2.9 You are concerned about the large number of software faults that are reported. In the last month you have had four people write to you directly as a result of faults in the software on which your services are based. Each such complaint involved your PA spending half a day investigating the cause and drafting a letter in reply; two incidents involved your spending half a day discussing the matter with clients.

2.10 You are also concerned that it has taken 3 months longer than expected to get the WIZZ-PAY service fully converted and operational. This has damaged your credibility with the client. WIZZ-PAY involved an unplanned upgrading of the computer hardware at a cost of £5,000 per month. The delay in bringing it on stream has delayed the receipt of revenue and damaged the company's cash flow.

2.11 The Finance Director is developing an improved management accounting system. This will calculate the contribution that each service makes to overheads. Details have not yet been finalized.

2.12 Directors all receive the same basic salary of £30,000 p.a.

2.13 Your PA's salary is approximately £17,500 p.a.

# Financial Director's brief

## *Joanna London*

### *1. Information to volunteer*

1.1   Your principal role is to conserve the company's working capital and to introduce an effective system of budgetary control.

1.2   You have experience of several companies that installed ISO9000/ BS5750-based quality assurance systems. They spent a lot of money, used up a lot of executive time, and generated a lot of paper but as far as you could see not one additional penny of profit was generated.

1.3   You believe that the accounts department is now very efficient. Monthly accounts are now available within 5 days of month-end.

1.4   The cash-flow situation is tighter than expected at the time of the buy-out.

1.5   You are now able to prepare management accounts for key services and a comprehensive system which establishes the profitability of each service will be available shortly.

### *2. Information to give if asked*

2.1   A major reason for the tight cash flow is that the new WIZZ-PAY service required the installation of additional computer hardware. The need for this was only realized part-way through the conversion of the service from its previous third-party operator. No allowance was made for this in the price agreed with the customer. This reduced the expected monthly profits by approximately £5,000 per month. In addition, the delay in bringing the service on stream lost profit and cash flow.

2.2   The majority of bank lending is through fixed-term loans. However, you also have a substantial overdraft, for which the company pays 3% over the bank base rate.

2.3   The new management accounting system will be based on making each service a profit centre. You are already able to prepare draft monthly accounts on this basis for a number of the services. An example of the accounts for third-party payroll services is attached (FDB1).

2.4   You believe that third-party payroll services are typical of the company as a whole.

2.5 The new management accounting system will allocate all direct costs to a specific service. In addition it apportions, on a pro rata basis, the computer and communications resources used.

2.6 Credits are a major problem. These result from a variety of causes. On a number of services (e.g. WIZZ-PAY) the company warrants the level of service that is to be provided and is contracted and obliged to pay compensation if certain tasks are not completed on time; this accounts for about 60% of credits.

2.7 Invoices are calculated manually from information printed out by the computer and sometimes errors result (about 5% of credits). Customers hardly ever complain that they have been undercharged. You imagine that as many invoices are sent out undercharged as overcharged.

2.8 The total value of credits given in March was approximately £11,500.

2.9 The manual processing of credits is time-consuming and takes one accounts clerk approximately 1 week per month to handle.

2.10 Since having to pay compensation to SUPER-SAL users, you have taken out insurance at a cost of £5,000 p.a. This is to cover contingent liabilities – not any contractual compensation arrangements.

2.11 The average salary of accounts clerks is £15,000.

2.12 National Insurance, etc. adds the equivalent of 12.5% of salary to the cost of employing staff.

2.13 As well as a basic salary, all directors receive a company car costing approximately £4,000 p.a. and the company pays an additional 2.5% of salary into a pension fund.

## FDB1 Breakdown of costs and revenue by service for the month of March

| | WIZZ -PAY £ | TWL pay £ | SUPER -PAY £ | Total third party payroll £ |
|---|---|---|---|---|
| Invoiced revenue | 44,298 | 36,450 | 19,425 | 100,173 |
| Less credits | 2,575 | 690 | 850 | 4,115 |
| Net revenue | 41,723 | 35,760 | 18,575 | 96,058 |
| *Direct costs* | | | | |
| Special hardware costs | 4,950 | 0 | 0 | 4,950 |
| Share of product manager | .5 | .25 | .25 | 1 |
| Product manager costs @ £21,500 p.a. | 10,750 | 5,375 | 5,375 | 21,500 |
| Data control staff | 1.25 | .75 | .5 | 2.5 |
| Data control cost @ £13,750 each pm | 17,188 | 10,313 | 6,875 | 34,375 |
| Data preparation hours | 295 | 225 | 205 | 725 |
| Data preparation costs @ £6.50 per h | 1,918 | 1,463 | 1,333 | 4,713 |
| Special stationery | 400 | 200 | 150 | 750 |
| Courier costs | 1,950 | 125 | 0 | 2,075 |
| Postage costs | 525 | 375 | 450 | 1,350 |
| Total direct costs | 37,680 | 17,850 | 14,183 | 69,713 |
| *Recoverable costs* | | | | |
| Computer time (hours) | 22 | 20.5 | 15 | 57.5 |
| Computer cost @ £152.00 per hour | 3,344 | 3,116 | 2,280 | 8,740 |
| Communications network usage (units) | 32,250 | 31,250 | 20,750 | 84,250 |
| Network cost @ 0.005 £/unit | 161 | 156 | 104 | 421 |
| | 3,505 | 3,272 | 2,384 | 9,161 |
| Total costs | 41,185 | 21,122 | 16,566 | 78,874 |
| Contribution to overheads | 538 | 14,638 | 2,009 | 17,184 |

# Technical Director's brief

## *Dave Brown*

### *1. Information to volunteer*

1.1 Your principal task is to maintain the software of existing systems. With any spare resources you also develop new systems – such as WIZZ-PAY.

1.2 You take quality very seriously and devote a lot of resources to ensuring quality. Your Senior Programmer is responsible for quality control.

1.3 You have already organized some training on quality assurance and you have already investigated the possibility of implementing TQM within the Systems and Programming team.

1.4 You believe that increasing resources to handle all the extra work being placed upon your department is more important than spending on external consultants.

1.5 The computer hardware is now obsolescent and the techniques that must be used to develop and maintain software are out-of-date. The purchase of new hardware and software development tools would allow your staff to become much more productive and ensure more reliable software.

1.6 You feel that your department is frequently blamed for the mistakes of others.

### *2. Information to give if asked*

2.1 Maintaining existing systems – correcting software faults when they are discovered and making minor changes (e.g. when the Chancellor changes the rules about PAYE) – takes up about four programmers. This leaves yourself and the Senior Programmer to work on new services.

2.2 Approximately two-thirds of maintenance work is correcting faults and one-third is making minor changes.

2.3 The Senior Programmer spends 75% of his time on quality control of software i.e. testing software to ensure that it works correctly. This covers fault correction, minor changes and new services.

2.4 The Senior Programmer has recently been on a 1-week course in software quality assurance at the National Computer Centre – cost

£1,250. He has also recently attended a seminar at the Institute of Software Engineering – cost £295.

2.5   The department now has fewer than half the people it had 10 years ago with which to support more services than ever before. You suspect that this results in inadequate testing of software.

2.6   Although you have been visited by many sales staff, trying to sell you productivity tools and software testing systems, you have no firm estimates of cost or clear identifications of the benefits that would be achieved.

2.7   A big problem is that you often have to work to very tight deadlines on work that has not been fully specified. A good example is the WIZZ-PAY system. This was supposed to be a simple conversion job requiring about 2 months of work by yourself and the Senior Programmer. In fact it required whole sections of the software to be rewritten. Moreover, the marketing department kept asking for changes, so you frequently had to rewrite sections that had already been changed. You managed to complete the work in 4 months – but only by taking staff off essential maintenance work. Just when you thought that you had finished, the marketing department asked you to prepare user manuals – this took you and the Senior Programmer another month.

2.8   The experience of WIZZ-PAY is not unique. You estimate that about 10% of all the development work (new services and minor changes) that you do is wasted because it has to be redone (free of charge) to accommodate changes in requirements.

2.9   You are now trying to clear the back-log of faults and minor changes that have built up in the other services, as well as handling all those that are being generated by the WIZZ-PAY service.

2.10  Many so-called software faults aren't actually faults in the programs but the result of operators not running them correctly. Given time, you could make the systems foolproof. You have personally been working with the Operations Director on this over the last year and have spent about half your time rewriting some sections of software and preparing operating instructions in order to help prevent further operator errors.

2.11  Programmers' salaries average £18,000 p.a. The Senior Programmer's salary is £21,500 p.a.

# Operations Director's brief

## *John Smith*

### *1. Information to volunteer*

1.1 The operations department is the heart of the business. Not enough attention has been devoted to meeting its needs.

1.2 You have basically an excellent staff. In the past they have been poorly paid, poorly trained and poorly managed. You are trying to put these problems right.

1.3 Your department is often wrongly blamed for what are really the faults of others; for example, incorrect processing of data where there are no operating instructions to guide staff in what were the correct procedures.

1.4 Some of the computer hardware is old and becoming unreliable. It always seems to fail at the most critical time and this can result in your missing deadlines with all sorts of consequences.

1.5 Services have rarely been designed with the needs of operators in mind. As a result, they are difficult to operate and costly errors sometimes result.

1.6 The workload of your department is very 'peaky'. Everyone seems to want payrolls on the same day of the week and everyone wants accounts to be processed immediately after the end of the month. Marketing don't seem to try to spread the workload.

### *2. Information to give if asked*

2.1 Until recently the Operations Department was not involved in the preparation of tenders or sales proposals. This has now been rectified. You have now started to spend about half a day per week checking the implications of tenders and proposals before they are issued.

2.2 You have instigated a training programme designed to ensure that there are no errors in operation. Each operator now spends about half a day per month being trained. About one-third of this is related to quality control.

2.3 Until recently there were virtually no written operating instructions. Everything relied on the operator's memory. To put this right you have personally been working with the Systems and Programming Director on this over the last year and have spent about 20% of your time preparing operating instructions. Also, your Operations Manager spends about 10% of his time on the same task.

2.4   You frequently have to rerun work. Sometimes your operators discover the problem; sometimes the problem is found by Data Control and sometimes by the customer. You have started to keep a rerun Diary. A page from a recent month is attached (ODB2). You believe this month was quite typical.

2.5   Organizing reruns and the necessary resetting of files is one of the major tasks of the Operations Managers. It occupies about 20% of their time.

2.6   The Operations Managers are paid approximately £19,000 p.a.

2.7   You normally operate the computers for a single shift every working day and operate a planned second shift at month-end (the peak for accounting work) and on Thursdays (the peak for payroll). You operate the computers for additional time (for which operators are paid a 50% premium) at peak periods and to overcome any breakdowns.

2.8   Last month your operators worked 67 hours overtime. Operators are typically paid about £250 per week for a 39-hour week.

2.9   Hardware breakdowns (computer and communications) have variable effects. For example, if part of the system fails, processing can sometimes continue on another job. However, downtime gives a reasonable guide. Last month there were 29 hours of downtime.

2.10 The computer was used for the equivalent of 232 hours during the last month.

2.11 The 'peaky' nature of processing is shown on the attached diagram (ODB1) Peaks are at:
(a) the start of the month;
(b) Thursdays (marked with a 'T');
(c) after periods of hardware breakdown (marked with a 'B').
The moving mean shows the monthly workload pattern.

2.12 An example of poor systems design is the SUPER-SAL service, which provides no feedback to operators on whether funds have been correctly transferred. Operators have to follow an exact procedure and the only way that you know it has worked correctly is if nobody complains. The trouble is that, when they do, Zentech have to pay compensation in the form of credits to the customer. You are trying to get the worst of these problems corrected.

2.13 The standby arrangements are written into contracts with some clients. They are only used if the computer is going to be down for more than 4 hours. They have only been used twice this year. On every other occasion when hardware failed, it was expected that the problem would be rectified more quickly.

2.14 The data preparation staff (keypunch and terminal operators) are almost all paid piecework based upon the number of keystrokes they make. There are few actual keying errors since everything is done twice – once to enter the data and a second time to verify. Comparison between the two is automatic and error correction is quick and simple. Data preparation costs about £6.50 per hour.

2.15 You are responsible for ordering computer stationery. Unfortunately, you are not always informed that software is due to be changed. As a result, you sometimes find special stationery becomes obsolete. You recently had to throw away £2,000 worth of stationery because of such a change.

## ODB1 Hours of computer usage: February–March

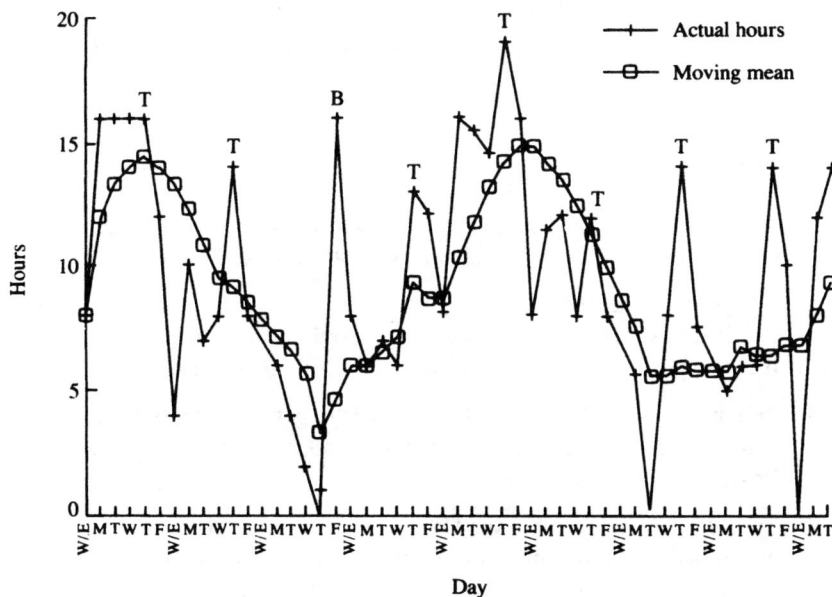

## ODB2 Rerun Diary

| Date | System | Discovered or reported by | Cause of problem | Hours machine time wasted |
|---|---|---|---|---|
| 2/3 | WIZZ-PAY | Operators | Software fault | 2.0 |
| 2/3 | 2C-ACCOUNTS | Operators | Incorrect operation | 1.5 |
| 9/3 | Jenkinsons | User | User error? | 0.5 |
| 12/3 | WIZZ-PAY | Data Control | Software fault | 3.5 |
| 14/3 | Barchester | User | Incorrect operation | 4.0 |
| 17/3 | NOMFLOW | Operators | Hardware breakdown | 1.0 |
| 17/3 | TWL Account | Data Control | User error | 0.25 |
| 18/3 | WIZZ-DEB | Data Control | Software upgrade | 0.75 |
| 18/3 | NOMFLOW | Operators | Hardware breakdown | 0.5 |
| 18/3 | SUPER-SAL | User | Incorrect operation | 2.5 |
| 23/3 | Several | Operators | Hardware breakdown | 3.25 |
| 25/3 | Roamshire | Data Control | User error | 0.25 |
| 26/3 | D-DEBIT | Data Control | Incorrect operation | 2.00 |
| Total | | | | 22 |

## Marketing Director's brief

### *Martin Banks*

#### *1. Information to volunteer*

1.1   You see your role as making Zentech fully customer-oriented and ensuring that the customer always gets what he/she wants.

1.2   You believe a quality assurance system would be especially valuable to the Systems and Programming and Operations departments, which you feel are poorly organized, inflexible and give poor service.

1.3   You are concerned about the time it takes to get new systems operational and the lack of control that seems to be exhibited within the Systems and Programming department.

1.4   You are now responsible for Data Control and the Help Desk. You are concerned about the number of software errors and operational mistakes that occur. These soak up large amounts of your staff's time.

1.5   You are particularly concerned about the long time that is required by Systems and Programming to correct errors and make minor changes.


## 2. Information to give if asked

2.1   The Help Desk provides a first line of support to users and customers. If they cannot resolve the problem they pass it on to the appropriate Data Control person. The Help Desk staff combined salaries are approximately £30,000 p.a. Their telephone costs are approximately £2,000 p.a.

2.2   Data Control staff check that incoming documentation and data from customers are correctly coded before passing it for preparation and/or processing. They also check that the results are correct before returning them to customers. About 25% of their time is involved with sorting out errors in preparation and/or processing. Another 25% is spent sorting out problems incurred by users and reported to the Help Desk.

2.3   Data control staff salaries average £18,500 p.a.

2.4   Product Managers are supposed to be there to assist you to plan the marketing of each type of service. In fact they spend much of their time (50%) organizing the resolution of customer problems and the correction of preparation/processing errors.

2.5   Product Mangers' salaries average £23,000 p.a.

2.6   Not all customer problems relate to mistakes by the company. In many cases users do not know how to operate the system properly. You have made Product Managers responsible for ensuring that customers operate the system correctly. They now spend about 10% of their time training users. During the last 12 months only 59 days of such user training were charged for.

2.7   Some faults reported over 4 months ago have still not been resolved. This has caused you to lose a major sale, which would have generated over £50,000 p.a. revenue.

2.8   Data Control staff suffer from a problem of peaks and troughs. They have to work particularly long hours at month-end when customers are preparing their monthly accounts. They do not receive overtime pay.

# Zentech Computer Services Ltd
# Quality cost calculations

## Notes on quality costs

The following estimates have been calculated from the information provided in the interview Briefs and are referenced, e.g. MD-2.1, Managing Director's brief part 2.1, and cross-referenced where appropriate, e.g. (FD-2.12). The quality costs have been categorized as prevention (P), appraisal (A), internal failure (IF) and external failure (EF).

| Case study section | Description and calculations | Annual costs | Cost category |
|---|---|---|---|
| **Managing Director's brief** | | | |
| MD-2.1 | QA activities = 10% of time<br>Salary = £30K (*see MD-2.12*)<br>+15% NHI, pension etc. (£4,500)<br>(*see FD-2.12/13*)<br>+car (say £4000 p.a.)<br>= £38,500 p.a. | £ 3,850 | P.1 |
| MD-2.3 | Compensation | £ 1,250 | EF.2 |
| MD-2.5 | Courier costs<br>£2,075 for third-party payroll for month<br>(*FDB1*)<br>= £24,900 p.a.<br>Third party payroll = 33% of company business | £74,700 | IF.2 |
| MD-2.9 | Investigating faults<br>4 * 1/2 day = 10% of time of PA<br>PA costs £17,500 p.a. (*MD-2.13*)+12.5%<br>(*FD-2.12*)<br>= £19,687 * 10% | £ 1,968 | IF.3 |
| MD-2.9 | 2 * 1/2 day = 5% of MD<br>MD = £38,500 p.a. (*see above*)<br>5% * £38,500 | £ 1,925 | IF.3 |
| MD-2.10 | Extra processing cost – not recharged | £60,000 | IF.2 |

## Financial Director's brief

| FD-2.6 | Credits–£11,500 p.m. (*FD-2.8*)<br>= £138,000 p.a.<br>60% = contractual compensation | £82,800 | EF.2 |
|---|---|---|---|
| FD-2.7 | Losses through undercalculating invoices<br>5% of £138,000 (*see above*) | £ 6,900 | IF.1 |
| FD-2.9 | Processing credits<br>1/4 of one accounts clerk at<br>£16,000 p.a. plus 12.5% (£2000) (*FD-2.12*)<br>= 1/4 * 18000 | £ 4,500 | EF.4 |
| FD-2.10 | Contingent liability insurance | £ 5,000 | EF.5 |

## Technical Director's brief

| TD-2.2 | Software fault correction<br>2/3 of 4 programmers = 2.67 programmers<br>Programmers cost £18,000 p.a. (*TD-2.11*)<br>plus 12.5% (£2,250) = £20,250 each p.a. | £60,750 | IF.2 |
|---|---|---|---|
| TD-2.3 | Software quality control for all software<br>developed by whole department –<br>equivalent to 4.5 programmers<br>= 75% of Senior Programmer's time<br>Senior Programmer costs £21,500 (*TD-2.11*)<br>plus 12.5% (£2,687) = £24,187 (*FD-2.12*)<br>Therefore 75% costs £18,140 p.a.<br>Of this, 59% (2.67/4.5) (*TD-2.2*)<br>is QC on fault correction | £10,702 | IF.4 |
| | The remaining 41%<br>is QC on minor changes and new work | £ 7,437 | A.1 |
| TD-2.4 | QA training for Senior Programmer | £1,545 | P.3 |
| TD-2.8 | Rework = 10% of all development work<br>undertaken by 1.83 (4.5–2.67) programmers<br>    (*see above*)<br>0.18% of programmer costing *at least*<br>£20,250 p.a. (*see above*) | £ 3,705 | IF.2 |
| TD-2.10 | Operating instructions<br>1/2 of director at £38,500 p.a. (*see above*) | £19,250 | P.4 |

### Operations Director's brief

| | | | |
|---|---|---|---|
| OD-2.1 | Reviewing proposals<br>OD cost £38,500 p.a. (*see above*)<br>1/2 day/week = 10% of OD's time | £ 3,850 | P.2 |
| OD-2.2 | Operator training<br>1/2 day p.m. = 2.5% of time for 5 operators<br>1.3 of this = 0.83% of ditto<br>Each operator costs £13,000 (£250 * 52)<br>+12.5% (£1,625)<br>= 0.83 * £14,625 * 5 | £   610 | P.3 |
| OD-2.3 | Operating instructions<br>20% of OD's time at £38,500 p.a. (*see above*) | £ 7,700 | P.4 |
| | 10% of Operations Manager's time<br>at £19,000 p.a. (*OD-2.6*)+12.5% (*FD-2.12*)<br>= £21,370 p.a.<br>Therefore 10% = | £ 2,137 | P.4 |
| OD-2.4 | Reruns = 22 hours p.m. (*ODB*)<br>Each hour's time costs £152 (*FDB1*)<br>= 3344 p.m. | £40,128 | IF.2 |
| OD-2.5 | Reruns = 20% of OD's time<br>at £21,370 p.a. | £ 4,274 | IF.2 |
| OD-2.9 | Downtime = 29 hours p.m. @ £152 per hour<br>(*FDB1*)<br>therefore cost = £4,408 p.m. | £52,896 | IF.5 |
| OD-2.13 | Hardware standby arrangement<br>(*see Case Study Fig. 8.1*) | £75,000 | P.5 |
| OD-2.15 | Write-off stationery | £ 2,000 | IF.1 |

### Marketing Director's Brief

| | | | |
|---|---|---|---|
| Mkt-2.1 | Help Desk salaries = £30,000+12.5% | £33,750 | EF.1 |
| Mkt-2.2 | Data Control staff cost 8 * £18,500<br>(*MD-2.3*)<br>+12.5% (*FD-2.12*) = £166,500 p.a. | | |
| | 50% = checking input and output | £66,600 | A.1 |
| | 25% = preparation or processing errors | £33,300 | IF.3 |
| | 25% = resolving user problems | £33,300 | EF.1 |

Mkt-2.3    Product Managers cost 4 * £23,000 (*FD-2.5*)
           +12.5% (*FD-2.12*) = £103,500 p.a.
           50% = organizing correction of problems        £51,750    IF.3

Mkt-2.6    User training = 10% of Product Managers'
           time = 10% of 220 * 8 days = 176 workdays
           Of this, 33% (59 days) = recharged

           Product Managers costs = £103,500 p.a. (*see
              above*)

           User training = 67% * 10% * £103,500           £ 6,935    P.4

Mkt-2.7    Lost sale revenue = £50,000 p.a.
           If costs same as third party payrolls, then
           contribution = 17%                             £ 8,500    EF.3

# Zentech Computer Services Ltd
# Quality cost report

## Estimate of quality costs for year (in £)

| | MD's brief | FD's brief | TD's brief | OD's brief | Mkt Dir's brief | Quality costs | Total quality costs (%) |
|---|---|---|---|---|---|---|---|
| **Prevention costs** | | | | | | | |
| P.1 Quality planning | 3,850 | | | | 3,850 | | |
| P.2 Quality review | | | | 3,850 | | 3,850 | |
| P.3 Quality training | | | 1,545 | 610 | | 2,155 | |
| P.4 Quality improve programme | | | 19,250 | 9,837 | 6,935 | 36,022 | |
| P.5 Standby capacity | | | | 75,000 | | 75,000 | |
| Prevention costs | 3,850 | | 20,795 | 89,297 | 6,935 | 120,877 | 15.64 |
| **Appraisal costs** | | | | | | | |
| A.1 Inspection and testing | | | 7,437 | | 66,600 | 74,037 | |
| Appraisal costs | | | 7,437 | | 66,600 | 74,037 | 9.58 |
| **Internal fail costs** | | | | | | | |
| IF.1 Scrap | | 6,900 | | 2,000 | | 8,900 | |
| IF.2 Replace, rework and Repair | 134,700 | | 64,455 | 44,402 | | 243,557 | |
| IF.3 Trouble shooting | 3,893 | | | | 85,050 | 88,943 | |
| IF.4 Reinspection | | | 10,702 | | | | |
| IF.5 Downtime | | | | 52,896 | | 52,896 | |
| Internal fail costs | 138,593 | 6,900 | 75,157 | 99,298 | 85,050 | 404,998 | 52.40 |
| **External fail costs** | | | | | | | |
| EF.1 Complaints | 3,893 | | | | 67,050 | 70,943 | |
| EF.2 Warranty claims | 1,250 | 82,800 | | | | 84,050 | |
| EF.3 Loss of sales | | | | | 8,500 | 8,500 | |
| EF.4 Recall costs | | 4,500 | | | | 4,500 | |
| EF.5 Product liability | | 5,000 | | | | 5,000 | |
| External fail costs | 5,143 | 92,300 | | | 75,550 | 172,993 | 22.38 |
| Total failure costs | 143,736 | 99,200 | 75,157 | 99,298 | 160,600 | 567,289 | 74.78 |
| Total quality costs | 147,586 | 99,200 | 103,389 | 188,595 | 234,135 | 772,905 | 100.00 |

Total quality costs as a percentage of sales revenue of £3,550,000 is 21.47%.

# 9 Quality costing at Windowco Ltd

## Introduction

Windowco Ltd manufactures window frames and doors from unplasticized polyvinyl chloride (uPVC) extrusions and mouldings. The company is the manufacturing arm of a small group of companies, all owned by Mr Des Hall. Windowco manufactures the windows which are then installed and sold by the two other companies in the group – 90% through Hall Double Glazing Ltd and 10% through Hall Trade Sales Ltd.

The company was founded in 1980 and operates from a modern purpose-built factory in an inner suburb of a large city in the north of England. It employs 15 of the group's 28 employees. The organization chart of the company and the group is shown in Figure 9.1. The group has experienced steady growth over the last decade, although in recent years the industry has become very competitive. Customers are heavily influenced by price considerations as the cost of replacing old doors and windows is relatively high. Low start-up costs have also encouraged some 'rogue' operators to enter the industry, with damaging effects on its reputation.

## Background information

### Sales

Almost all sales are for replacement windows, where a householder is replacing old rotten wooden windows with new uPVC ones. Typically, a contract will involve five windows. Of all the gross revenue, 45% is allocated to the two sales companies. Windowco receives the remaining 55% to cover all its costs. The sales companies use a variety of methods to generate sales, including cold calling, telephone selling, direct mail and local advertising. An excerpt from a sales brochure is shown in Appendix A.

In a typical week Windowco will produce and sell 100 windows and five doors (i.e. 105 units). A typical unit costs the customer £200. All are made to order to the style and dimensions specified by the customer.

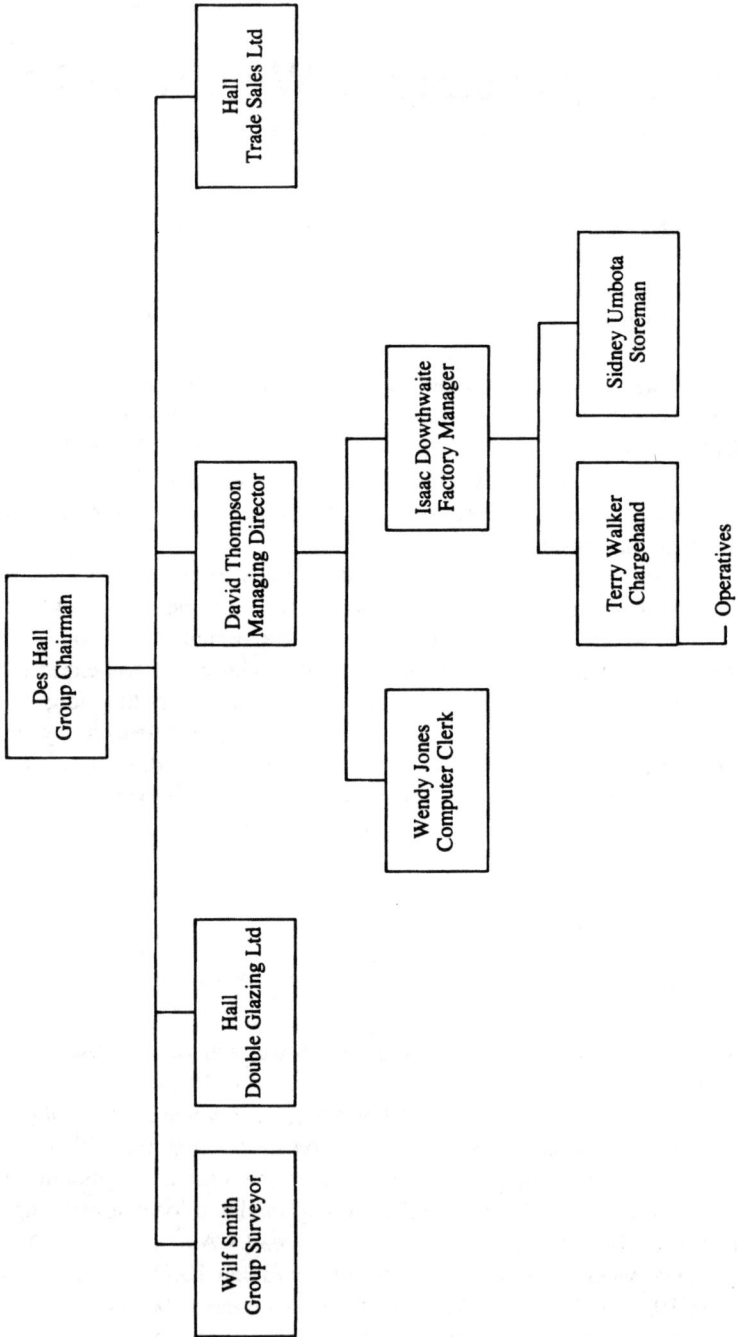

**Figure 9.1** *Windowco Ltd: organization chart*

## Order processing

Des Hall checks all customers' orders coming into Windowco. He spends an average of 1 hour per week on this activity.

Once the order has been accepted by Des, it is keyed into a personal computer for conversion into a Job Sheet. Conversion is performed by a proprietary program called Windowmaker. This produces a Job Sheet which identifies each piece of uPVC that must be cut and a complete Bill of Material identifying all handles, locks, etc. An example of a Job Sheet can be found in Appendix B. The computer is operated by Wendy Jones.

The Windowmaker program correctly processes about 98% of units. The remaining 2% have to be adjusted by hand by Wendy. Occasionally, she also has to make corrections to the survey details before keying them into the computer. Wendy spends about 10% of her time making these adjustments and corrections.

## Operations

The manufacture of windows and doors is relatively simple.

1 The operator draws the necessary material from stores and cuts lengths of profile to the dimensions specified on the Job Sheet.
2 Drain slots and handle holes are drilled into the appropriate cut lengths, using a special drill or router.
3 The welder uses a thermal welding machine to fabricate the frames. (The pattern of the frame is shown on the Job Sheet.)
4 The frames are cleaned, i.e. the 'sprue' is cut away to make clean corners. This is done either with a machine or by hand, depending on the type of frame.
5 The sash and outer frame are hinged together and handles and locks are fitted, as specified on the Job Sheet.
6 The completed window is moved to the side of the factory, ready to be collected by the installers (who work for Hall Double Glazing Ltd).

Glazing is purchased from an outside company. Upon receipt, it is stored at the side of the factory ready for the installers to collect along with the window. The installers fit the glass after the frames have been installed in the customer's home. Doors require uPVC door panels to be cut to size and inserted within the frame.

The factory staff are almost all young and low-paid. Four factory staff are involved in the initial manufacturing (cutting, drilling etc.) and 8 work on fabrication and assembly processes. Operators record their production times on time sheets, an example of which is shown in Appendix C. There is a high staff turnover in the industry and Windowco is no exception. Staff turnover is about the same as the industry average. The Chargehand spends about half his time checking the work of the other production staff and resolving any production problems. The rest of the time he is producing. An analysis of the time sheets for the last 3 months is shown in Appendix D. This gives a breakdown of the time spent on specific production activities.

The Factory Manager generally believes that he has a well-run factory. Amongst his most pressing problems are:

1 The fact that Wendy doesn't give him notice of what he has to do – so that some weeks he could complete all the work by Friday morning, whilst other weeks he has to work overtime and weekends. He estimates that on 1 week in 3 he could complete all the necessary units by Friday lunchtime or earlier. He normally tries to 'spin it out' till 4.00 p.m. on the Friday.
2 Wendy's alleged inaccuracy with the computer. He personally checks every Job Sheet and 'frequently' encounters incorrect Job Sheets which he adjusts himself. On average, he spends 30 minutes per week correcting Job Sheets.
3 The untidiness of the installers – particularly when they come in on a morning to collect their day's work. Often they break glass while sorting through to collect their units. This delays the installation of the unit whose glass was broken, as well as incurring a replacement cost. This happens at least once per week at a direct cost of circa £12.50 per time.

Managing Director David Thompson spends more than half of his time on the telephone dealing with customers' or installers' problems. Also, he frequently has to visit customer premises to sort out problems with installations or to pacify dissatisfied customers.

### Costs

Sales and Purchase Ledgers are processed each month and simple management accounts prepared. Full accounts are only prepared by external accountants at the year-end. Simplified accounts for the last financial year for Windowco are given in Appendix E, which also shows the principal costs.

The Factory Manager, Managing Director and Computer Clerk are regarded as 'factory overheads'. All other staff (including the Chargehand) are regarded as 'direct labour'. The Factory Manager and Managing Director both have company cars. There has been no change in the number of factory employees over the last year.

The offcuts from lengths of profile can be sold as scrap. About 12% of the uPVC purchased is wasted. The company made £1,350 last year from the sale of uPVC scrap.

### *Quality performance*

Until recently there was no formal quality assurance system. As a result, the local authority (which requires BS5750/ISO9000 certification as a condition of tender) ceased purchasing from the company. Windowco sold £19,500 worth of units to this authority last year.

This loss of business prompted the company to employ consultants to help it install a BS5750/ISO9000-based quality assurance system and the company has recently been successfully assessed. Installing the system cost £1,800 in consultants' fees, £1,250 in external training courses and approximately £500 in form and label printing. The assessment process cost £2,335. The annual cost on continuous surveillance is expected to be £1,100.

The company's policy is to replace a unit where there is a manufacturing fault. However, Mr Hall frequently gives instructions for replacement units to be made even where (in David Thompson's opinion) the fault is that of the salesmen or installers. David Thompson estimates that in the last month, for all reasons, he has had to remake approximately 25 windows that had already been installed or had been sent out for installation. In almost all these cases, new glass had to be ordered.

In addition to the above, the Factory Manager estimates that on three occasions a week a unit is found to be faulty before it leaves the factory and must be remade. Reasons for this include:

1 Poor-quality fittings (e.g. door handles) are often used. Frequently they are found to be scratched or corroded when they have been fitted. Often keys don't work and thus the whole lock has to be replaced.
2 The welding machine needs to be replaced. Its thermostat is unreliable, resulting in variable weld quality. The problem is usually identified by one of the staff 'down line', in which case the unit is scrapped and a replacement made. The temperature control on the welder will then be adjusted to try and get everything back 'in tune'.
3 Mistakes by the workshop staff.

A requirement of BS5750/ISO9000 was that the company installed a weld-test machine. This is used each day to monitor weld quality, although with no clear benefits. The cost of the machine was £550 second-hand, and the first calibration of the gauge cost £125. The gauge has to be recalibrated every

6 months. Each test requires an employee to spend about half an hour and uses about £2 worth of material.

An unsatisfactory unit does not always result in it having to be remade. Sometimes the customer is given a discount instead. At the end of the year the total value of such discounts is split 50/50 between Windowco and the other two companies. Last year Windowco's share was £13,500.

Remaking a unit does not mean that all is lost. Some of the material can be recovered or cut and reused to make smaller units. Others may be sold off in an occasional factory sale.

Until 3 years ago the company used uPVC profile from another manufacturer. Much of this material is now becoming discoloured due to the effect of weathering. The group is obliged by its Five-Year Sales Guarantee to replace all faulty units. The manufacturer has now ceased production of this profile and claims that he is not responsible for the discoloration.

Under the new BS5750/ISO9000 quality system, David Thompson acts as Quality Manager. He estimates that it takes up about 20% of his time.

As part of the quality system, David Thompson keeps a diary of quality problems. A typical week's entries are attached as Appendix F.


### Other points

There was a problem last year when a workman was injured by a sheet of glass falling on him. As a result, the company was prosecuted and fined £1,000. The case also cost £1,250 in legal fees. Replacing the broken glass cost £55 and required the installers (two) to spend an extra day on the installation.

A few months ago the company tried to sue a customer for non-payment. The customer claimed that the windows supplied were 'not fit for the purpose intended' and the court found in favour of the customer. Windowco had to write off the debt (£1,150) and pay all the costs (£2,750). The resultant bad publicity in the local free newspaper corresponded with a significant dip in sales. It is estimated that the case cost the company 25 contracts.


## Assignment 1

You have been advising Windowco Ltd on the documentation and imple-mentation of a new quality assurance system, designed to enable the company to gain BS5750/ISO9000 certification. The company has been successfully assessed and has gained certification.

The Managing Director of the group of which Windowco is a part, Mr Des Hall, has now asked you to prepare an estimate of their current quality costs. You believe that the information in your existing files, summarized in the attached Windowco Case Study, is sufficient for this purpose.

Your task is to review the Case Study and estimate the current annual costs of quality in Windowco, using the prevention–appraisal–failure (P–A–F) model.

# Appendix A: Windowco replacement windows

## Elegance and style

A wide range of window styles, featuring slender sight lines in a choice of plain, patterned, Georgian or lead glazing, is available to satisfy your individual requirements.

## Designed for life

Only the finest materials are used during the manufacture and installation of your uPVC windows. They will not rot, warp, corrode; they will never need painting, and will retain their pristine condition.

## Comfort and security

Your uPVC windows are complemented by a sealed-unit double glazing, to provide excellent thermal and noise insulation which will conserve energy and help to reduce heating bills. The most advanced multipoint window locking system is incorporated to provide high levels of security.

## Superior weather protection

Your windows are individually manufactured to the most exacting standards, so that they will withstand the most severe climatic conditions.

## Made by craftsmen

Your windows are manufactured and installed by trained craftsmen with years of experience, who take a professional pride in each and every installation.

# Appendix B: An example of a Job Sheet

Trade job

Assembly list

| | | | | |
|---|---|---|---|---|
| Batch no. 44 | | | No. | |
| Job no.: | 2951 /001 | | 1200 | |
| Account: | XXXX | | | |
| System: | SYO1 Regency casements(T) | 350 | Top | |
| Design: | 4 Casements MW 4 | | 410 | Fixed |
| O/A size: | 1200w × 800h | | | |
| Frame: | 1200w × 760h | | | |
| Glass: | 4–20–4 Unglazed | | | |
| Quantity: | 1 | | | |
| Regency cill: | RPC 01 | | | |
| Outer frame: | RPF 01 | | Viewed from the outside | |
| Regency transom: | ROT 21 | | | |
| Regency vents: | RPZ 11 | | | |
| Espags. Y/N: | Espags . . . . | | | |
| Espag handles: | Locking | | | |

| Description | Stock no. | Qty | Size | Saw | Pane |
|---|---|---|---|---|---|
| Slimline O/frame | RPF 01 | 2 | 1200W | | |
| Slimline O/frame | RPF 01 | 2 | 760h | | |
| Transom RPT 21 | RPT 21 | 1 | 1128w | | |
| Z Section Z11 | RPZ 11 | 2 | 1142w | | Top |
| Z Section Z11 | RPZ 11 | 2 | 314h | | Top |
| T Reinforce ali. | RPR 24 | 1 | 1108w | | |
| G 16 | RPG 16 | 2 | 2913 | | Top |
| Ext D/G bead white | RPB 28 | 1 | 5398 | | |
| Regency Cill 150 mm | RPC 01 | 1 | 1300w | | |
| End caps 150 mm | RPC 03 | 2 | | | |
| Drainage . . . . . . . . | Concealed | | | | |
| Rej screws | RPR 10 | 4 | | | |
| Espags | Espags | | | | Top |
| Espag 1000+keeps | RPE 10 | 1 | | | Top |
| White key locking | Locking | 1 | | | Top |
| F/Stay 250 mm | ETH 01 | 2 | | | Top |
| Double-sided foam | RPG 22 | 1 | 2475 | | Top |
| Double-sided foam | RPG 22 | 1 | 2923 | | Fixed |

| Glass | Qty | Width × Height | Pane |
|---|---|---|---|
| 4-2-4 Unglazed | 1 | 1033w × 205h | Top |
| 4–20–4 Unglazed | 1 | 1114w × 347h | Fixed |

# Appendix C: Extract from a time sheet

| Windowco Ltd – time sheet | | | |
|---|---|---|---|
| **Operator:** Steve Jones | | **Date:** 23.11.9X | |
| **Job no.** | **Operation** | **Number** | **Time (min)** |
| 3487 | Cut uPVC to length | 10 | 15 |
| | Check lengths | | 5 |
| | Recut | | 10 |
| 3398 | Recut uPVC to length | 4 | 10 |

# Appendix D: Time sheet analysis

| Production activity | Percentage of Total time |
|---|---|
| Draw materials from store | 2 |
| Cut materials | 10 |
| Check cut-lengths | 2 |
| Recut materials | 4 |
| Drill uPVC lengths | 15 |
| Check drilling | 2 |
| Redrill uPVC | 5 |
| Weld | 10 |
| Check weld | 3 |
| Reweld | 5 |
| Clean frame | 3 |
| Assemble units | 25 |
| Check assembly against Job Sheet | 4 |
| Reassemble faulty units | 10 |
| Total | 100 % |

Analysis does not include remakes.

# Appendix E: Windowco Ltd – Trading account (in £)

*Revenue*

| | | | |
|---|---|---|---|
| Total group revenue | | 948,000 | |
| Less group margin (45%) | | | −426,600 |
| Revenue attributable to Windowco | | | 521,400 |
| Less share of discounts | | −13,500 | |
| Other income – sale of scrap, etc. | | 1,500 | |
| | | | 509,400 |

*Gross revenue*

| | | | |
|---|---|---|---|
| Direct labour | | | |
| Basic salary | 104,000 | | |
| Overtime | 24,650 | | |
| NHI etc. | 16,150 | | |
| | | 145,400 | |
| Materials used | | | |
| Profile | 126,500 | | |
| Glass | 66,750 | | |
| Other materials | 34,600 | | |
| | | 227,850 | |
| Total cost of goods sold | | | 373,250 |
| Net factory revenue | | | 136,150 |

*Factory overheads*

| | | | |
|---|---|---|---|
| Management and supervision | | | |
| Salaries | 62,800 | | |
| Bonuses | 3,400 | | |
| NHI | 9,420 | | |
| | | 75,620 | |
| Motor car costs | | | |
| Depreciation | 4,100 | | |
| Running costs | 3,250 | | |
| | | 7,350 | |
| Plant costs | | | |
| Depreciation | 5,900 | | |
| Maintenance | 3,900 | | |
| | | 9,800 | |
| Rent and rates | | 14,550 | |
| Heat, light, electricity | | 8,200 | |
| Telephone | | 1,150 | |
| Postage and office supplies | | | 1,650 |
| Cleaning and janitorial | | 3,775 | |
| Legal accounting consultancy | | 6,500 | |
| Travel | | 575 | |
| Other costs | | 1,450 | |
| | | | 130,620 |
| Factory profit | | | 5,530 |

# Appendix F: Fault diary

| Day | Customer | Problem | Action |
|-----|----------|---------|--------|
| Mon | Mrs V Jones, 14 Jubilee Way French windows wrong-handed | Has she changed her mind? Order not signed by customer | Replace |
| Tues | Jenkinsons Ltd Weld cracked | Manufacturing fault | Replace |
| Tues | Mrs N Wilson, 18 Wilson St | Condensation in kitchen | 50% discount |
|  | Bulwell, Fir Tree Way (14) | Discoloration Units 3 years old | Replace two units |
| Wed | Mr J Arkwright 147 Mill St South | Frame scratched Installers? | Replace |
| Thurs | Andersen, 228 Willow Rd | Lock jammed Misuse? | Unjam |
| Thurs | Wilson-Brown, Linford Lodge, Picketts Way | Scratches | Offer discount |
| Fri | Bronswells, 729146 Harrison St | Draught Unit undersized Survey? | Replace |

# Windowco Ltd: Quality costing notes: a P–A–F quality cost report

## P–A–F quality cost notes

### 1. Scrap

|  |  |  |
|---|---|---|
| (a) Offcut and wastage from uPVC profile 12% of £126,500 | £15,180 | |
| Less recovery | £1,350 | |
| | £13,830 | |
| (b) Glass breakage – 50 occasions *£12.50 | £625 | |
| | £14,455 | |

### 2. Cost of customer complaints

(a) Remakes of complete units: 25 each month = 300 units per annum
Total units manufactured = 5250 per annum
Therefore remakes = 300/5250 = 5.7%
5.7% of total cost of goods (£373,250)                £21,275
N.B.: Does not include effect of requiring extra overtime to be worked

(b) Managing Director spends at least 50% of time resolving quality problems
Assume Managing Director salary + bonus = £30,000 p.a.
add 15% for NHI, etc = £4,500
add car costs (50% of £7,350) = £3,675
Therefore cost of MD is £38,175
50% of cost of Managing Director                £19,087
N.B.: Does not include costs to rest of group

(c) Share of discounts given to customers                £13,500

(d) Lost sales as result of court case
Net revenue of 5250 units = £136,150 = £26 per unit
Therefore lost profit on 25 sales (each of 5 units)
lost as result of court case                £3,250

£57,112

### 3. *Cost of internal wastage*

(a) Approximately 150 units require remaking
Assume fault discovered halfway through process.
Equivalent of 75 units
Therefore internal remakes = 75/5250 = 1.4% of
workload
Equivalent of 3.5 working days. Thus 3.5 working days
of overtime result from internal wastage
Normal working days cost £104,600 for 250 working
days: i.e. £418 per day.
Assume overtime paid (on average) at time-and-a-half
Therefore overtime day costs £627
Therefore cost of internally discovered mistakes
= 3.5 * £627                                                    £2,195
N.B.: Assume material losses already covered in point
1 (d) above.

(b) Wendy's hand adjustments and correction to survey
details:
10% Wendy's time
Assume Wendy costs £11,250 including 15% for NHI      £1,125

(c) Factory Manager correcting Job Sheets
30 min per week or approximately 1.3% of his time
Assume he costs £20,000 p.a. plus 15% for NHI etc.,
plus car costs (1.3% of £20,000 + £3,000 + £3675)       £347
                                                             ───────
                                                             £3,667

### 4. *Costs to rest of group*

(a) Installation commission of 20% on 300 units that need
to be remade (@ average price of £200)
= 300 * 200 * 0.20%)                                     £12,000

### 5. *Inspection costs*

(a) Checking customers' orders.
Des Hall spends 1 hour per week or approximately 2.5%
of his time.
Assume he costs £40,000 p.a. inclusive of NHI and all
benefits.
2.5% of £40,000                                           £1,000

(b)  Assume Chargehand costs £200 per week
Therefore Chargehand costs (200 * 52) = £10,400 p.a.
plus 12.5% for NHI etc. = total of £11,700
Time spent by Chargehand on inspection costs (50%)              £5,850

(c)  Checking of Job Sheets
(say) 1 min per sheet, 105 * 50 sheets per annum
= 5250 minutes = 87.5 hours
= 2.24 weeks of Factory Manager
= 2.24/48 = 4.6% of his time
He costs £26,675
4.5% of £26,675                                                £1,227

(d)  Weld testing requires 1/2 hour per day
1/2 hour * 250 days p.a. = 125 hours p.a.
Assume operative costs £150 per week plus 12.5%
= £169 per 39-hour week = £4.33 per hour
Therefore labour costs of weld testing                           £541

(e)  Material cost of weld testing = £2 * 250                      £500

(f)  Acquisition and installation of test equipment               £550
                                                                ———————
                                                                 £9,668


## 6. *Quality assurance costs*

(a)  Design and installation of QA system
£1,800 + £500                                                  £2,300

(b)  Quality training courses                                    £1,250

(c)  Quality auditing
External assessment fees = £2,335
plus expected annual surveillance fee = £1,100                £3,435

(d)  Calibration costs (£125 * 2)                                  £250

(e)  Quality Manager costs
20% of £38,175 (see point 2(a))                              £7,635
                                                              ————————
                                                              £14,870

## Example of a quality cost report

| Group: HALL GROUP | | Division |
|---|---|---|
| Unit: WINDOWCO | | Period: |
| Year: 199X | Costs | Worksheet ref. |

| | Costs | Worksheet ref. |
|---|---|---|
| **Prevention costs** | | |
| Calibration and maintenance of quality measurement, test and control equipment | 250 | 6.4 |
| Quality training | 1,250 | 6.2 |
| Quality auditing | 3,435 | 6.3 |
| Quality manager | 7,635 | 6.5 |
| Quality improvement programme | 2,300 | 6.1 |
| **Total prevention cost** | 14,870 | |
| **% of total quality cost** | 13.3% | |
| **Appraisal costs** | | |
| Preproduction costs | 2,227 | 5.1 + 5.3 |
| Inspection and testing | 6,391 | 5.2 + 5.4 |
| Inspection and test equipment | 550 | 5.6 |
| Materials consumed during inspection and testing | 500 | 5.5 |
| **Total appraisal cost** | 9,668 | |
| **% of total quality cost** | 8.6% | |
| **Internal failure costs** | | |
| Scrap | 14,455 | 1.1 + 1.2 |
| Replacement, rework and repair | 3,667 | 3.1 + 3.2 + 3.3 |
| Troubleshooting or defect/failure analysis | 19,087 | 2.2 |
| Modification permits and concessions | | |
| Downgrading | 13,500 | 2.3 |
| **Total internal failure cost** | 50,709 | |
| **% of total quality cost** | 45.4% | |
| **External failure costs** | | |
| Products repeated and returned | 33,275 | 2.1 + 4 |
| Loss of sales | 3,250 | 2.4 |
| **Total external failure cost** | 36,525 | |
| **% of total quality cost** | 32.7% | |
| **Total quality cost (TQC)** | 111,772 | |

Typical ratios

**TQC as a percentage of:**

| | | |
|---|---|---|
| Sales revenue 521,400 | $\dfrac{TQC \times 100}{\text{Sales revenue}}$ | 21.4% |
| Value added 293,550 | $\dfrac{TQC \times 100}{\text{Value added}}$ | 38.1% |
| Direct labour costs 145,400 | $\dfrac{TQC \times 100}{\text{Direct labour costs}}$ | 76.9% |

Distribution:
Issued by: LP/PR                                    Date: 20.3.199X

## Assignment 2

Using the case information and the following additional notes, construct appropriate process cost models for Windowco Ltd.

### *Process cost model*

*Additional notes*

1  Many of the non-conformance costs have already been calculated (see P–A–F Quality Cost Notes 1.1, 1.2, 2.1, 2.2, 2.3, 2.4, 3.1, 3.2, 3.3, 4).
2  The majority of activity costs can be estimated from the Time Sheet Analysis, Appendix D, and the Windowco Trading Account, Appendix E.
3  Four major subprocesses can be analysed:
   (a)  order subprocess
   (b)  initial manufacturing subprocess
   (c)  fabrication/assembly subprocess
   (d)  installation/after-sales subprocess
4  Other processes, e.g. quality assurance process, cannot be analysed in full due to insufficient information in the case study. Hence the prevention and appraisal costs of quality assurance will not appear in these process models.
5  Labour costs:

| | |
|---|---|
| Initial manufacturing | £48,467 |
| Fabrication/assembly | £96,933 |
| | £145,400 |

6  Other material costs (Appendix E) include welding materials, £5,190, of which £1,038 is used during rewelding.
7  The four installers, who work for Hall Double Glazing Ltd, earn £12,000 p.a. basic. The cost to the company is £16,500 p.a. per person inclusive of NHI and bonuses.
8  Des Hall spends an estimated 5% of his time dealing with customers' complaints. His total salary and benefits cost to the company is £49,750 p.a.

# Windowco Ltd process cost models

## Windowco Ltd process cost model. Flowchart 1: order processing subprocess

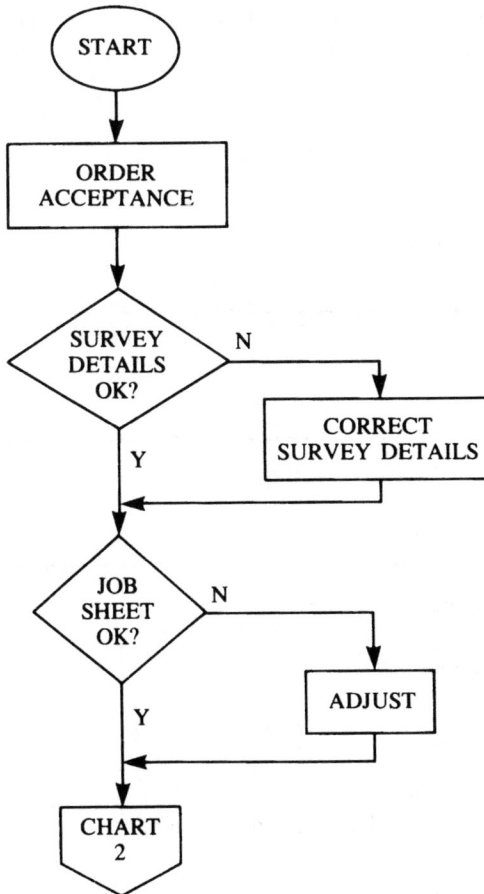

## Windowco Ltd process cost model.
## Subprocess – order processing, flowchart 1

| Activity | Cost of conformance | Cost of non-conformance |
| --- | --- | --- |
| Order acceptance | 2.5% Des Hall's time | |
| Job sheet preparation | 90% cost of Wendy Jones | Hand adjustments Correction to survey. details (10% Wendy's time) |
| Job sheet check | 4.6% David Thompson's time | |
| Job sheet adjustment | | 1.2% Dave Thompson's time |

| Cost report | Date |
| --- | --- |
| Order processing | Annual costs (£) |
| *Cost of Conformance* | |
| Order acceptance | 1,000 |
| Job sheet preparation | 10,125 |
| Job sheet check | 1,227 |
| Total conformance cost | 12,357   (89.4%) |
| *Cost of non-conformance* | |
| Hand adjustments to job sheet and correction to survey details | 1,125 |
| Job sheet adjustments | 347 |
| Total non-conformance cost | 1,472   (10.6%) |
| Total process cost | 13,824   (100%) |

# Windowco Ltd process cost model. Flowchart 2 – manufacturing subprocess

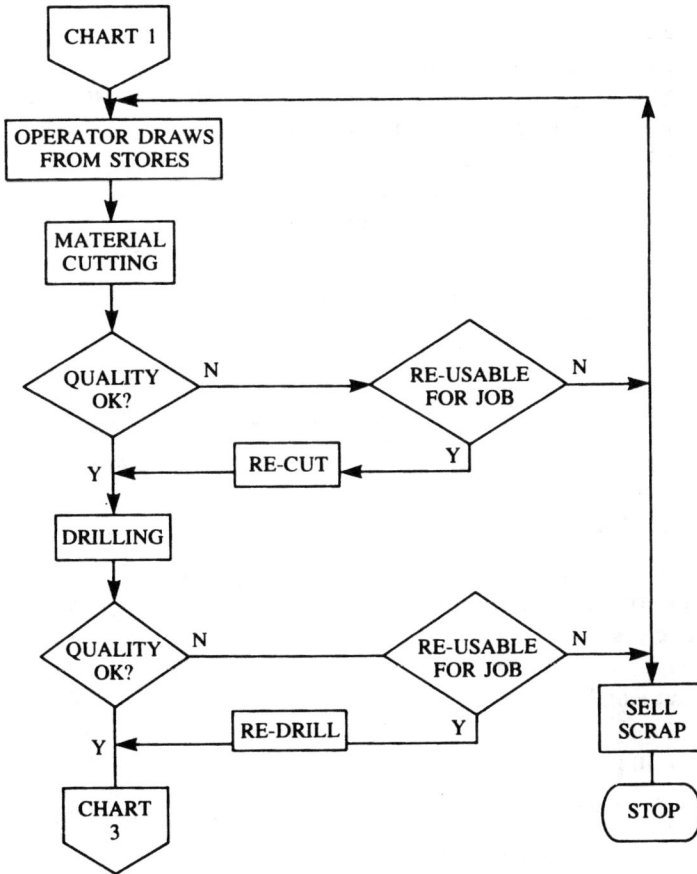

## Windowco Ltd process cost model.
## Subprocess – manufacturing, flowchart 2

| Activity | Cost of conformance | Cost of non-conformance |
|---|---|---|
| Draw material from stores | 2% labour costs + uPVC costs | |
| Cut material | 10% labour costs | uPVC waste offcuts |
| Collect, check cut lengths | 2% labour costs | |
| Recut material | | 4% labour costs |
| Drill | 15% labour costs | |
| Check drilling | 2% labour costs | |
| Redrill | | 5% labour costs |

| Process cost report manufacturing | Date Annual costs (£) | |
|---|---|---|
| *Cost of conformance* | | |
| Draw material from stores | 969 | |
| Material costs | 112,670 | |
| Cut material | 4,847 | |
| Check cut lengths | 969 | |
| Drill | 7,270 | |
| Check drilling | 969 | |
| Total conformance cost | 127,694 | (87.5%) |
| *Cost of non-conformance* | | |
| uPVC waste | 13,830 | |
| Recutting material | 1,939 | |
| Redrilling | 2,423 | |
| Total non-conformance cost | 18,192 | (12.5%) |
| Total process cost | 145,886 | (100%) |

# Windowco Ltd process cost model. Flowchart 3 – fabrication/assembly subprocess

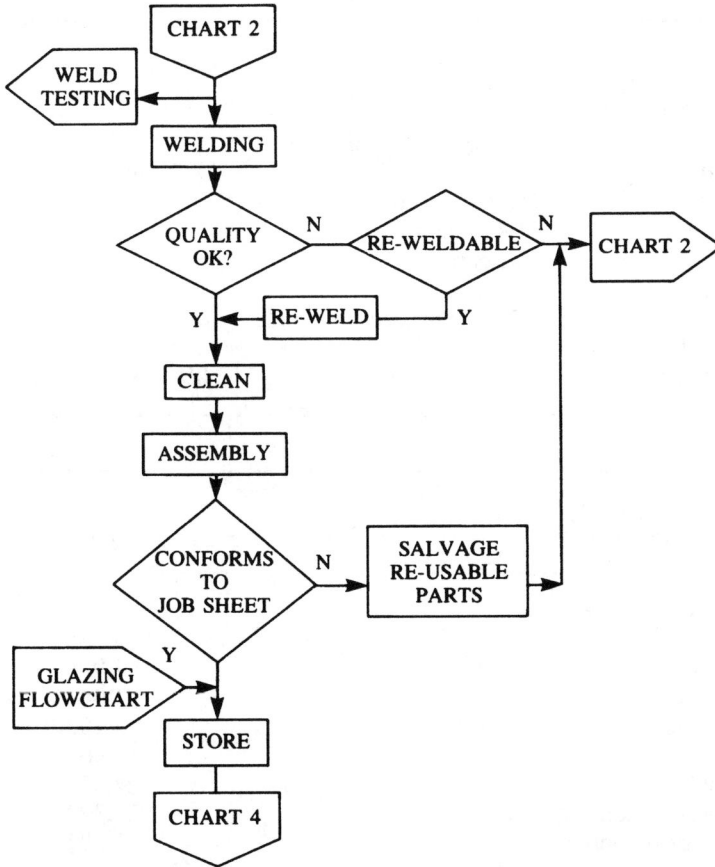

```
                    ┌──────────┐
                    │ CHART 2  │
                    └────┬─────┘
        ┌──────┐         │
        │ WELD │◄────────┤
        │TESTING│        │
        └──────┘    ┌────▼─────┐
                    │ WELDING  │
                    └────┬─────┘
                         │
                    ╱QUALITY╲   N    ╱RE-WELDABLE╲   N   ┌─────────┐
                    ╲ OK?   ╱──────► ╲           ╱──────►│ CHART 2 │
                         │            └────┬────┘        └─────────┘
                       Y │◄──┌────────┐    │ Y
                         │   │RE-WELD │◄───┘
                         │   └────────┘
                    ┌────▼─────┐
                    │  CLEAN   │
                    └────┬─────┘
                    ┌────▼─────┐
                    │ ASSEMBLY │
                    └────┬─────┘
                    ╱CONFORMS╲   N    ┌──────────┐
                    ╲   TO   ╱──────► │ SALVAGE  │
                    ╱JOB SHEET╲       │RE-USABLE │──────►
                         │            │  PARTS   │
      ┌──────────┐     Y │           └──────────┘
      │ GLAZING  │       │
      │FLOWCHART │──────►│
      └──────────┘  ┌────▼─────┐
                    │  STORE   │
                    └────┬─────┘
                    ┌────▼─────┐
                    │ CHART 4  │
                    └──────────┘
```

## Windowco Ltd process cost model. Subprocess – fabrication/assembly, flowchart 3

| Activity | Cost of conformance | Cost of non-conformance |
|---|---|---|
| Weld | 15% labour costs and materials | |
| Weld check | 3% labour costs + weld quality monitor | |
| Reweld | | 5% labour costs |
| Clean | 5% labour costs | |
| Assemble | 25% labour costs and parts | |
| Check against job sheet | 7% labour costs | |
| Reassemble faulty units | | 10% labour and parts |

| Process cost report fabrication/assembly | Date Annual costs (£) | |
|---|---|---|
| *Cost of conformance* | | |
| Weld | 9,693 | |
| Weld check | 2,908 | |
| Weld quality monitor | 1,041 | |
| Weld materials used | 4,152 | |
| Clean | 2,908 | |
| Assemble | 24,233 | |
| Assembly materials/parts | 27,322 | |
| Check against job sheet | 3,877 | |
| Total conformance cost | 76,134 | (81.2%) |
| *Cost of non-conformance* | | |
| Reweld | 4,847 | |
| Reweld materials | 1,038 | |
| Reassemble faulty units | 9,693 | |
| Reassembly materials | 2,088 | |
| Total non-conformance cost | 17,666 | (18.8%) |
| Total process cost | 93,800 | (100%) |

## Windowco Ltd process cost model. Flowchart 4 – installation/after-sales subprocesses

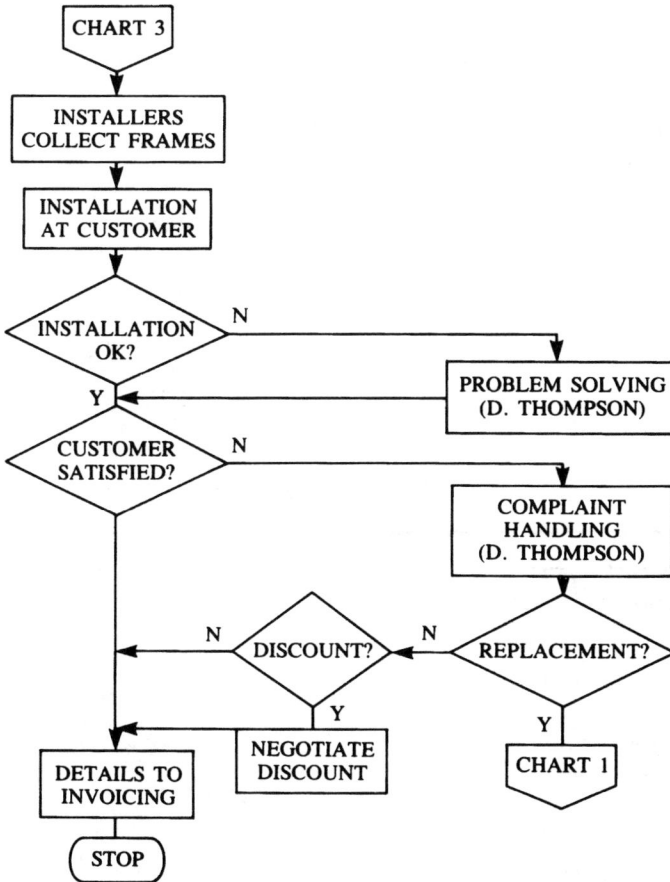

## Windowco Ltd process cost model
## subprocess – installation/after-sales, flowchart 4

| Activity | Cost of conformance | Cost of non-conformance |
|---|---|---|
| Collect frames | 5% labour cost * | Glass breakages |
| Installation | 80% labour cost * | |
| Installation check | 5% labour cost * | |
| Problem-solving | | 50% D. Thompson's time |
| Complaint-handling | | 5% Des Hall's time |
| | | Replace 300 units |
| | | Discounts |
| | | Court case |
| | | Loss of sales as result of court case |

*Estimated costs (not given in case).

| Process cost report installation/after-sales | Date Annual costs (£) | |
|---|---|---|
| *Cost of conformance* | | |
| Collect frames | 3,300 | |
| Installation | 52,800 | |
| Installation check | 3,300 | |
| Total conformance cost | 59,400 | (45.1%) |
| *Cost of non-conformance* | | |
| Glass breakages | 625 | |
| Problem-solving | 19,087 | |
| Complaint-handling | 52,512 | |
| Total non-conformance cost | 72,224 | (54.9%) |
| Total process cost | 131,624 | (100%) |

# 10 Performance through Total Quality: the Shorts experience

## Introduction

Shorts Brothers launched their Total Quality programme in 1987. Since then all personnel have received quality improvement training and over 1300 quality improvement projects have been completed, with estimated benefits exceeding £46m per year. The company's efforts recently received national recognition, with Shorts winning both the British Quality Award and the Northern Ireland Quality Award.

These results were achieved in spite of the uncertainties of privatization and the disruption caused by a fundamental reorganization of the company. This case describes the major initiative within Shorts, the performance improvements to date, and future plans for the Total Quality programme.

The Shorts experience shows that performance improvement through Total Quality requires the commitment and involvement of personnel at all levels. Furthermore, sustained quality improvement is achieved only when it clearly supports the business objectives as perceived at different levels throughout the company.

Shorts Brothers PLC are the largest industrial employers in Northern Ireland, with some 8400 personnel. The company has been engaged in the aviation business for over 90 years and its activities include the design and manufacture of civil and military aircraft, major components for other aerospace companies and close air defence weapon systems. Today, Shorts are part of Bombardier Inc., a Canadian-based international corporation engaged in the design, manufacture and marketing of transportation equipment, aerospace and motorized consumer goods. These products are sold worldwide into increasingly demanding and competitive markets.

During the 1980s, increasingly fierce competition highlighted the importance of and the need to reduce the 'cost of poor quality' within the company. The search for new methods led the company to investigate TQM in early 1987. Shorts needed an approach that would be meaningful to every aspect of its business, including clerical, commercial, design and manufacturing areas. In view of previous experiences, the chosen method would also have to provide a sound basis for identifying the most important opportunities for improvement and for defining the true cause of a problem before attempting to resolve it.

A review of the quality improvement literature, and of the approaches adopted by some of their customers, suggested the most appropriate methodology to meet their requirement. The company recognized the need for initial training to be consultant-led in order to provide credibility and a breadth of experience which did not exist within the company at that time. They chose, therefore, a consultancy which could help implement the chosen approach and in May 1987 gained Board-level approval for the programme. Detailed planning started immediately.

A team consisting of Shorts personnel and consultants was formed to devise an implementation programme for the Total Quality activities. The team defined the organizational structure needed to direct continuous improvement throughout the company. This consisted of a Company Quality Council, two Divisional Councils and 18 Functional Quality Teams (FQTs). The planning team also specified the initial membership of each of these groups, ensuring the involvement of senior management in each team.

The Company Quality Council is chaired by the President and comprises Vice-presidents from each Division who provide overall leadership and direction for the programme. The Divisional Councils are chaired by their respective Vice-presidents who, with senior management, meet to set objectives and monitor progress in their respective divisions. The Functional Teams are chaired by a senior manager and comprise departmental managers who lead Total Quality in their functions.

A Total Quality Centre was established to act as a focal point for training and support, and to take the leading role in assisting the Company Council develop a Total Quality strategy. It was staffed by six full-time secondees from a wide range of company departments who would serve 12–24 months, acting as planner, trainer, facilitator and coordinator.

The planning phase lasted less than 2 months. In hindsight it might have been beneficial to have spent more time analysing the objectives since the focus was almost solely on training and techniques. If more attention had been given to solving the everyday problems faced by team members, Shorts may have had a more widespread uptake in the first few months. However, they had a structure in place to manage the programme, and the training of the teams became the first priority.

## The training programme

The company fully understood the need for top-level understanding, commitment and involvement in the programme. Thus the training pro-gramme was very definitely a 'top-down' process. It began with the President and his Management Committee and moved systematically through the company until all personnel were trained.

### Quality Council and FQT Training

The first training session took place in October 1987 and consisted of a 3-day off-site workshop for the members of the Company Quality Council. It was followed by 12 similar workshops for the other Quality Councils and FQTs. Over 200 Vice-presidents and Senior Managers were involved in the training, which was completed during September 1988.

Each workshop covered the theory, practice and tools of quality improvement. On the final day of training, each group elected a chairperson and secretary, set an agenda and held their first meeting to discuss opportunities and priorities for improvement. These meetings continued on a weekly or biweekly basis after the workshops.

### Project Team Leaders

Each project team has a Team Leader to guide and control the team's efforts. All Team Leaders attended a 4-day off-site course on tools, techniques, leadership and presentation skills. These courses were scheduled concurrently with the training for Councils and Functional Teams so that Team Leaders were available to lead nominated projects. The first course took place in July 1987 and since then 49 courses have been held, providing a pool of over 750 trained leaders. The initial training courses were consultant-led with increasing involvement of Total Quality Centre personnel. Since 1989 all courses have been run by Shorts staff, forming a successful and visible part of Shorts ownership of the process. Team Leader training is an ongoing task which is currently provided on a point-of-need basis.

### Management and senior executives

The remainder of Senior Management and Senior Executives attended a 1-day on-site training session. These were highly interactive and focused on the need for Total Quality. Practical exercises were also introduced to familiarize the participants with the basic quality tools.

A total of 68 courses were held involving 1000 personnel over the period April 1988 to July 1989. Participants were very enthusiastic and, despite some initial anticipated cynical reasons, the majority of people left the session eager to put their new-found knowledge into practice.

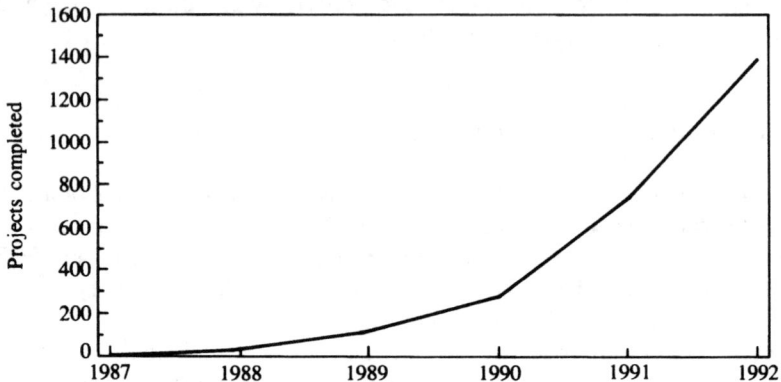

**Figure 10.1** *Projects completed*

### *Senior technical, admin and supervisory staff*

A further 40 1-day sessions were held during 1989 to cover 700 personnel. The enthusiastic input from shopfloor supervisors was very encouraging, although concern over the imminent privatization and possible redundancies was becoming apparent. This was partially compensated for by the increasing number of completed improvement projects throughout the company (Figure 10.1).

## Privatization – obstacle or respite?

During June 1989 the company underwent a major reorganization in which the existing three divisions were transformed into five largely autonomous Business Units and the Corporate functions. This fundamental change in structure resulted in the relocation of personnel and was the precursor to privatization.

It was fortunate that the previous training phase had been completed before the full effect of the reorganization had been felt. Quality improvement ceased almost completely as the Total Quality organizational structure became obsolete. However, the resulting 2-month pause allowed the company to examine progress so far and to design a new organizational structure which focused more intently on the Business Unit objectives. Commercial awareness and accountability have since increased and reduction of quality costs has taken on new strategic importance.

Thus, during September 1989 Total Quality was relaunched with a new relevance to the company's goals. The revised organizational structure now consists of five Divisional Quality Councils, and a Corporate Quality Council, supported by 36 FQTs. Once this structure was in place it was possible to reallocate the existing 100 Total Quality projects, some of which had lost their teams during the reorganization. Total Quality was now restored to life and Shorts embarked on the most ambitious training phase yet–to educate the remainder of the workforce.

## 1900 down, 7100 to go!

In preparing to train the workforce, the company was very aware of potential barriers to progress, e.g. trade union resistance, the fear of redundancies, and the false impression that this was a managers' programme since the training so far had been for senior staff.

Trade union resistance was avoided by involving them in discussions about the aims of the programme and by giving shop stewards the opportunity of participating in the training in advance of their members. This resulted in the trade unions giving the programme their full support.

At this stage, Shorts changed the format of the training sessions. They realized that, if training was to be interesting and relevant to non-managerial staff, it had to be sharply focused on the particular opportunities in their work areas. The solution was to involve local managers in delivering the training. To maximize the impact of this training phase, they completed the training of one Business Unit before starting another. This allowed the Business Unit goals to be integrated with the training material and also enabled them to perform brainstorming in a real situation with each group.

Training of all personnel was completed in October 1990, after some 400 training sessions, in which 20 000 brainstorm ideas were generated. A high level of awareness was created amongst the workforce and a great majority of people were enthusiastic about the programme.

Because of the focus on training and the fact that some of the earliest improvement projects were chosen more as training exercises than as attempts to improve the business, there was a growing feeling that Total Quality was 'interesting' but nothing to do with 'real' work. At this stage the Total Quality Centre staff, who attended both Council and FQT meetings, gently steered each meeting towards activities that were more relevant to the business objectives. This approach resulted in an increased focus on meaningful projects.

## Total Quality projects–a means of reducing costs

For many historical reasons Shorts had not proved to be a profitable business for at least the 5 years before privatization in 1989. Indeed, the financial performance was steadily deteriorating, despite the fact that order books had never looked more healthy.

It was decided that the Total Quality programme should be used to identify areas where better management would result in cost reduction. After their training, the Quality Councils and FQTs met regularly with a prime objective of identifying the most significant opportunities for improvement in their areas. Each team created a list of possible projects by brainstorming, through an analysis of their quality costs and by focusing on the customer–supplier interfaces within their own department. In essence this meant finding areas where large financial savings could be made by improving a process, getting things right first time, improving efficiency, motivating people, improving technological capabilities, and so on.

The potential savings of each project were estimated, as was the cost of each project, and those with the greatest return were given priority. In many cases these projects spawned smaller, more manageable projects. Projects also resulted from the extensive brainstorm lists generated by the non-managerial staff during their training sessions. During these sessions it was stressed that the Total Quality programme was not only trying to save money but was also a useful and important vehicle with which to transform the company culture. This meant not only listening to ideas but acting on them.

Having chosen a project, a suitable Team Leader was selected from the pool of already trained personnel. A project team, consisting of on average four to six people with an interest in the problem, was then assembled. Their role was to analyse the problem and suggest a plan of remedial action. This was then presented to the relevant Council or FQT for authorization.

One major difficulty learned with project teams was providing them with enough time to complete the project. It was vital that adequate priority was given to Total Quality activities, that the team was empowered to make decisions; and that progress was monitored to ensure that blocks to progress were removed. Without this, teams could become demoralized and flounder.

Experience at Shorts has shown that, across the 1300 projects completed, the majority of teams have enjoyed their involvement and found continuous improvement both challenging and rewarding. Team members have been 'amazed' at the progress made in the novel 'no-blame' environment of their meetings and have developed a greater respect for their colleagues from other departments.

## Recent developments with the programme

The company continually reviews the effectiveness of its approach to ensure that the programme continues to support the needs of the business. Recently the supporting role of the Total Quality Centre has become focused on the divisional needs by the provision of a dedicated member of staff. The divisional representative now plays a pivotal role by providing timely, accurate information on performance against Total Quality Plans, acting as a source of ideas for improvement techniques and providing examples of best practice in other companies.

As a means of furthering industrial and academic links within Northern Ireland, Des Bell (a Shorts manager and former member of the Total Quality Centre team) has been seconded to Shorts Quality Unit, at the Ulster Business School, as a Senior Fellow in Quality Management. The role facilitates the promotion of TQM in Northern Ireland and the transfer of knowledge in various aspects of TQM to local industry. Furthermore, through his research activities, Des will be able to provide Shorts with evidence of current best practice and how the Total Quality programme can be further developed.

The company has also begun to benchmark in an effort to discover best practices and to compare its performance against selected metrics. A wide range of areas are being benchmarked and medium- and long-term targets are being set based on these activities.

No Total Quality programme is complete if it does not address the supplier issue. The company is currently attempting to reduce the supply base and to build long-term partnerships with a number of preferred suppliers. Shorts staff now liaise closely with suppliers, providing support and a range of training services such as quality improvement workshops, symposia and seminars. Suppliers are invited to send delegates to the Team Leader Training courses and are encouraged to participate in joint improvement teams in an effort to encourage them to embrace Total Quality.

Shorts have also begun to incorporate advanced quality techniques into the programme. The Manufacturing Division has recently introduced a Process Review Programme aimed at systematically improving their manufacturing processes. The programme is based on Statistical Design of Experiments and is aimed at reducing variation and eliminating defects at source. They have also begun to establish a proactive approach to business process improvement and process optimization which will be deployed throughout the company.

# Performance improvements to date

### Business results: financial measures

From the outset the company realized that the Total Quality programme would only survive if it could provide tangible benefits for the company. At the end of the first year, during which time the emphasis had been on training, only

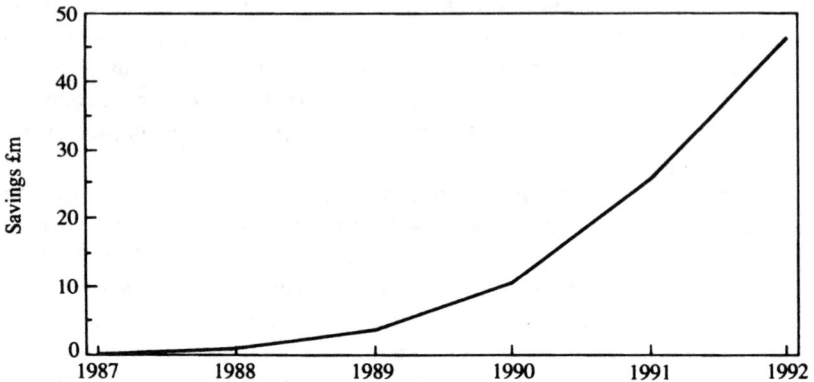

**Figure 10.2** *Savings in millions of pounds*

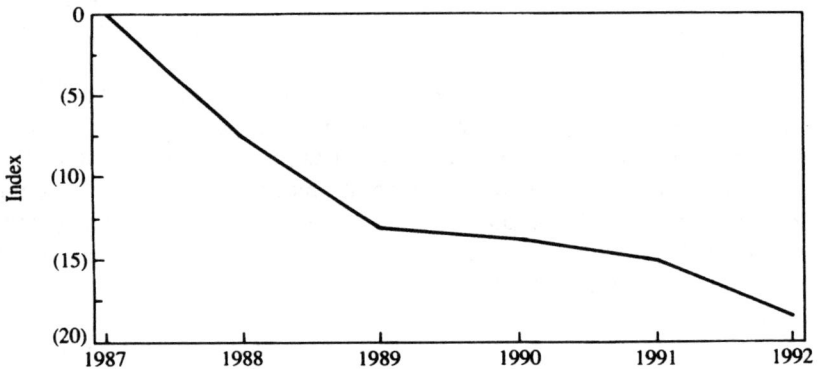

**Figure 10.3** *Reductions in quality costs as a percentage of turnover*

one project had been completed, with a saving of less than £30 000 per year. Five and a half years on, after a fundamental shift towards project support, Shorts have completed over 1300 projects, with an estimated benefit of over £46m per year Figures 10.1–10.3).

It must be stated, however, that success is not simply measured by the magnitude of the savings. The important factor is that the savings, no matter how small, continue to mount up.

Company turnover has more than doubled since 1987. Although the order book has expanded, the company has not had to increase the number of employees over the period, resulting in turnover per employee more than doubling.

### Business results: non-financial measures

The Total Quality programme has resulted in a number of other benefits. Process improvements enabled Shorts to deliver 59 wing sets in 1991, representing a 50% increase from 1990. The work-hours required to produce a complete wing set have been reduced by 50%, leading to a doubling of efficiency levels. Overtime has been reduced by 10% in the same period and the learning curve is better than anything previously achieved on similar contracts in Shorts' history.

The level of shortages within the assembly areas had caused numerous delays and diversions for many years in Shorts. Through reducing non-conformances, and other contributors to the problem, shortages have reduced by a factor of more than 25 over a period of less than 2 years (Figure 10.4). Focusing on improving the accuracy of the management information systems

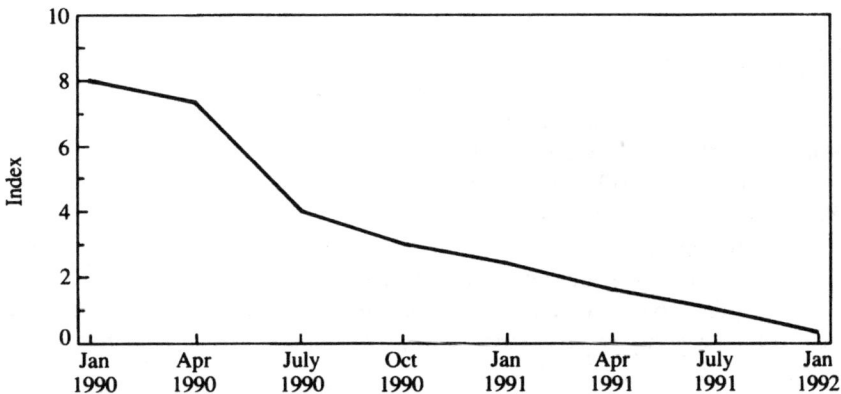

**Figure 10.4** *Company shortages 1990–1992*

has enabled them to achieve previously unheard-of accuracy levels for inventory, typically between 98 and 100% (Figure 10.5). In addition, all areas of the company have vigorously pursued stock value reductions, with achievements of 40% or more being typical.

Improvements in production control and master scheduling systems have enabled Shorts to plan activities more accurately. When combined with manufacturing leadtime reductions (some sheet metal parts have had leadtimes reduced from 4 weeks to 4 days) and assembly hour reductions of up to 34%, Shorts have been able to meet delivery schedules and other key milestones ahead of programme.

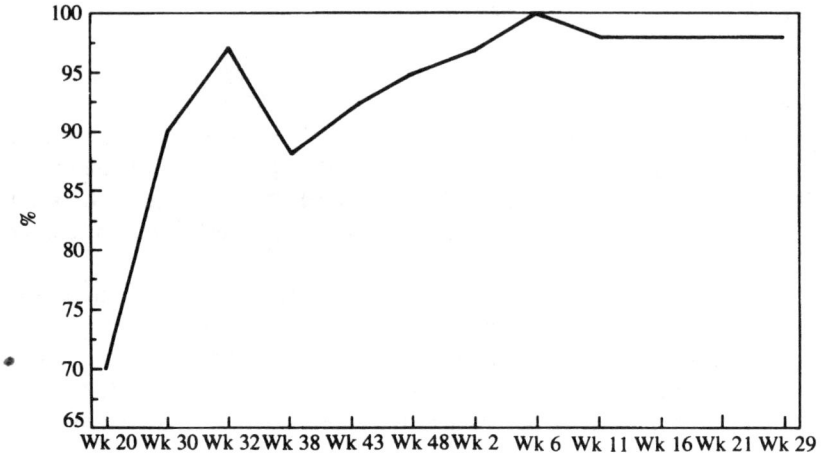

**Figure 10.5** *Inventory accuracy 1990–1991*

### People satisfaction

The Total Quality programme has generated many changes whose value would be difficult to measure in monetary terms, e.g. improved service levels and improved industrial–academic liaison. A major benefit is that all employees are now aware of the competitive threats facing Shorts and the benefits presented by Total Quality. Through the training process they are capable of applying simple problem-solving tools in their day-to-day work. They also understand the concept of the internal and external customer and realize the necessity of satisfying their needs if the company is to become a leader in each sector of its business.

Perhaps the biggest change is that of attitude. Not only has the workforce attitude changed, but that of the middle and senior managers as well. Although this culture change is by no means complete, there is objective evidence that the company is moving in the desired direction, e.g. over 4200 management and staff are involved in improvement activities at any one time. The company believes that through sustaining this commitment and working as a team it will continue to effect the required cultural change.

### Customer satisfaction

Shorts fully appreciate that to survive and prosper, it is necessary to guarantee customer satisfaction. They have focused on the chain of events from the supplier, through internal customers and suppliers, to the end-customer in an attempt to ensure they meet customer requirements.

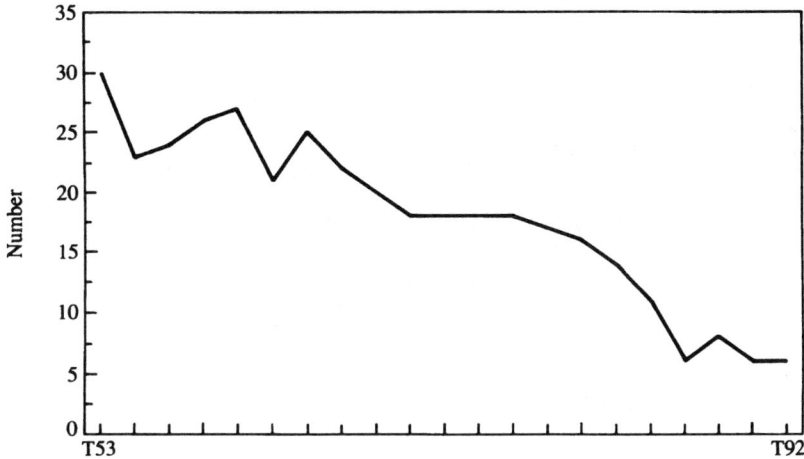

**Figure 10.6** *Concession reductions*

They begin by agreeing customer requirements during the bid phase of the programme. These are regularly reviewed through customer conferences and involve customer representatives in the multidisciplinary design-build teams. This approach has enabled the company to reduce engineering change levels and product development cycle time by up to 44%. In addition, customer complaints, on one programme alone, have reduced by a factor of 10 over a 2-year period, and there has been a dramatic reduction in the number of concessions (Figure 10.6).

Customer satisfaction teams have developed key performance indicators that, when combined with industry standard measures, enable Shorts to compare themselves with competitors. Using these mechanisms to identify where to improve is beginning to show results, e.g. Shorts product support activities were recently rated second among the manufacturers of turboprop aircraft by *Commuter Regional Airline News* (Figure 10.7). The Sherpa Combined Logistics Support Group were given an overall rating of 'outstanding' (the highest rating attainable) for each year of service with the US Airforce in Germany. In addition, Super Sherpa achieved 99% despatch reliability, and Starburst missile system was 100% operational during the Gulf Crisis; the company received many letters of commendation praising its efforts.

Shorts have also won nine Boeing Pride in Excellence Awards and were the first company in Europe, and only the second in the world, to be approved to the new Advanced Quality Standard D1–9000. Currently Shorts is the only company to gain Boeing D1–9000 reapproval.

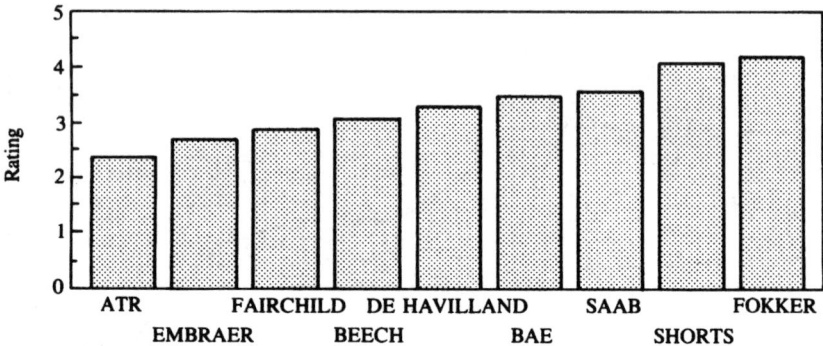

**Figure 10.7** *Perceptions of product support: manufacturers of turboprop aircraft*
*Source: Commuter Regional Aircraft News*

### *Impact on society*

The Total Quality programme has brought indirect gains in terms of enhanced company image as a result of publicizing the programme. Some may say that TQM is simply a marketing issue, but at Shorts they realize it is a competitive and survival issue.

Members of Shorts staff have had the opportunity to attend and present papers at international conferences. This both publicizes the fact that Shorts are involved in TQM and gives the staff the chance to discover what other companies are doing and how their approach may help. This has already proved beneficial, e.g. the first Total Quality Plan was developed in 1990 as a result of attendance at a US conference. This was one of the most significant developments of the programme as there now exists a series of clearly defined and challenging divisional and company goals forming part of the Company Business Plan. This has resolved the conflict of 'real work' versus TQM activities.

Other benefits include the winning of a 1989 LTK National Training Award for the Total Quality training programme, the 1992 British Quality Award and the 1992 Northern Ireland Quality Award. These reflect the widespread support and commitment from all personnel to the Total Quality programme.

## Lessons learned

Shorts Total Quality programme has survived during the most turbulent period of the company's history. The results so far are encouraging but they feel they still have a great deal to do, especially in transforming the organization to world-class status.

Five and a half years into the programme, Shorts management can look back and assess how things were done, how they could have been done better, what were the problems encountered, and the lessons learned:

- The Company's Chief Executive must be absolutely committed to TQM if there is to be even the slightest chance of sustained success. Shorts President has provided visible support to the programme and has played a key role in its implementation.
- The Shorts Total Quality team feel that they failed to publicize Total Quality successes on a wide-enough scale. Until recently, employees were generally unaware of Total Quality success stories outside their immediate work area. This led to a belief that TQM was not happening and was just another of those good ideas that never reached fruition. They now realize that employee achievements and contributions must be recognized. They also need to be aware that the programme is working and that things are changing. Shorts have recently introduced a quarterly magazine which informs everyone of progress. Dedicated displays, the company newspaper, divisional newsletters and team meetings are also used to publicize Total Quality activities.
- Total Quality, like any other business activity, is a dynamic process which must be regularly reviewed to maintain its success and relevance to company goals.
- The more effort put into the planning phase of a TQM programme, the greater the likelihood of success. Plans must be practical and reasonable, with sufficient resources and commitment to implement them. It is comparatively simpler to rally support for a TQM programme than it is to maintain that support when operational problems occur or interest fades. Nothing short of sustained commitment will provide the necessary results.
- The top-down approach to training appears to be the best method of creating sustained improvement within a large organization, even if it does slow the message reaching every level in the company. The need to devolve responsibility and accountability cannot be overemphasized; employees at every level want to get involved and have a major contribution to make.
- Total Quality makes good business sense. Shorts estimate that the benefits to date exceed the total programme cost, including training, by a factor of 13.

## The future

The Total Quality Plan was reviewed recently and endorsed by the President and Company Quality Council. The plan prioritized the following areas for attention for the following year.

### Strategic framework

The company will incorporate a strategic Total Quality framework into their Total Quality Plans, based on the European Model for Self-Appraisal. This will help to integrate the various major initiatives currently underway or planned. Further performance measures, which will assess the effectiveness of the Total Quality Strategy, will be established and monitored and a self-assessment of each division will be undertaken using the elements of the strategic framework.

### People involvement

Shorts management plan to raise employee involvement level to 60% through the provision of suitable training, involvement in Total Quality projects and the suggestion scheme.

### Benchmarking

Each division will develop its respective benchmarking methodologies and action plans based on its findings, to ensure the achievement of company-wide world-class business practices.

### Customer focus

The customer focus teams for each division will further develop relevant satisfaction metrics, thus identifying further opportunities for improvement.

## Concluding remarks

- To date, the results are encouraging, both financially and in the way the company deals with its people, but the management know they have more to do before Shorts become a Total Quality company.
- If the company claims that people are its greatest asset, it must mean it and show it. Long-term survival depends largely on the ability to harness the knowledge and enthusiasm of the entire workforce. Total Quality is the vehicle for achieving this aim at Shorts.

● It is clear that the Total Quality programme has played, and will continue to play, a vital part in the transformation of Shorts. To build on what they already have achieved will require the continuing support of personnel at all levels. Only through this support do the management feel they can progress towards Total Quality.

## Acknowledgement

This is from a case study by Desmond A. Bell.

# Part Four
# The Organizational, Communication and Teamwork Requirements

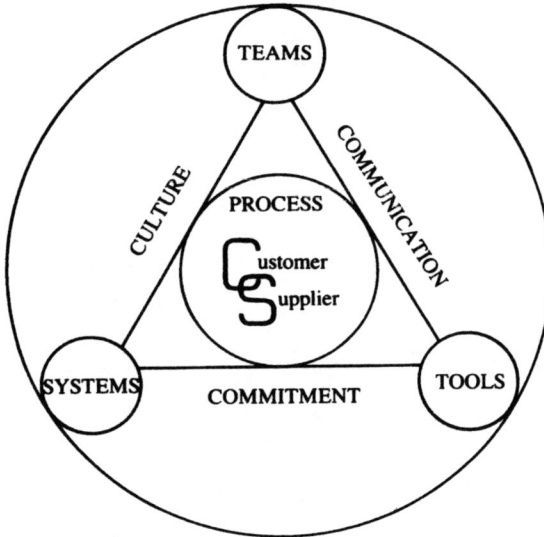

# 11 Organizing for success at Pirelli Communication Cables

## Introduction

TQM is now recognized by enlightened companies as being of strategic importance in the drive for market share. Such companies may engage in a programme of publicity, employee briefings, training courses, new working practices and have a commitment to achieving excellence, and yet the much-sought-after benefits do not materialize. Instead of order there is confusion, instead of progress there is stagnation, instead of success there is failure, resulting in frustration and a belief that TQM is not the way forward to the cultural change necessary for continuous improvement.

To be successful, some companies believe that an organizational structure must be established at the outset of introducing TQM in order to create a framework which will enable quality improvement to develop and flourish. The structure itself is considered a key factor in achieving success and must be given priority attention by senior management. Such a company is Pirelli Communication Cables, a division within the Pirelli General PLC group responsible for the design, manufacturing and installation of both optical and copper communication/control cables in the UK and world markets. Pirelli Communication Cables implemented a TQM-based organizational structure in March 1989. This case describes the details which have involved all employees in the company.

## Organizational structure

The structure for implementing quality improvement throughout the company is shown in Figure 11.1. The structure has been designed to harness the total potential to improve at every level of the organization and, being simple, is well-understood by all employees. This means that each individual in each department can readily become involved in the quality improvement process.

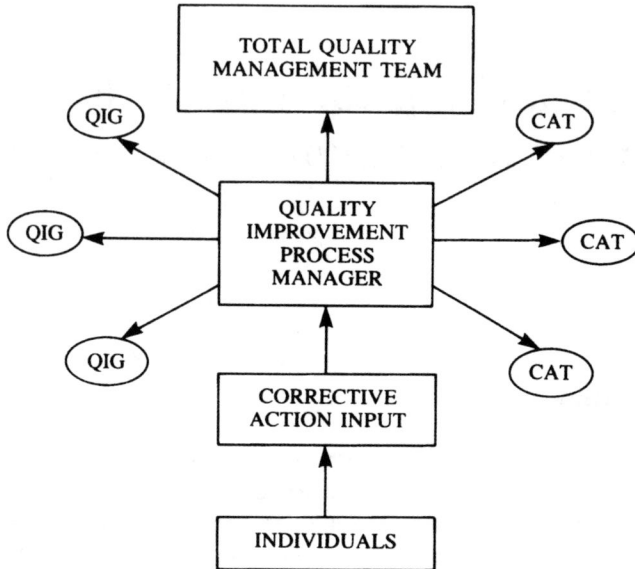

Key:
QIG   Quality improvement group
CAT   Corrective action team

**Figure 11.1** *Organizational structure for quality improvements*

The following sections describe the five key elements of the structure and explain how the element activities were integrated together to achieve continuous quality improvement. It will be shown that by implementing this structure, and by using the methodology and tools/techniques referred to, Total Quality concepts have been established throughout Pirelli Communication Cables.

## Total Quality Management Team

The Total Quality Management Team (TQMT) consists of the General Manager, the first-line reporting managers and a specialist for facilitating the operation of the Quality Improvement Groups (QIGs) and the Corrective Action Teams (CATs). This facilitator is known as the Quality Improvement Process (QIP) Manager within Pirelli Communication Cables, to place emphasis on the nature of the activities involved.

The TQMT determines policy, establishes direction, provides support and, by example, demonstrates commitment to quality improvement. It is important that the TQMT does not act as a corrective action team or deal with specific quality issues; these are dealt with at other forums convened for that specific purpose. The TQMT operates as a steering group for the implementation of TQM, and the responsibilities for the various tasks involved are divided among the TQMT members. This is considered an essential requirement as all senior management must be actively involved and the various tasks have been divided as follows:

| | |
|---|---|
| General Manager | Chair, Management commitment |
| Marketing Manager | Communications |
| Technical Manager | Special events |
| Financial Controller | Cost of quality |
| Operations Manager | Tools and techniques |
| Purchasing Manager | Performance measures |
| Personnel Manager | Education, recognition |
| QIP Manager | QIGs, CATs |
| Quality Manager | Secretary, planning |

The General Manager has led the way and has ensured that the TQMT members demonstrate *commitment* by acting as role models at all times. *Communications* have been specifically addressed to determine the most effective methods and media to be used to ensure all employees are kept informed of progress. Monitoring the *cost of defects* has proved to be a powerful management driver for quality improvement and *performance* has been measured whenever possible to provide a basis for QIG, CAT and individual improvement initiatives. The *education* and *recognition* of personnel has been a major task to organize and a master plan has been established to ensure timely progress was maintained. *Tools and techniques*, such as Statistical Process Control (SPC), have been introduced where appropriate and *special events* arranged, such as the initial launch of TQM and the issue of news bulletins. The task-holders have become local experts in their particular areas of responsibility and they facilitate the implementation of the action plan agreed at the TQMT meetings.

Terms of reference have been established for the TQMT in Pirelli Communication Cables, as detailed below. These have been published throughout the company to ensure the function and role of the TQMT is fully understood.

## Terms of reference for the TQMT

1 To determine policy for quality improvement within the company.
2 To establish an environment where QIGs and CATs can flourish.

3 To establish procedures for measuring ongoing performance and cost of quality and ensure corrective actions are taken where appropriate.
4 Actively to support the implementation of the established policy consistently and on a continuous basis, ensuring that all disciplines/work areas are fully involved in quality improvement.
5 To hold meetings at 3-week intervals during normal working hours for approximately 1 hour to determine the implementation programme and monitor progress. Minutes will be issued of each meeting held to record decisions and actions agreed.

## Quality Improvement Process Manager

The QIP Manager facilitates the day-to-day operations of the QIGs and CATs and, as such, has a major role in the ongoing success of the quality improvement process. The individual chosen was carefully selected: he was an efficient organizer, an able motivator, enthusiastic and had well-proven management experience. He was also sufficiently senior in the organization to have the authority to ensure actions would be taken where required.

The QIP Manager is responsible for establishing the QIGs in the first instance and was actively involved in the training programme at the initial launch. Three days of training have been developed, as shown in Figure 11.2.

Once the groups were established, the QIP Manager provided assistance to the group leaders, ensured operating procedures were being implemented, monitored progress through the QIG meeting minutes, arranged for TQMT members to attend QIG meetings from time to time to demonstrate

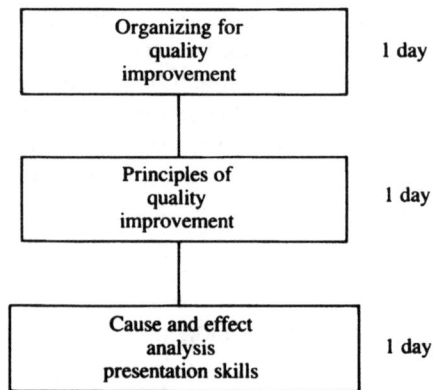

**Figure 11.2** *QIG training programme*

management commitment and interest, and organized quarterly reviews with all QIG leaders. A report is presented at each TQMT meeting to ensure top management visibility is maintained.

The second major role for the QIP Manager has been to facilitate the operation of the corrective action system and the CATs. A single interface is provided for the company in terms of processing, reporting and communicating corrective actions. This ensures that there is no duplication of effort and priorities can be established to deal with the major problems first. Corrective Action Requests (CARs) can arise either from QIGs or individuals and assistance is provided to identify the process owner and, where appropriate, to select the CAT leader. A database of personnel with specific skills is held for reference in selecting CAT members; this ensures that the 'experts' are known and serve on CATs where required. The QIP Manager keeps the TQMT informed of all CARs in progress and priorities will be decided by the TQMT when necessary.

## Quality Improvement Groups

QIGs operate at all levels in the organization on a departmental basis. The QIG leader is generally the supervisor of the work area concerned, which in some cases may be a senior staff member. A team approach is adopted, however, and all QIG members are equal as far as the group operation is concerned. A QIG leader's guide has been published to provide ideas for discussion at the QIG meetings and guidance on specific topical issues.

QIGs create the framework where personnel involvement can be maximized in striving for improvement and excellence. The groups address quality issues within their specific departments/work areas, with the object purpose of reducing waste and error, enhancing performance and proposing corrective actions for those issues which cannot be resolved by the QIG concerned. They create an opportunity to resolve many of the frustrating, niggling quality issues which affect the smooth running and efficiency of day-to-day operations.

Benefits for those participating include improved morale, increased job satisfaction, stimulation of teamwork and development of skills.

In Pirelli Communication Cables a total of 25 groups has been established covering all departments on site. The number of personnel who have completed 3-day training courses for QIGs equates to 50% of the workforce; all these personnel, both white- and blue-collar, are active members of QIGs. It is planned to train the remaining 50% of the workforce to enable these people to become involved on a rotation basis.

Improvement is managed by the QIGs on a project-by-project basis. A simple recording and control system is operated by the QIG leader, which enables progress to be monitored.

## Corrective Action Teams

CATs address specific CARs with the purpose of establishing a permanent and cost-effective solution. The QIP Manager facilitates the appointment of the CAT leader where appropriate; the leader will be selected for his/her skills or knowledge in dealing with a particular problem. The CAT leader selects his/her team, which should comprise no more than five members; reference to the database of skilled personnel is made to assist in this exercise. It is important that the team members invest adequate time and effort to team activities and must not compromise progress by nominating deputies. For this reason, the CARs must be carefully prioritized and resources allocated to ensure a successful closure of each request.

The CAT will address only the problem allocated for investigation and resolution. When the work is complete, the CAT will be disbanded and the CAR closed down. The QIP Manager is responsible for managing the total activity to ensure maximum use is made of the company resources. The QIP Manager will decide when a CAR can be addressed by an individual or when a CAT is required. The TQMT members may be consulted in particular cases to assist in making this decision.

CAT members are trained in tools and techniques in a similar manner to the QIGs (see Figure 11.2). More advanced courses are also being organized for the next phase of implementing TQM.

## Individuals

It is important that all employees, from goods-in to goods-out, from marketing to design, from reception to delivery, are totally involved in the QIP process. The structure has, therefore, been designed to enable all individuals to contribute by applying the quality improvement principles to their own job. Every individual receives 1 day of training in these principles to provide a common understanding throughout the business of what is required. Individuals are encouraged to strive for excellence and improvement on a day-to-day basis and to raise issues either through their local QIG or by raising a CAR.

## The reasons for success at Pirelli Communication Cables

Management commitment, publicity, training and improved working practices are all important elements of a TQM programme but in themselves they are insufficient to ensure success. The successful implementation of TQM requires a defined organizational structure which demands and harnesses the full potential of the workforce. This can be achieved by establishing teams and groups to manage quality improvement across the company, thereby organizing for success. In this way the considerable benefits of the TQM route, i.e. achieving excellence in all aspects of business and employee performance, will be realized.

A defined organizational structure is essential if TQM is to be successfully implemented. This case shows that Total Quality has to be managed and that this can be achieved by means of senior management involvement through, in the case of Pirelli, the TQMT, by appointing a QIP manager to facilitate day-to-day operations, by establishing QIGs throughout all departments to manage local improvements, by organizing CATs to address specific company-wide problems, and by involving all employees through individual efforts and through QIGs and CARs.

TQM must be seen as a fundamental part of the business operation and not as an add-on extra. Continuous hard work, determination and persistence and a total commitment from the top down are all essential ingredients which, together with the defined structure, will ensure success in the greatest of all ambitions – to become the best. In this way the considerable benefit of the TQM route – achieving excellence in all aspects of business and employee performance – has begun to be realized at Pirelli Communication Cables.

# 12 Organization and teamwork for quality at Thomas Cork SML

## Introduction

Thomas Cork S M Ltd is part of the Hartz Mountain Corporation of Harrison, New Jersey, the world's largest supplier of pet accessories. The company's principal business is the supply of complex ranges of non-food products to supermarkets. It is located in a modern purpose-built warehouse complex in Nottingham, UK, and provides a comprehensive distribution service with full merchandising support at store level.

Orders are picked in individual units, priced according to customer requirements and shipped direct to stores. The warehouse currently processes between 1 and 1.5 million units per week. Store deliveries are made by the company's own team of merchandisers who merchandise customers' fixtures and place a reorder for the next delivery.

The company operates throughout the UK and the Republic of Ireland. It employs 600 people, almost half of whom work on sales and merchandising. It currently markets and distributes around 2000 lines. These include Hartz pet accessories, Cover Girl cosmetics, Stylers haircare, Scholl footcare, Supermark stationery, Stitch & Sew sewing accessories, Rhymers babycare, Duracell batteries and a comprehensive range of housewares.

The common feature of these ranges is complexity. Many of them are own-branded ranges for which the company is responsible for marketing and buying. Products are sourced from the UK and from around the world. The company's customer base includes Sainsbury, Tesco, Asda, Gateway, Safeway, regional multiples and Co-ops.

The company sends its merchandising teams to set up and manage display stands as part of each store's operation, adapting their approach according to the company they happen to be servicing. It is a complex and subtle relationship, in which the merchandisers have to justify by sales the space they occupy, while maintaining a wide range of products, some of which move only slowly, but are essential to the overall impression of comprehensiveness and variety.

Managing Thomas Cork calls for a knowledge of the needs and expectations of its suppliers and the retailers, plus an insight into the needs and expectations of the retailers' customers, too. The demands include the utmost reliability of supply and the absolute minimum of defects and deficiencies.

Apart from the problems relating to managing 2000 products across a number of ranges, because the company's merchandisers operate within customers' stores, it has to accommodate individual customers' requirements and work within their systems. This inevitably adds considerably to the complexity of the business. For example, Thomas Cork supplies both Gateway and Tesco with more individual product lines than any other suppliers.

## The need for quality management

The Chairman and Managing Director were concerned for some time about growing complexity and the problems being encountered in day-to-day management. It seemed that an inordinate amount of time was being spent on fire-fighting, and 'getting it right first time' simply did not appear to be part of the company vocabulary. The company had survived, even prospered, by 'crisis management'.

About three years ago the Chairman/Managing Director was invited to a seminar on Cost-Effective Quality Management, sponsored by the Department of Trade and Industry. He had previously heard a good deal about Quality Management but had tended to associate this with manufacturing companies. This particular seminar soon convinced him, however, that the principles applied equally to companies involved in activities such as distribution and service.

Following discussions within the board room, they concluded that a Quality Management Programme could be very beneficial to the company and decided to proceed. Their objective was to change the culture of the business so that all the principles of Quality Management would become a natural part of the day-to-day activity, thereby enhancing the efficiency and profitability of the company.

At this stage, the Board made a number of decisions on how they should implement the programme:

1 They would take on a Quality Consultant to advise on technique and to provide guidance and assistance to help drive the programme along.
2 They agreed that the programme would be successful only if it had the total commitment of both Directors and Senior Management and that this group of people should be involved in the Quality Programme through all its stages.

3 They decided not to work to a fixed timetable, but considered that it was essential to have made sufficient progress at each stage in order to create confidence in the benefits of the programme, before moving on to the next stage.

The question now was, how should the Board of the company proceed to introduce their ideas?

## The introduction

The programme began with a 2-day introduction for Directors, at which the principles and techniques of TQM were explained by the consultant. They then proceeded to redefine the company's policy and objectives. A similar exercise was carried out with the company's Senior Management and they too came up with views on the company's policies and objectives, not always the same as the Directors. This was immediately followed by a joint meeting with Directors and Senior Management, at which the final Policy Document was agreed.

A Programme Management Team (PMT) was set up at this stage to oversee the introduction of the Quality Programme. The Chairman/Managing Director acted as Chairman of the PMT and a coordinator was appointed to look after administration and to coordinate the work of the Team. All Directors and Senior Management were coopted on to the PMT.

The next stage was to identify the key problem areas which were preventing the company from operating effectively. Two exercises were carried out. The first was a Needs and Expectations exercise, which involved a large number of people from all levels and all departments within the business. Who – they asked themselves – receives my work and that of my department, and are we supplying them with what they really need and want?

The Financial Controller recalled the excitement of senior managers when they realized their opportunity to speak directly and freely to the Board. That sense of involvement and participation was extended downwards; for example, the Director responsible for transport went out with one of the lorry drivers – and came back with a checklist of questions and ideas.

The second exercise was devoted to identifying the amount of management time spent on fire-fighting. These two exercises highlighted a comparatively small number of problems which appeared to account for a large proportion of the difficulties.

In all, six key problems were identified, but it was realized that they could not all be dealt with simultaneously and it was decided that three Action Teams should be established to tackle the most pressing problem areas. Each of the Action Teams had its own Chairperson (who reported to the PMT) and

Coordinator. Each team was made up by representatives from a number of departments and these were selected from different levels of management to ensure good cross-representation within the processes involved and to bring together the people best equipped to find a solution, without regard for rank or departmental boundaries. This was particularly important as it ensured that departments were working in close cooperation with common objectives. During the early stages the consultant attended PMT and Action Team meetings to provide guidance and assistance, particularly on problem-solving techniques.

The role of the Coordinator was very important. He or she was responsible for arranging meetings, for administration and, generally, acting as progress-chaser. The first task for each of the Action Teams was to define its objectives and then to tackle the particular problem allocated to them. It was also decided that all of the management needed to be informed about the programme, to stimulate their interest and to enlist their support. This was done at a 2-day management conference.

We now move into the most difficult phase of the programme. Remember, the management were already stretched trying to cope with complex day-to-day problems, endless fire-fighting and simply the job of surviving. To this the Board were to add the burden of Action Team and PMT meetings. These involved a lot of people and took up a great deal of time. Far from improving job satisfaction, the initial stage of the programme brought little but frustration and all that was offered in return was hope that things could only get better.

The Senior Management faced the problems of deciding what was important now, and how they should tell people of the important issues and stress the benefits of quality improvement.


## The implementation

The importance of the PMT Coordinator and the Consultant became apparent at this stage. It was necessary to maintain strict discipline to ensure that meetings were held as planned and that reports were submitted on time.

They found that it is necessary to keep the 'day-to-day management function' and 'the improvement function' separate in the early stages of a TQM programme. Ultimately, ongoing improvement must be the major management focus, but it is unrealistic to assume that such a cultural change can be brought in overnight. Thomas Cork's experience was that this change can be brought about by having two parallel structures working together. Soon the members of the Management Team started to question the need for two structures and resolved to create one integrated operation.

The company found that, for successful projects, training is needed in team skills. Although the management recognized that individuals are different, it was very useful to formalize the process of recognizing these differences and to concentrate on the inherent strengths and weaknesses of different personality types. Training in these concepts, together with frank discussions about the dynamics of the management team concerned, led to much stronger and more constructive management team operations.

They found it was crucial specifically to spell out the role of the PMT (or Quality Council) and to spell out the role of the Action Team. This allowed the PMT to establish a specific brief for each Action Team so that their activities became very focused. It was easy for Action Teams to drift from specific topics to attempt to resolve every issue facing the company.

One area which needed strong management was that when an Action Team had completed its task, it should be thanked publicly and disbanded. It is easy to allow an Action Team to continue after its first task has been completed, which can be quite a mistake.

People also needed constant reminders of the benefits which could be derived from the programme. The management quickly learnt that, just because they were dealing with problems in a more constructive manner using the newly acquired problem-solving techniques, there were no quick solutions and it was quite some time before workable solutions began to see the light of day. This undoubtedly was the low point of the programme. All the effort and cost of the programme – but none of the benefits.

Slowly but surely, however, Thomas Cork began to get results. Solutions were found and, more importantly, people began to understand that, by working through problems or tackling new opportunities with well-constructed Action Teams, they could get much better results and improve efficiency and customer service. Individual managers began to set up ad hoc Action Teams to tackle problems and opportunities using the same techniques. They were also becoming more proactive in seeking opportunities to improve efficiency.

Once the full commitment of the management was secured and they began to see the benefits of the programme in terms of reduced fire-fighting and increased efficiency, it was decided that all employees should be involved. This was done by holding a Quality Week, during which all employees attended Quality Meetings. They worked with comparatively small groups so that each employee had an opportunity to participate directly in these meetings. A special edition of the company's newspaper, featuring Quality Week, was also published.

This last phase of the Quality Management Programme was launched and the company is still steadily developing programmes to involve all of the staff.

There is still a long way to go but they are already seeing important contributions, particularly in the warehouse and in the sales and merchandising operations.

As far as the management is concerned, the principles of Quality Management have become a way of life. The Quality Programme is no longer run on a stand-alone basis but has been integrated into the normal management process. The PMT has been disbanded and its functions have been taken over by the Management Committee.

The managers of Thomas Cork SML are eloquent about the pain and frustration of TQM but they are unanimous that the suffering is worthwhile in the long run. 'It's not a bed of roses', warned the Chairman and Managing Director, 'or an instant revolution. We were warned that things would get worse before they got better – and that's certainly true – but I have no doubts about the benefits.'

He cites product launches as one of the areas of greatest progress. 'In the old days, there was not enough coordination of planning between departments, work fell behind schedule, and there were crises that could be solved only by throwing money at them. Sometimes, too, salesmen would make overambitious promises, and leave others to make them good. The company has now taken to heart the lesson preached by our quality consultants: that planning is the only worthwhile management activity, because it eliminates personal control (failure to delegate effectively) and fire-fighting (reacting to crises as they break).'

Interdepartmental action teams now plan every product launch in detail well in advance, according to a basic master plan. Salesmen who make rash promises are themselves made responsible for forming the action team which will fulfil them.

The Operations Director has launched a 'needs and expectations' exercise in the warehouse, where pickers have the monotonous but vital front-line job of making up the orders. It is also too easy here for a picker to be blamed for picking and packing the wrong item, when at least part of the responsibility lies with the person who put it in the wrong tray – or, more likely, with the system of working.

The Financial Controller is able to quote figures. 'We estimated the annual cost of wasted time in doing jobs twice as something between half and three-quarters of a million pounds,' he says. 'In the first 2 years of our quality programme, we have reduced these costs by half a million!'

It is this cost-effectiveness that has persuaded the Operations Director that Total Quality is more than just another gimmick. He no longer sees quality solely in terms of the product or service to the customer, but as 'part of everything everybody does'. Fundamentally, he believes, it is a matter of attitude.

## What the company has achieved

1 There is a much greater spirit of cooperation between departments, with all departments working with a common purpose.
2 There has been a substantial reduction in time spent fire-fighting.
3 The company has been able to achieve a significant reduction in costs.
4 It has been possible to improve the company's profitability considerably, despite the quite difficult problems caused by the recession.

## What advice may be given to companies embarking on a TQM programme?

1 Leadership must come from the top.
2 There must be complete commitment to the programme by all management.
3 The organization of the teams and the choice of personnel is crucial to success.
4 Be prepared to pass through a pain barrier before beginning to see any real benefit from the programme.
5 Avoid creating an unduly high level of expectation, otherwise there will be much disappointment and frustration during the early stages.

And finally:

● *A Quality Programme is hard work but well worth the effort.*

# Part Five
# TQM – Its Implementation and Integration into Strategy

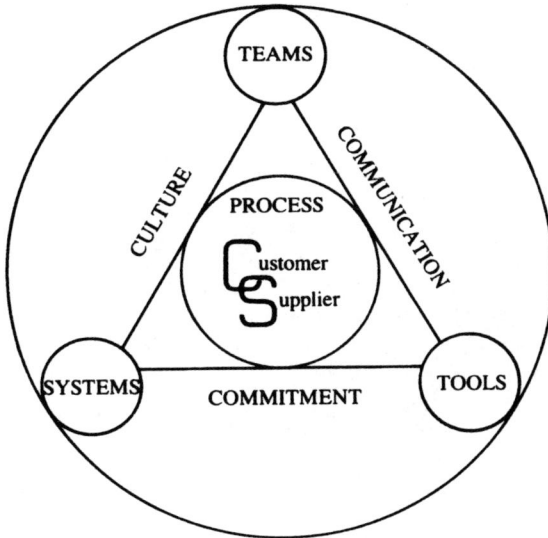

# 13   Implementing TQM at Newtech Tools Ltd

## Introduction

Newtech Tools Ltd was set up over 40 years ago by the present Chairman and Managing Director, Jim Pearson. Jim is the major shareholder in the company, with a 51% stake. Three other members of the Pearson family own the remaining 49%. The company manufactures a wide range of standard and special tooling for the white-goods, automotive and machine-tool industries. The firm employs 156 staff, the majority of whom are skilled operatives. In recent years, there have been some staff cutbacks, mainly as a result of recession in the industry and increased use of new technology, such as computer numerically controlled (CNC) machines.

Newtech has occupied the same premises in Shipley for the last 20 years, although three major expansions at the factory floor area have taken place. The last of these was in 1986 and the site is now fully developed. The factory generally provides good working conditions but the phased development of the site has resulted in a layout that sometimes hinders efficient production. The increased demand for space over the years has resulted in some departments having a cramped layout. As a result of the above factors, plans are well-advanced to relocate the company in new purpose-built premises on a nearby industrial estate.

Newtech enjoys a good reputation for the quality and reliability of its products. With the exception of two periods, one in the early 1970s and the other from 1980 to 1983, demand for the company's products has been high and profitability has been about average for the industry. The general high level of activity has left management little time to develop a coherent business strategy.

## The management

Newtech has three executive directors: Jim Pearson – Managing Director; John Pearson – Technical Director; and Tom Hines – Marketing Director.

The production function is headed by John Pearson, who oversees the organization (see Appendix A). John works in close liaison with the works manager, Ken Simpson, and head of the production planning and control section, David Smith. Supervision at shop-floor level is effected by departmental foremen and chargehands.

The majority of the senior managers have been with the company for many years, although John Pearson, Jim's son, recently joined the company from a larger machine-tool company. John has recently completed a part-time MBA and had submitted a dissertation on TQM. He was very keen to introduce some new ideas on quality within the company.

## Human resources

The company has a very traditional management style. Employees are generally kept well-informed of developments but there is very little active participation in the company decision-making process. The culture is best described as one of benevolent paternalism.

The company recognizes the Associated Engineering Union (AEU) for the purposes of collective bargaining. Terms and conditions of employment of all employees up to supervisory level are negotiated with the union. Any day-to-day problems are dealt with by the two shop stewards and departmental foremen. The management team meet with full-time union officials on an annual basis to review pay and conditions.

Generally speaking, labour relations are very good and the company has experienced only one strike in its 40-year history. This was during the recessionary period from 1980 to 1983 when the company was trying to enforce wage restraint as part of a cost-cutting programme. This was heavily resisted by the whole workforce.

In the last few years there has been a rapid decline in union membership in the company. Membership now stands at less than 50% and this has presented a major problem to the union and management. Sole bargaining rights for the AEU is now inappropriate. A Works Council has been set up in the last year to represent a cross-section of the workforce. This Council meets with the management at regular intervals to review the progress of the company. It is intended to negotiate directly with the Council at this year's review of pay and conditions.

The company does not employ any separate personnel manager. This role is performed by John Pearson. John is very keen on developing people and has completely redesigned all the apprentice training programmes and trainee programmes. The main emphasis on these new programmes is on multi-skilling and giving people 'richer' job opportunities. The design of appropriate development plans for the more experienced workers is currently being addressed, although this is proving difficult, given the financial constraints and production demands.

Staff turnover and absenteeism rates in the company are very low. Many staff have achieved 25 years' service with the company. This stability has many advantages, but it does present a problem in offering promotion opportunities to younger employees.

## The production facilities

The company is organized on a job shop basis. There are four main departments – turning, milling, grinding and final assembly. A heat treatment section is situated between the turning and milling departments. The layout gives the usual problems associated with this configuration but a general lack of space compounds the problem. In particular, difficulties arise in accommodating the high level of work-in-progress that the system generates. Outline details of the plant are given in Appendix B. Capital investment has been heavily cut back in recent years, partly as a result of the low return achieved on investments and the high cost of capital in the late 1980s and early 1990s.

## Sales and marketing

Tom Hines heads up a small sales and marketing section. Tom has been with the company for just over 4 years, having previously been the Marketing Manager in a larger machine-tool company. Tom has a good network of contacts in the industry and spends most of his time visiting customers. Customers value this attention and Tom takes a substantial number of orders during customer visits. There is no formal mechanism which enables the company to assess its capability to meet the customers' delivery requirements when taking these orders.

The majority of customers' enquiries come via the post. Two sales staff are responsible for preparing smaller-value quotations. Large-value quotations are handled by Jim Pearson. Newtech wins approximately one-third of all the work quoted for. Quoted prices are based on experience and the quoted lead times reflect the state of the company's order book.

The company exports approximately 10% of its output, mainly to Europe. This is a growing business and some problems have arisen in servicing this customer base. European customers do not receive the attention (customer visits etc.) that their UK counterparts receive.

## Production planning and control

The company manufactures its own product range, together with a wide range of special made-to-order tooling.

For the standard product range, the marketing department produces sales forecasts, based on sales representatives' estimates, for each item in the product range. The forecast gives the expected monthly demand for a 3-month period. The production planning and control department uses this information to produce a master production schedule for the standard product range. Each job is given an internal works order number and the release authorization note, drawings and specifications are sent to the works manager for release into the factory according to the schedule. A route card showing machining details and times etc. accompanies each job. Standard products are put into stock when finished to await call-off by customers. Generally the stock turnover is good, although some items are slow-moving.

In the case of 'specials', a slightly different system operates. Upon receipt of a customer's order, a copy is sent to the production planning and control section where it is assigned a works order number. This copy order is accompanied by detailed drawings and specifications from the customer. These documents, together with a release note, are sent to the works manager who checks and clarifies, if necessary, the instructions received from the customer. The whole set of documents is sent to the foreman at the department carrying out the first machining operation. Instructions concerning the sequence of operations are not included. Similarly, times for each operation are not given.

The foremen issue drawings and verbal instructions to the chargehands who in turn load each machine according to the number of jobs currently on the machine. Foremen also inform the storekeeper of the raw material requirements and other consumables. With the exception of steel bars, consumable parts are regularly reordered by the storekeeper who operates a basic two-bin system. Steel bars are subject to closer control by the works manager to ensure that advantage is taken of any quantity discounts.

## Quality

Newtech does not have a separate quality function. Operators are trained to inspect their own work at every stage of the production process. The chargehands and foremen coordinate and facilitate this process and deal with any difficult inspection problems. Foremen are also responsible for ensuring that the products conform to specification before being passed on to the next phase of production. There are few documented procedures detailing test and inspection methods. Most test and inspection equipment is calibrated as the need arises.

The company prides itself on its quality record, with customer returns consistently below 0.2% of sales. Many of these returns are simply the result of customers' overstocking. Indeed, the marketing department uses this as a marketing tool as the figure is thought to be well below that of many competitors.

## Problem areas

### *Human resources*

Newtech has an ageing workforce. There has been very little recruitment of apprentices and young trainees in the last few years. The problem is even more acute at management level. Jim Pearson, Ken Simpson and David Smith, together with the Chief Works Accountant, Eric Hall, are all due to retire within the next 3 years. The succession question has not even been raised, let alone answered.

The general morale in the company is currently quite low. The industry has faced a difficult 4 years and the drive for greater efficiency and lower cost production has resulted in significant downsizing. The worst is now over but raising morale is a serious challenge for the management.

### *Production planning and control*

The wide product range makes effective planning and control difficult to achieve. Important customers frequently telephone urgently required orders into Newtech's marketing department. These are given priority over other jobs and tend to disrupt production schedules. This causes friction between marketing and production. The average lead time is 6 weeks but priority jobs are rushed through the system in 7–10 days. Similarly, Tom Hines frequently takes orders during his visits to customers and offers unrealistic delivery dates. Tom and Ken Simpson have frequent arguments over this issue.

There is a wide variation in machine utilization, again due to the nature of the work. Some machines are working at less than 50% capacity, whilst jobs are queuing at other machines. Similar jobs show considerable time variation at different points through the production process. Machine operators do not appear to record consistent times, which adds to the control problem.

The ageing plant profile is causing some problems. There is a backlog of repair and maintenance problems and it is increasingly difficult to obtain spares for some of the older machines. All maintenance is carried out on a 'need' basis.

A persistent problem has been Newtech's failure to meet the customer delivery dates. This has been the subject of much management attention and, although the situation has greatly improved, with 90% of the orders being delivered within 7 days of the customer's required delivery date, there are still jobs that are sometimes delivered many weeks after the due date. The total production cycle time appears to be a contributing factor. Some jobs simply get bogged down in the large volume of work-in-progress.

### Purchasing

Steel bars of various sizes and specifications are the main purchase. Over 25 different types of steel are stocked in various sizes. In recent years the company has been concerned at the large amount of money tied up in steel stocks; some sizes and specifications are particularly slow-moving. In the past, the purchasing strategy tended to be based on placing sufficiently large orders to obtain the maximum discount. However, this has now gone to the other extreme, with orders being put in for small quantities. This has increasingly led to stock-out situations, which has disrupted production schedules.

### Quality

Newtech has started out on an ISO9002 programme, but the diverse system of informal procedures is hampering progress. The majority of these procedures are still undocumented. The programme is receiving assistance under the government's Quality Initiative and local consultants are helping the company. Responsibility for quality within the company is understood but not always unambiguously defined. John Pearson has overall responsibility for quality and liaises frequently with customers on this matter. All employees have received some quality awareness training and there is a general desire for a greater involvement in improvement activities.

Although the number of customer returns is very low, the system is geared to defect detection rather than defect prevention. Senior management is aware of several quality-related problems within the company. For example, many jobs have to be returned to the turning department for reworking as a result of a lack of quality consciousness on the part of some operators. Time pressures have not allowed this problem area to be fully resolved.

In the last 2 years, Newtech has come under increasing pressure to use Statistical Process Control (SPC) techniques, to install a documented quality system, and even consider TQM. John Pearson, in particular, has argued the case for TQM since joining the company. Senior management had generally been able to sidestep these pressures, using the company's good record on customer returns as an argument. There is genuine reluctance within the company's older managers to implement a fully documented quality system because of the time and cost involved. It is simply seen as an additional level of bureaucracy which is particularly inappropriate to a small firm. However, the ISO9002 programme is making steady if somewhat slow progress. The company is a year into the programme and it anticipates gaining registration within the next 12 months. Similarly, the senior production staff are very opposed to the introduction of SPC. As the Works Manager said, 'When you work to a couple of tenths (0.0002"), who needs SPC?' However, the company's main customer, Cram International PLC, has recently adopted a tougher line on this subject. John Pearson was recently invited to a seminar on TQM arranged by Cram International and this reaffirmed his belief in TQM. The quality 'pressure' reached a critical peak with the receipt of the letter shown in Appendix C.

## Management action

As the quality pressures appeared to be mounting at an uncomfortable rate, Jim Pearson decided to call a special meeting of the senior management team to review the present situation. Jim opened the meeting as follows:

> Gentlemen, I have called this meeting at short notice as we must give serious consideration to the customer pressure we are currently facing. We can no longer use our past good-quality record as an excuse for fending off these quality pressures. Some action is required and . . .

(The name Newtech Tools Ltd is fictitious and any similarity to other companies trading with a similar name or engaged in a similar business activity is purely coincidental.)

# Appendix A Organization chart for the production function

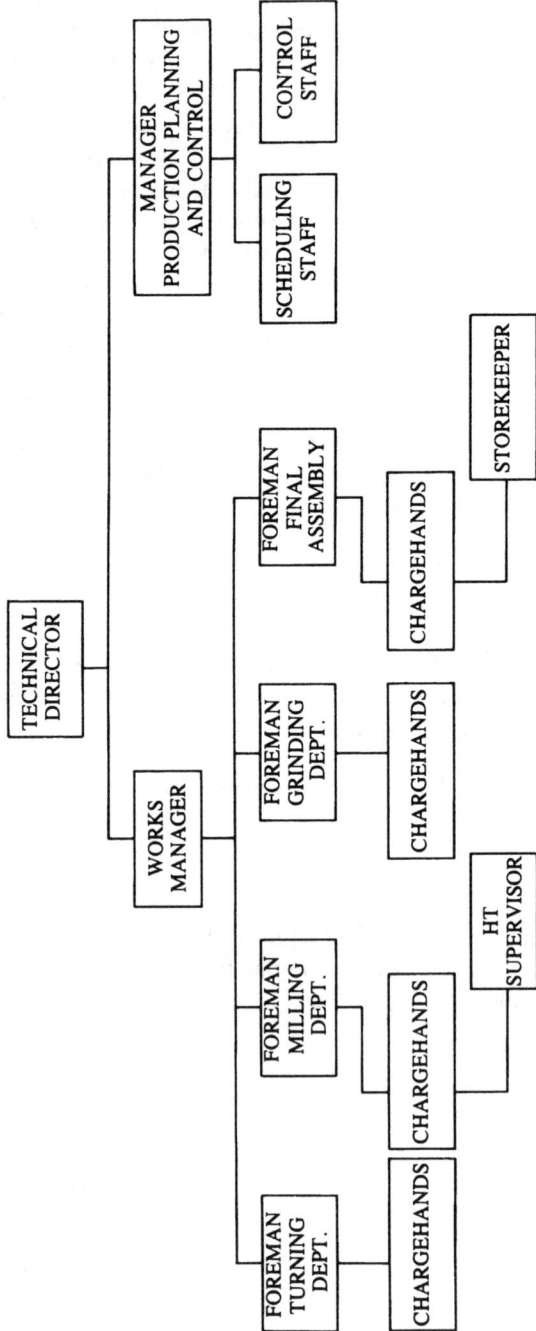

# Appendix B Outline of the main plant details

| | |
|---|---|
| 8 | CNC lathes |
| 14 | Semiautomatic capstan lathes |
| 15 | Centre lathes |

| | |
|---|---|
| 6 | Universal milling machines |
| 8 | Vertical milling machines |
| 5 | Horizontal milling machines |

| | |
|---|---|
| 5 | Slatting machines |
| 2 | Key seating machines |

| | |
|---|---|
| 12 | Drilling machines |

| | |
|---|---|
| 8 | Internal precision grinding machines |
| 10 | External precision grinding machines |
| 10 | Universal grinding machines |
| 7 | Surface-grinding machines |
| 4 | Centreless grinding machines |

| | |
|---|---|
| 5 | High-speed saws |

| | |
|---|---|
| 2 | Gas carbonizing furnaces |
| 5 | Salt bath furnaces |
| 6 | Tempering furnaces |

| Age profile of plant | Number of machines |
|---|---|
| <5 years old | 8 |
| 5–10 years old | 20 |
| 10–15 years old | 20 |
| 15–20 years old | 38 |
| >20 years old | 46 |

# Appendix C

*Cram International PLC*
*Randle Street,*
*Enfield,*
*Middlesex*

| | |
|---|---|
| *Telephone* | *0471-813433* |
| *Fax* | *0471-813255* |
| *Telex* | *047108* |

27 April 199X

Newtech Ltd
South Street
Shipley

*For the attention of Mr J Pearson, Technical Director*

Dear Sir,

We have recently received adverse publicity concerning the wholly unacceptable level of quality currently being experienced by Cram International.

As we indicated in the recent seminar which you attended, the time for action is long overdue, and it is for this reason that we write to you to confirm our quality policy and the actions which we propose to take in both the short and long term to ensure a rapid and major improvement.

1 No new vendor will be added to our approved supplier listing without passing a TQM audit.
2 All existing vendors will be the subject of a TQM audit. Any deviations located are to be rectified within an agreed timescale.
3 All vendors are to be the subject of follow-on audits at regular intervals.
4 Suppliers who cannot or will not meet the required standard will be eliminated.

*Our objective is 100% defect-free supplies delivered on time. The policy is to utilize only those suppliers who can meet this criteria.*

This quality drive is not a vendetta against our supply base; it is to be regarded as a supplier development programme, without which the current level of unacceptable quality will always prevail.

Cram International are fighting for survival in an international market place. Should we not quickly move to the level of quality required, then we will continue not only to fail to satisfy our customer but ultimately to lose our market.

We hope that you will support us in this project and that we will have your complete cooperation.

Yours faithfully,

I G Stephenson
Purchasing Manager

# 14 TQM implementation in British Gas West Midlands

## Introduction

This case study reflects the situation that existed in British Gas West Midlands in 1989. The statistics referred to, therefore, are relevant to that year and do not take into account growth that has occurred since 1989.

British Gas West Midlands is one of 12 regions within British Gas PLC. British Gas was privatized in 1986 and is a very successful company. In terms of turnover it is ranked the seventh largest company by any measures of performance.

British Gas West Midlands has approximately 1.7 million customers. The area it serves stretches from Congleton in the north to Hereford in the south, Rugby in the east and to the Welsh Borders on the western side of the region. The region has a Chairman who is responsible for the management of the business and a team of Regional Directors who are responsible for specific areas of activity. An idea of the scale of the operation is given by the statistics below.

British Gas West Midlands Region:

- Has 1.7 million customers;
- Has 6600 employees (2267 industrial staff and 4333 administrative staff);
- Reads over 3.5 million meters per year;
- Issues nearly 7 million accounts per year;
- Handles over 2 million telephone calls per year;
- Sells over 1750 million therms of gas per year;
- Sells over 160 000 appliances per year;
- Carries out over 1.3 million service requests per year;
- Has over 21 000 km of mains.

The introduction of TQM into a service company of this size, with the large administrative organization that supports the operation, is a major undertaking. The decision to introduce TQM into British Gas West Midlands was a proactive one and not simply the result of customer or other external pressure. The aim was to make British Gas West Midlands excellent in the eyes of everyone who came into contact with the company.

## The initial stages

In the summer of 1988 the Regional Chairman and Directors of British Gas West Midlands met over a number of weekends to formulate a Total Quality Strategy, which would move the region towards its excellence goals and would harness the commitment and enthusiasm of the entire workforce.

The strategy had three basic objectives. These were to make British Gas West Midlands by 1991:

- First for customers.
- First for employees.
- First within British Gas PLC.

The financial measures for becoming the leading region within British Gas PLC were identified and it was recognized that these would be reached only if the objectives relating to customers and employees were achieved. To become an excellent company they needed to look deeply into the way in which they managed the business and involved staff. To achieve the necessary changes, there had to be a major cultural change within all levels of management and across the whole of the workforce, not only at the external customer interface but also within all administrative and support activities.

A strategy called 'The Way Ahead' was developed, with five key elements identified:

1 *TQM* was seen as central to all the elements and would bind activities together to achieve the goal.
2 *Human Resource Development* – a coordinated approach to provide the opportunity for all employees to develop their own potential both at a personal level and for the benefit of the region.
3 *Effective communications* – a major review of the way in which the organization communicated both orally and in writing to employees and customers.
4 *Role in the community* – a more active role in supporting events and institutions within the West Midlands region was required, e.g. work with schools, the arts, local charities and the community at large.
5 *Information technology* – computer and support systems were needed in order to achieve the maximum advantage from available technology.

These elements were called mandates and each Regional Director accepted responsibility for developing these key areas of the business. It was also agreed that the Regional Chairman and Directors would be responsible for the management and steering of the process.

Before launching the programme, a set of main TQM principles was established. These formed the framework for involving and informing all employees and they are detailed below.

- TQM is not just concerned with products or quality of service. It embraces every aspect of business activity.
- TQM is a long-term continuous process with no end-date. It is not a short-term training programme, but a significant business strategy in its own right. Importantly, it recognizes that quality improvement never ends and that it must match ever-increasing customer requirements and expectations.
- TQM involves all employees in the problem-solving process.
- TQM presents a disciplined teamwork approach to problem-solving.
- TQM is about prevention and embraces the concept of continuous improvement.
- TQM embodies and supports the British Gas-published principles and standards of service and the Way Ahead objectives.
- TQM is at the core of the Way Ahead process and the objective that customers will regard the company as excellent in service, sales of both appliances and energy, distribution work and in every customer contact.
- TQM is encouraging every employee to provide an excellent service to the external customer and to their colleagues, the internal customers.
- TQM is 'getting it right first time, every time, in everything done'.

A Quality Statement was formulated against this framework (Appendix A). The company was attempting radically to change the corporate culture and the way the organization operated. This change process required careful planning.

## Total Quality survey

The starting point for the Total Quality process was to establish the current position in British Gas West Midlands. To this end two extensive surveys were carried out in March 1989. The first part of the survey was concerned with customers and was structured to collect information relating to the main areas of the external customer. The second part of the survey was concerned with employees and was structured so that they could collect in-depth information about what employees thought about the company. For both surveys, a personalized letter from the Regional Chairman was sent with the survey form, explaining the importance of the survey and requesting their cooperation.

Group discussions were also carried out with both customers and employees to explore some of the issues in more detail. Twelve customer-group discussions were held throughout the West Midlands region at local hotels and a cross-section of customers were invited to attend. In addition, 12 employee-group discussions were held at various locations and a cross-section of employees were invited to attend. The data collected from the surveys and group discussions was extensive and enabled the identification of aspects of the company's activities where priority attention was required. The information was fed back to all the management teams.

## Customer survey

The survey involved a random sample of 8000 customers (e.g. domestic, industrial and commercial, local authorities, etc.), and was structured to collect information about their views and perceptions on a whole range of activities, including:

- Company image.
- Level of service provided.
- Staff attitudes.
- Meeting customer requirements.

### Customer survey results

The results of the survey showed that the majority of customers were satisfied with the company. However, it was recognized that there was still much work to do to reach the desired level of customer service. One of the many interesting aspects to come out of the survey was that many customers thought British Gas West Midlands was better than other major organizations they dealt with and it was interesting to note that generally customers had a better view of the service provided than did employees. The results are summarized in Figure 14.1. A total of 32% of customers indicated only average or below average levels of satisfaction.

## Employee survey

The survey involved 650 employees across all levels of the organization and was structured to collect information regarding:

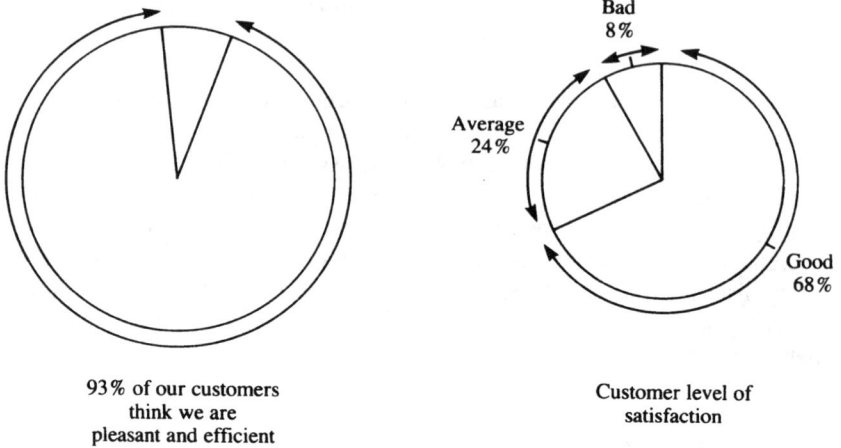

93% of our customers
think we are
pleasant and efficient

Customer level of
satisfaction

**Figure 14.1** *What customers said*

- Their views of the organization.
- The management style.
- Communications.
- Employee perception of customer requirements.
- Understanding of their involvement in quality.

### Employee survey results

The results of the employee survey gave a valuable insight into employees' perception of the company across the areas indicated. The diagrams shown in Figure 14.2 give an indication of some of the results. The first shows that 45% of employees considered communications were not good enough. Since the survey, team briefings have been introduced and communication has improved. The second and third charts show employees' awareness of quality before the TQM programme was introduced.

The information proved to be extremely valuable in structuring the content of the Total Quality training material. The TQM survey is also used on a regular basis to monitor the progress of Total Quality in British Gas West Midlands.

## Publication of results

The survey results were assembled in a summary booklet with a message from the Regional Chairman and circulated to all employees. (A copy of the message from the Regional Chairman is shown in Appendix B).

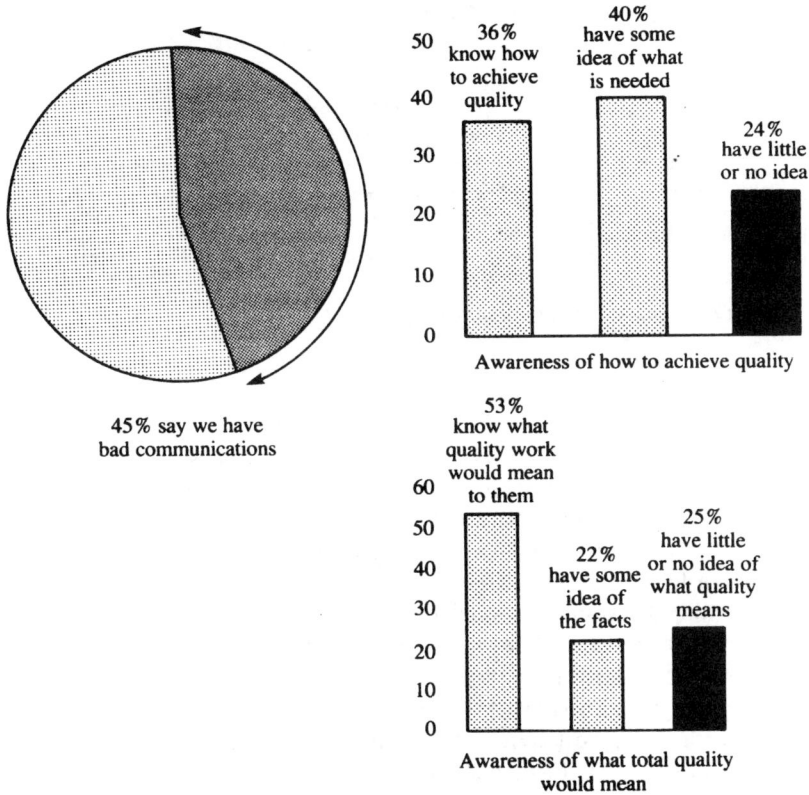

50  36%         40%
    know how   have some
    idea of what
40  to achieve  is needed
    quality
                            24%
30                          have little
                            or no idea
20

10

0

45% say we have        Awareness of how to achieve quality
bad communications

        53%
        know what
        quality work
        would mean
60      to them
                            25%
50                          have little
                22%         or no idea of
40              have some   what quality
                idea of     means
30              the facts

20

10

0
        Awareness of what total quality
                would mean

**Figure 14.2** *What employees said*

Although a commitment was given to employees that the results of the surveys would be made available for all their staff, it is obvious from this quotation from a survey form that all were not convinced: 'If the results of the survey are not to the Director's liking, I would not be at all surprised if they are never released for public scrutiny'. To demonstrate commitment, this quotation was printed on the inside cover of the booklet.

## Organizing for TQM

Having established where they were now, the organizational and resource implications in achieving the objectives had to be examined.

Various options were considered, including individual managers introducing the concepts into their own functional area in their own way and own

Organization chart

```
                    ┌──────────────────┐
                    │ Regional Quality │
                    │   Coordinator    │
                    └──────────────────┘
   ┌──────────┬──────────────┴──────────┬──────────────┐
┌─────────┐ ┌─────────┐          ┌──────────────┐ ┌─────────┐
│ Quality │ │ Quality │          │   Quality    │ │ Special │
│Development│ │ Support │          │Administrative│ │Projects │
│Assistants│ │ Manager │          │  Assistant   │ │Assistant│
└─────────┘ └─────────┘          └──────────────┘ └─────────┘
```

**Figure 14.3** *Quality coordination department*

timescale. However, the view was taken that to ensure the success of the process it was necessary to introduce TQM consistently and evenly throughout the organization. To support this objective a major decision was made to create a Quality Coordination Department which would be responsible for the introduction and coordination of the process.

A senior line manager was appointed as Regional Quality Coordinator and reported directly to the Regional Director of Engineering, who had overall responsibility for the TQM mandate. To assist him, a Quality Support Manager, two Quality Development Assistants, a Special Projects Assistant and a Quality Administrative Assistant were appointed (see Figure 14.3). Only personnel of the highest calibre, who showed enthusiasm and commitment to quality, were appointed to the team.

This team of six provides support to the process and is responsible for coordinating workshops, formulating training plans and collating statistical information. In addition to this, the team continually review the content, structure and emphasis of workshops.

## Quality Advisers

Following the formation of the coordination team, 12 full-time Quality Advisers were appointed, seconded from each of their four main functions. Their responsibilities included formulating departmental implementation plans and providing training, advice and assistance to their functional line managers during the training process. In addition to this they facilitated the establishment of Quality Teams. Although working within an overall brief from the Regional Quality Coordinator, the Quality Advisers are responsible to their appropriate departmental manager for implementation. The Quality Advisers were selected from middle management ranks and from a variety of backgrounds. The most important credential was an enthusiasm for quality.

This resourcing represented a major commitment by British Gas West Midlands to ensure that the process was introduced consistently and evenly throughout all activities.

Once the team was established, all members had to undergo extensive training in the following areas:

- History and background of TQM.
- Concepts and philosophies.
- Presentation skills.
- Quality team problem-solving methods.
- Leader training.
- Facilitation skills.

Following training, the team were heavily involved in developing workshop material.

The company was now ready to launch its TQM programme. How could it do this and achieve the active involvement of all of its 6600 employees?

## The launch

In the months following the decision to introduce TQM in British Gas West Midlands, detailed consideration was given as to how to announce the start of the process. There were many ways to do this but in the end it was decided that the launch had to be on a scale in line with the importance and commitment given by the Regional Chairman and Directors. It was decided to launch the initiative over 8 days in the autumn of 1989. The belief was that all 6600 employees should be told that something important was happening and that they played a very crucial role in the plan and, equally importantly, that the process would start at the top of the organization.

Having made this decision, the logistics of transporting employees from all parts of the West Midlands region were examined. The venue chosen was a large hotel near Kenilworth in Warwickshire. Although the hotel was large enough to accommodate the conference, a marquee capable of seating 800 people every day for lunch had to be erected in the grounds.

The transportation of the entire workforce involved approximately 16 coaches every day picking up employees from various locations throughout the West Midlands region. In some cases at the extremes of the region, staff boarded the coach at 7.30 a.m. and were involved in a 2-hour journey to get to the conference.

For the purpose of the launch, the concept of a live television studio was used, with the theatre being modelled to reflect this. The day was hosted by a local television presenter. The Regional Chairman and Directors outlined the objectives of the Way Ahead strategy and the plans for the future in a series of interviews. The interviews were reinforced by televised footage which was projected on to a large screen at the rear of the theatre.

The decision was taken very early in the planning stage that the audience would be a complete mix of the workforce. There were no special days or reserved areas for managers and there were no reserved seats. Quite clearly, this gave out some very powerful signals to the workforce that everyone was equally important to the initiative.

The bringing together of the entire workforce in a 'live presentation situation' for the first time represented a very high investment and was not without its risks. Overall, the exercise was tremendously successful. A survey of all employees who attended the conference was carried out. The reaction to the event from the majority of employees was extremely positive.

## The education process

In order to bring about the major cultural change necessary to make British Gas West Midlands an excellent company and to involve all employees in the process, a comprehensive education model was designed. A workshop attended by between 15 and 18 employees was central to the model. The workshop was highly participative and encouraged all people to become involved in the TQM process. The Regional Chairman, together with the Regional Directors, took part in the first workshops. The same workshop structure and content were then cascaded down to all levels of staff within the organization.

A decision was made that these workshops would be held off the company premises at local hotels throughout the region. The same approach was followed for all categories of employees and there was no differentiation between management and other levels of staff with respect to the facilities offered.

Coordination of booking and timetables was carried out by the Quality Coordination Department. In their contact with hotels, very strict standards were required in respect of service, organization and domestic arrangements, in line with what one would expect when attending a Quality workshop.

The plan was to ensure that between February 1990 and March 1991 all of the 6600 employees would attend a workshop. By the end of October 1990, 408 workshops had been held, involving 5600 employees (3462 administrative and 2138 Industrial staff).

# The workshop

The workshops had a central theme and core messages which ensured that there was a common understanding throughout all departments and functions. However, the contents were tailored to meet the specific needs of individual departments and line managers were fully involved in this process. The workshop consisted of formal input, discussion and a large number of syndicate exercises and feedback. A workshop summary booklet was issued to everyone. Workshops were frequently opened by the Regional Chairman or Directors, where the objectives of the day were outlined. If they were unable to attend, a video of the Regional Chairman was used.

There are some very important features of the workshops to note. The first is that they were management-led and line managers and supervisors played a leading role at the workshops. Although there was specialist advice available in the form of the functional Quality Advisers, the line managers presented the bulk of the material and led the discussions. The second important feature is that the workshop started the Total Quality process and the issues and problems identified were taken away by managers for consideration and, where possible, action. All participants were asked what prevented them from providing a 100% quality service in everything they did.

There were two types of workshops – 1-day and 2-day workshops.

## *Two-day workshop*

The 2-day workshop was designed for management levels. The main elements covered were:

- The concepts of TQM.
- Threats and opportunities facing British Gas West Midlands.
- Management style and personal quality.
- Identification of quality issues.
- The role of quality teams.
- Understanding of the tools and techniques to be used.
- Identification of Quality Focus Costs.
- Measuring progress.

Particular emphasis was placed on management style and the role that managers play in encouraging an environment in which everyone can contribute to the Total Quality philosophy. The concept that managers are the role model was actively pursued.

*One-day workshop*

The cut-off point for the 2-day workshop occurred below supervisory/
management level; the reason for this was that less emphasis was placed on
Quality Focus Costs and management style. However, the same concepts and
philosophies were developed.

The main elements of the 1-day workshop were:

- Concepts of TQM.
- Threats and opportunities facing British Gas West Midlands.
- Concepts of 'getting it right first time, every time'.
- Personal quality.
- Measuring progress.

Particular emphasis was placed on the concept of TQM, how the individual
could become involved in the process, the importance of the internal
customer, and administrative support activities. At the start of the workshop,
everyone was given a folder containing a pen and a copy of the company
principles. In certain functions joint workshops for external contractors and
company staff were held.

The workshops were very participative and created a forum in which people
were encouraged to speak openly and frankly regarding issues that concerned
them. At the end of the workshop everyone was given a small red lapel badge.
The reaction from the workshops was extremely enthusiastic and employees
found the workshops both enjoyable and rewarding.

## Problem-solving and feedback

At the start of the workshops, managers promised workshop members that all
issues and problems raised would be given consideration and that there would
be feedback on the actions to be taken. It was also mentioned that in some
cases no action would be taken, but importantly there would also be feedback
on this, and why. It was crucial to the success of the process that managers
honoured this commitment. Workshop participants were invited to join small
action teams to help find solutions to the problems identified.

Three types of Quality Action Teams were established:

1 *Functional Quality Teams*: These teams were set up by local managers and
were concerned with issues that could be solved at local level. Following
discussion, local managers decided the make-up of the team, which
normally consisted of around five people. The teams disband once work on
the problem is complete.

2 *Cross-functional Quality Teams*: These teams operated in the same way as Functional Teams at local level, except that they were made up of people from different functions.

3 *Task Forces*: These teams were concerned with policy issues and were set up by Regional Directors or Regional Managers. Again, once work on the issue/problem is completed, the team disbands.

Some of the quality opportunities for the teams are shown in Appendix C. The list is a summary of some of the key issues raised in the workshops and some specific areas selected by management.

Employees who agreed to be Quality Team Leaders were given training on problem-solving techniques which could be used to assist in finding the solution to the problem. The problem-solving tools and techniques used are:

- Brainstorming.
- Pareto.
- The fishbone diagram.
- The six-word diagram.

As a rule, the teams met for about 1 hour each week. Once the problem had been addressed, the group presented their findings to the appropriate management group and, on conclusion of the project, disbanded. There was flexibility in this regard where the local manager considered it appropriate. The teams were involved in specific tasks selected by management and terms of reference were drawn up for the leader.

The Quality Advisers were also available to provide further training in tools and techniques, for the team members, to help solve the problems.

By now, all employees had received some TQM training. The company was well into its TQM programme. Measuring and maintaining progress are now the key issues.

## Quality costs

Quality costs are an effective way of monitoring progress and provide a focus for quality improvement activities. There is an opportunity for all organizations to reduce operating costs by 'getting it right first time'. A considerable amount of investigatory work was carried out to quantify the 'cost of lack of quality' in the company.

Research carried out worldwide indicated that the cost of quality could represent between 20 and 40% of a company's operating costs. The first thing to do was establish whether this was true of British Gas West

Midlands. It was quickly realized that the general concept was as applicable to them as to any other company, but that there were some major differences.

Those differences primarily related to significant elements of costs which were outside the company's direct control, for example, costs associated with the purchase and distribution of gas from the National Transmission System. In quantifying operational costs which they believed the Total Quality process could influence, they excluded those costs which they felt were outside their control. The costs that could be influenced were called Quality Focus Costs. Work was then carried out to develop and prove a method of quantifying and measuring those elements, within the overall total of the Quality Focus Costs.

As a result of this work, financial targets for the savings were set, and these were built into the business plan.

## Quality Awards

To maintain the high profile of the TQM Programme, it was decided to introduce a Quality Awards scheme.

The main purpose of the scheme was publicly to recognize employees who consistently demonstrated a high commitment to quality. In introducing the scheme the company did not want to establish a bureaucracy and so the nomination procedure is simple. Anyone from first-line supervision can nominate someone for a Quality Award. These nominations can be from within the nominator's own department or he or she can nominate someone from any other function. There are guidelines laid down for nominations, but within them the complete range of activities can be recognized. There have been award winners from both administrative and industrial functions, including porters, mains layers, telephone enquiry staff and transport clerks. There have also been awards to small teams (2/3 people) who have been brought together for specific projects.

Each quarter, nominations are invited and around 30 awards are made. The award consists of an invitation to attend the theatre with a partner and during the evening one of the Regional Directors presents the winners with a Quality Award Certificate and a £50 voucher. At the end of the year all award winners go into a draw made by the Regional Chairman, from which 12 holiday vouchers to the value of £750 are awarded. The presentations are given a very high profile in the house magazine.

During 1990 a total of 152 employees received awards. The interest which the scheme has generated has been extremely enthusiastic and enables the company to recognize quality achievements.

## Ongoing support

TQM features in the majority of publications to employees, e.g. house magazine features, management bulletins and regular video news programmes. There are regular updates on the progress being made and the work of Quality Teams.

Support given to the process by the Regional Chairman, Directors and Senior Managers is ongoing. This support takes the form of opening workshops, attending presentations and promoting the concept of TQM in visits to company offices.

The indications are that support and enthusiasm are widespread throughout the organization and this is reflected in many of the initiatives underway. The company is very aware at this stage that it is vitally important for managers to continue to demonstrate their commitment to TQM.

## Achievements

It is only fairly recent that the initial acknowledgement has been made that TQM would be the most appropriate way to move the business forward. During this time progress has been rapid and some notable achievements have been made:

- The establishment of the Regional Management Committee as the Quality Council, a Quality Coordination Team and Quality Advisers.
- Carrying out a major Total Quality Survey involving customers and employees.
- A major launch of plans to all employees.
- Introduction of the Quality Award scheme.
- Designing and developing a TQM workshop to involve all employees.
- Running TQM workshops for all 6600 employees.
- Developing an awareness of TQM, its importance to the business and that everyone must be involved in the process.
- The establishment of numerous Quality Teams and a formal reporting mechanism for issues, problems and subsequent feedback.
- The introduction of an Employee Enquiry Line.
- Introduction of Team Briefings.
- Identification and quantification of the 'cost of lack of quality.'
- Developing an understanding within the culture that managers are the role models.
- Performance indicators showing improvements across a number of activities and an improvement in the company's image ranking from eighth to third, compared to 29 other companies (1991 rating).

● Creation of an environment in which people feel able to put forward suggestions and raise issues and problems.

British Gas West Midlands will now have to address how they should pursue the next phase of their TQM programme. They have created the necessary awareness and enthusiasm. Some early benefits have started to filter through. However, the whole of the British Gas business faces a period of uncertainty, with calls to split it up and create more competition in the industry. Maintaining the momentum of the TQM programme in this climate will require even more dedication and enthusiasm.

## Valedictory

It is four years since the launch of TQM in British Gas West Midlands and there have been a number of significant advancements. To date a total of 142 quality teams have been established with 109 reporting their findings and recommendations. Savings totalling £1 million per annum have been identified with a potential total, if applied across the Region, of £2.9 million.

In addition there has been significant measured improvement in management/employee relationships and a recognition by all employees of the important role individuals play in delivering quality service.

There has been the establishment of a clearly defined strategy for managing the process with the formulation of a Quality Council and local Quality Improvement Panels.

There is now new clear evidence that the TQM strategy adopted by British Gas West Midlands is paying dividends in all aspects of the business.

## Acknowledgements

This is from a case study by Danny Burke, National Total Quality Team, British Gas PLC. Special thanks must go to Arthur Tyrell, Operative Director and the TQ team in West Midlands Region.

# Appendix A: Quality statement

British Gas West Midlands has set itself the objective of becoming an excellent company in the eyes of both our customers and employees. To achieve this objective requires the commitment and enthusiasm of every one of our employees to 'get it right first time' in every aspect of our work.

Every person who works for us, regardless of the duties and activities he or she performs, is responsible for quality by:

- identifying the requirements of both internal and external customers;
- meeting the agreed requirements of these customers both now and in the future;
- promoting through contact with customers our image as a quality company.

In order to create an environment which encourages the involvement of all our people, managers must:

- encourage participation and an open style of management and communication;
- develop teamwork and the opportunity for individual participation and involvement;
- involve our people in identification of issues and problems and seeking ways to improve working practices.

Through these principles they will achieve ongoing improvement in the quality of service and products that we provide to our customer. We will also achieve our objective of being regarded as an excellent company and by so doing achieve our objective of being first within British Gas PLC.

# Appendix B: Message from the Regional Chairman re TQM

Dear Colleagues,

You will recall that earlier this year we carried out an extensive survey of over 8000 customers and 600 of our employees. We needed to gather information from customers about the service we provide and from employees about their views of the region as an employer.

I promised then that the results, good and not so good, would be made known to you. The purpose of this special report is to give all of you an opportunity to gain an insight into how our customers see us and how we see ourselves.

On the whole, results are quite good, whilst there are areas in which we clearly need to work hard to become excellent.

In the coming months you will hear a lot about the major initiatives which we are introducing under The Way Ahead strategy to address the issues identified in the survey.

I am confident that with your help we will achieve our target of becoming excellent in all the services we provide to customers and also be regarded as excellent by employees.

Thank you for your support.


Donald A Young
Regional Chairman

# Appendix C: Quality Teams' summary of opportunity areas

*Information technology*
Image promotion within the department
Volume and cost of printed output (development machine)
Reason for increase in Query Master run-times
Causes of down-time to on-line services

*Distribution*
Office procedures in Coordination and Planning department
Communications with Central North District
Aspects of team morale in Coordination and Planning department

*Customer service*
Looking at methods of carrying out training
Paperwork on Regular Servicing Department at headquarters
Communications with Central North District
Identification of spare parts
Installation of central heating

*Customer accounting*
Meter accountability

*Finance*
Introduction of new starters

*Engineering*
Eliminating unnecessary call-out of standby staff

*Domestic sales*
Message handling in Central South District
Whom to contact at headquarters (identified by Central North District)

*Secretariat*
Positioning of waste skips at headquarters
Organization of shredding room at headquarters
Collection of property rents (architects)

*Industrial and commercial*
Training of staff
Commitment to customers
Image of the department
Advertising and promotion of services

# 15 Building a quality organization in Infomat

## Background

Infomat was founded in 1981. It is a relatively small company, employing around 50 people, based on a single site in Newbury. Since 1988, Infomat has been a subsidiary of Predicasts. The main concept of Infomat was to provide a competitor tracking, market monitoring service under contract to large organizations, i.e. a tailored or customized information service.

Major companies such as ICI, Unilever, British Telecom and Akzo utilize Infomat to gather relevant information on a daily or weekly basis. This information is distributed to clients either electronically or on paper. Typically, clients will pay between £5000 and £15000 per annum for the service.

Working with the client's staff, Infomat defines the information required by that client. A profile is established which is changeable, and may be refined at any time as the client's interests change. Most clients do not have a clear understanding of their real information needs and this part of the process is critical to the subsequent success of any service. The material delivered to clients is derived from over 600 publications, originally published in 12 different languages. The key articles are selected by multilingual graduate staff and then abstracted and indexed. The relevant articles are matched with the previously defined profile using the indexing system and made available to clients either daily or weekly.

As is typical with such companies, the staff are young – 85% are under 35 years old. The business is characterized by an open management style and, in 1990, it had a typical functional structure with sales and marketing, production and administration.

During the late 1980s the company grew rapidly and expanded, but suffered from significant staff turnover problems, especially in the production area.

## TQM implementation

The key dates in implementing TQM are shown in Table 15.1. These can be broken down into six stages:

1 Interest/awareness.
2 Researching.
3 The launch.
4 Implementation/operating.
5 Post implementation audit.
6 Certification.

## Interest/awareness

In late 1989, the Managing Director at Infomat became aware of the UK Department of Trade and Industry's (DTIs) Quality Initiative. After receiving several mail shots he attended an introductory seminar sponsored by the DTI.

**Table 15.1** *TQM at Infomat – key dates and events*

| | |
|---|---|
| November 1989 | TQM awareness begins |
| March 1990 | Attended introductory courses |
| April 1990 | Management-assessed cost of quality failure |
| June 1990 | MBA student/consultant project |
| August 1990 | Launched quality initiative to staff |
| November 1990 | Integrated teams developed<br>Changed organization structure |
| August 1991 | Adjusted pay scheme<br>Implemented new coding system |
| October 1991 | Created Quality Department |
| January 1992 | Launched/implemented improvement scheme |
| February 1992 | Post implementation audit |
| March 1992 | Feedback to staff |
| August 1992 | 400 improvements achieved |
| September 1992 | External training of all staff |
| December 1992 | Acquired by Esmerk Group |

This highlighted the cost of quality and some of the benefits of adopting a TQM approach. It stimulated the management team to undertake further research and analysis.

The first step was a planning meeting at which the costs of quality were reviewed. Like most business, Infomat underestimated it. The biggest single expense was the cost of lost business and lost opportunities. This was particularly true for subscription or repeat contract-based activities.

This analysis highlighted that client retention was a key parameter. Failure to retain hard-won clients meant wasted marketing expense and dissatisfied clients acting as 'negative salesmen'. The company realized the potential power of satisfied clients acting as reference sites and word-of-mouth advocates. Clearly if Infomat could retain all of its clients, including trials, it could cut out a major drain on the business. It would also cut marketing expenses, as new clients are far more expensive to win than increasing business from existing clients.

The other major cost of quality failure was fire-fighting and associated rework, rush jobs, scrapped photocopies, retyped letters, etc. The estimate of the cost of quality failure was 20% of turnover. This represented more than the annual profits and clearly justified further research and investigation. It also coalesced the Management Team around the advantages of the Total Quality approach.

## Researching

The advice in all the literature and the seminars indicated that a consultant was required to implement a TQM programme. As a small business operating on tight budgets, Infomat felt that it could not afford a typical TQM consultant costing several hundred pounds per day. A Business School provided a solution in the form of a suitably qualified MBA student to undertake a project for the company.

The key steps to this project were:

1 To identify the external clients' perceptions of quality.
2 To validate the current staff perceptions of quality and general attitudes.
3 To determine future actions.

The key step here was to start with the external clients' perceptions of what they required and to assess the extent to which Infomat was meeting those requirements. This highlighted a number of key points. Clients were seeking highly pertinent, timely, accurate, well-presented information. They also wanted the comfort of 'not missing things' and yet wished to avoid duplication of stories, unless there was additional relevant information.

Having determined these criteria, they were then validated using customer satisfaction surveys on a wider client base to determine the current level of conformance with the desired expectations. Simultaneously the researcher/consultant was assessing the internal perceptions of quality and staff attitudes in general. A key finding was the mismatch between external perceptions of service quality and the internal perceptions of quality, focusing on abstracting related quality issues.

The other findings made fascinating reading. There appeared to be two businesses, one in Sales and Marketing and the other in Production. Communications between departments and with management needed substantial improvement, morale in Production was low and there were high stress levels.

By tracking the clients' perception of quality, based on their criteria, the company sought to get early warnings of likely terminations through the customer satisfaction surveys and the use of a Quality Index. They reasoned that a better quality rating would lead to more satisfied clients and thus to higher retention rates. As quality was related to the relevance of the profile, to improve the quality of the service Infomat needed to:

1  Improve the understanding of clients' needs.
2  Improve the precision of the profiling.
3  Meet analysts' needs to know more about their clients.
4  Reduce the inefficiency of current processes.
5  Communicate more effectively between departments and as management.

## The launch

To launch the programme, Infomat closed the office and held a full off-site meeting with all staff. The results of the project work undertaken so far were shared with the staff and various videos available from the DTI were utilized to illustrate the costs of quality failure and the application of TQM techniques in other environments. An additional objective was to commence the process of identifying client–supplier relationships within the company. Cross-departmental groups were put together to start this process.

Following this meeting, the immediate issues raised by the staff discussions with the consultant were addressed individually and a new monthly newsletter written specifically for the staff was initiated. The Managing Director took on the role of Quality Manager and Facilitator to demonstrate commitment to the principles being adopted.

## Implementation/operating

During the latter part of 1990 it became clear that in order to improve analysts' understanding of their client needs, it was necessary to shorten the communication process. This was achieved by changing the organization structure by collecting the customer service staff within each analyst team. This was reinforced by introducing performance-related pay, related to the key performance indicator of the company, client retention.

Continued efforts were made to improve communications between individuals by getting them to focus on their personal client–supplier relationships. Despite various tools to assist in this process, this was difficult to implement and probably not fully understood.

Throughout this period extensive change was taking place. Infomat revised its coding system so that it could provide a more pertinent and relevant service. Even though the database users had been seeking a Predicasts compatible system vociferously for some time, it was only due to the contract clients' needs that such a change could be justified. This major project was completed in August 1991, 14 months after it had been identified that such a radical change was required. The effort involved in this change undoubtedly distracted the organization from the general TQM effort and a number of the initiatives lapsed at that time.

During the autumn of 1991, it became clear that the role of Quality Manager, which had been adopted by the Managing Director thus far, needed to be devolved to a manager who could commit him-/herself to it full-time. In November 1991 a new Quality Department was created from the customer service staff with a full-time manager reporting to the Managing Director. The remit of the Quality Manager was to focus on improving processes, documenting procedures and retaining clients. The revised structure also altered departmental and personal relationships. This was complex as it meant that individuals had to reassess how they related to their colleagues. Some people changed from immediate boss to 'most important clients' – a subtle change with significant behavioural implications.

This change provided new impetus to the programme and Infomat now have several different Quality Teams looking at specific problems and issues which occur within the business, e.g. improving journal pass-round to increase timeliness, reducing waste from printers, reducing the number of invoices which have to be reissued. In addition to these activities, the company staff and management attended at least eight different TQM-related seminars/courses and had 1 day's free consultancy training at Newbury for seven people, as part of the DTI's support. Infomat also initiated a complete skills analysis review and committed resources to ensuring that everybody in the organization had received the training required to undertake their tasks satisfactorily. In the short term this meant a sharp rise in training and development.

Despite encouragement and some involvement, there was a feeling that people still felt restricted and lacked the involvement which was desirable. To try to overcome this and to encourage greater involvement, an Implemented Improvement Scheme was introduced in January 1992. This provided authority for all individuals to spend a defined amount of money to improve their work-related activities without further reference and on completion of such an improvement the individual was rewarded by a small monetary payment. The objective was to generate over 1000 improvements a year. This had a successful launch, with virtually every member of staff contributing at least one improvement. Like all such schemes, it will undoubtedly need to be reviewed and renewed to ensure the real objectives are achieved.

The reaction to being offered a small financial reward to do what they considered to be their job anyway was one of frustration and a degree of cynicism. This was eventually countered by changing the system, allowing individuals to give their award to charity, if they so chose. Over time this developed into a normal part of the management process, with everybody participating, and became a major mechanism for measuring commitment.

## Post implementation audit

As can be seen from the above, substantial management time and financial commitment have been invested in the implementation of TQM. What has been the payback? In order to establish this, the same consultant who undertook the original research was invited back to undertake a post-implementation audit. This audit analysed the actions taken to date and the change in quantifiable measures, specifically client retention, staff turnover and staff attitudes.

### Client retention

Client retention between 1990 and the end of 1991 rose by 7%. Returns for the early part of 1992 indicated a further improvement on the 1991 position. This factor alone has produced a revenue payback in excess of £50K in the first year, with a long-term value, not on a discounted cash flow basis, of at least £150K. This single factor would justify the entire programme to date.

Additional qualitative evidence supports this view. 'The customers perceive that they are receiving more of a personal and quality service, their queries are being dealt with more quickly and they more readily communicate with Infomat. New customers also report greater confidence that they are dealing with a quality organization. The most compelling evidence for the success of the TQM programme is the increase in client retention. The fact that there is a recession when companies are looking to cut costs makes this result even better', says the Managing Director.

### Staff turnover

A measure of satisfaction is the number of staff leaving the company (Table 15.2). This dropped markedly from 17 in 1989 to five in 1992. Most of those leaving in 1991 and 1992 were due to familial commitments, e.g. having

**Table 15.2** *Staff turnover*

| Year | Number of staff leaving | | |
| | Production | Non-production | Total |
| --- | --- | --- | --- |
| 1989 | 11 | 6 | 17 |
| 1990 | 6 | 3 | 9 |
| 1991 | 3 | 3 | 6 |
| 1992 | 4 | 1 | 5 |

children or spouses moving. Other variables obviously affect this, however, notably the opportunities for other jobs outside the company, which in a recession must be limited.

### Staff attitudes

To gain a more accurate perception, the Internal Customer Satisfaction survey was repeated. This used precisely the same set of questions as in 1990. These covered job interest, responsibility, feedback and supervision. The statistical survey was supplemented with personal interviews of 16 employees.

The Internal Customer Satisfaction survey for the total organization, summarized in Table 15.3, suggests very few major changes, with marginally reduced satisfaction for salary and supervision. When the results are split between production and non-production staff, however, a slightly different picture emerged.

As in 1990, non-production scored consistently higher on all factors. In 1992, however, Production were more satisfied than they were in 1990 on all factors except two. Non-production achieved still higher 1992 satisfaction ratings. This could partly be due to the restructuring in the Non-production area. The difference between the two sets of numbers indicates that the company is substantially more cohesive than in 1990. This was highlighted again in considering the issues affecting staff. By comparing the nature of

**Table 15.3** *Internal Customer Satisfaction survey*

| | Percentage of respondents | | |
|---|---|---|---|
| *Question* | *Yes* | *No* | *Don't know* |
| Do you fully understand IQUIP?* | 63 | 25 | 12 |
| Do you think IQUIP is beneficial to you? | 54 | 27 | 19 |
| To the company? | 81 | 4 | 15 |
| Do you think there has been a significant change since IQUIP was launched? | 64† | 16 | 20 |

\* IQUIP = Infomat Quality Improvement Programme.
† Of this, 74–94% believe the change was for the better.

staff issues pre- and post-TQM, this highlighted a move towards a quality organization.

Table 15.4 illustrates the major issues. The management's conclusion was that the nature of the staff issues over the 18 months had changed. Again, the Managing Director said:

> If these issues are taken in conjunction with what the staff perceive to be the benefits of the TQM programme, it is fair to credit TQM as having resolved the majority of these issues. Due to TQM, Infomat's employees now understand

**Table 15.4** *Major issues*

| *Major issues – July 1990* | *Major issues – February 1992* |
|---|---|
| Communication<br>  between departments<br>  with management | Communication<br>  with management<br>  them-and-us with management |
| Training | Increased complexity of jobs |
| Equipment to aid with job | Too many changes |
| High stress level and low morale in Production | Management roles and responsibilities |
| Needs for feedback | Payment system |
| Cohesive company | |

what the final customer wants. We are a more cohesive company, with the 'them-and-us' attitude between Production and Non-production virtually vanished. The empowerment of individuals to take control over their environment has also alleviated stress, as well as enabling them to get the right equipment for the job.

There are, however, two caveats to these findings, expressed in the issues raised by staff and the perceived disadvantages of the Infomat Quality Improvement Programme (IQUIP). The first is how the quality changes have been implemented, e.g. 'quickly', 'greater complexity', 'increased paper-work'. The second is confusion regarding the Quality Programme and its component parts, e.g. only 60% fully understood the programme.

This was addressed by a systematic programme of communication to all staff together and then repeated in small work groups, explaining the real impact of client retention on the long-term health of the business. It also explained how the new flatter, team-based systems may introduce greater complexity but on the whole should produce better solutions. The need emerged for increased training. Staff felt uncertain of how to behave in teams when they had grown up with more rigid and hierarchical organization structures. To achieve this every member of staff, from the Managing Director downwards, attended three full afternoon training sessions to improve teamwork.

Despite the inevitable reaction from some about 'wasting time' on something they did not understand, this eventually resulted in a tremendous improvement in attitudes within the office and a greater understanding of the underlying processes of teamwork. It also led to a reassessment by individuals of their own roles and capabilities. Some people who had been in a leadership role voluntarily stepped down. In choosing their replacements, leadership/coordinator skills were considered ahead of pure technical ability.

## Certification ISO9002

By the beginning of 1992, Infomat felt that it had made enough progress to aim for certification of the quality system. The objective was set to obtain ISO9002/BS5750 registration by the end of 1992. To do this the company had to document all the processes and ensure that people were operating to those processes. Having documented the processes, Infomat was then in a position to *improve* them.

By September 1992, the company was able to retain an External Quality Consultant to audit the systems, as a precursor to finalizing the application for certification. He found that the processes developed conformed to the standard, and that he expected Infomat to obtain ISO9002 certification at the first attempt. In fact, this was overtaken by events, as the company was acquired in December 1992, before the certification visit could be completed. As many of the systems have now changed, they needed to be redefined and redocumented.

## Conclusions

The post implementation audit concluded that: 'all the findings suggested that the Total Quality Programme had contributed significantly to delivering quality to both the internal and external customer'. This was most reassuring. It was clear that Infomat had made progress but the audit also highlighted the need for further action. The confusion felt by staff was, once again, a measure of the failure of management to communicate:

● their vision of quality;
● the quality plan;
● the way in which specific actions conform to that plan;
● the payback from the increasing investment by all staff in the apparent 'time sink' of quality-related activities.

In order to overcome some of the negative perceptions a systematic process of communicating the results and benefits of the quality programme was begun. All staff were briefed twice, once in a full staff meeting and then in small groups about the detailed payback, the significance of client retention and the impact of the results so far.

Despite this, some scepticism continued. None the less, Infomat began to get greater involvement in the Continuous Improvement Programme. Improvements which had initially been regarded as trivial began to be appreciated. After 4 months the scheme was generating a steady average of 30–40 implemented improvements every month. This represents just under one improvement per month from each employee or around 10 per year. This far exceeds the impact of most suggestion schemes, which rarely exceed one per employee per year.

By the end of 1992 Infomat could also quantify the benefits in financial terms. They serviced an additional 18% turnover, but with a 20% cost reduction – clearly a sharp improvement in margins. No major cuts were made in staffing or in level of service, nor was it immediately obvious exactly how these savings were being achieved. It was a combination of many small improvements and a more systematic approach to problem-solving.

Infomat has made substantial changes since early 1990 from a functional-based hierarchically driven business into a client-focused, quality organization. There remain huge improvements in procedures and processes which are required to cut out waste and ensure greater consistency and reliability in the quality of the service we deliver. The challenge for all organizations, particularly those in the information service industry where virtually everything is intangible, is to develop organizations in which continuous improvement is embedded in the culture of the company.

Table 15.5 lists the staff perceptions of IQUIP. The major recommendations from the senior management of Infomat to other organizations are:

● Get commitment from the top.
● Estimate the costs of quality failure.
● Start with external clients' concept of quality.
● Identify key quality measures for all activities
    (a) externally;
    (b) internally.

**Table 15.5** *Staff perceptions of the Infomat Quality Improvement Programme (IQUIP)*

---

*Main benefits of IQUIP*

Better service to the client
Better quality work and product
Improved communication between departments/more cohesive company
Individuals are empowered to change things themselves
Increased problem-solving:
    Resolved at initial stages
    Able to vent problems and issues
    Staff more responsible for working environment
    Staff change things rather than complaining
Staff fully appreciate what quality is for the final customer
Staff are less stressed and more motivated

*Main disadvantages of IQUIP*

Greater bureaucracy and paperwork
Time-consuming
Ideas implemented too quickly
Lack of appropriate criteria for a good idea
Lack of company-wide commitment to IQUIP
Increased complexity associated with many changes
Quality programme lacks structure

---

- Measure internal staff attitudes.
- Identify barriers to improvement, and remove them.
- Communicate planned actions.
- Communicate achievements.
- Retrain staff for the new skills.
- Focus on teamwork.
- Rewrite/simplify procedures.
- Empower the staff.

## Acknowledgement

This is from a case study by Sebastian Crawshaw.

# 16　Goal deployment in Exxon Chemical

## Goal deployment – what is it?

### Definitions

*Goal*: point where race ends; object of effort; destination.
*Deployment*: taking up position; fanning out; spread; cascade.

These words represent a more meaningful translation of the term policy deployment or policy management, which itself is an American translation of the Japanese phrase *Hoshin Kanri*. *Hoshin Kanri*, translated literally, means 'direction needle management, administration or deployment'. For their purposes, Exxon Chemical take the words 'goal deployment' to refer to the process by which are developed strategic business plans that are cascaded and implemented throughout the organization (Figure 16.1).

### So – what's new?

For many people, first impressions of goal deployment are that it is not new and that 'we have been here before'. Organizations have always had business plans, quality plans, objectives and improvement targets. Very often, though, these have been only partially successful because they were imposed top-down, were divisive, contradicting or naive, were short-term, were focused on who and what, got lost as another flavour of the month, were just plain unachievable, or were never effectively communicated.

By contrast, the attributes of effective goal deployment are linked to the principles of TQM in that they depend, for example, on two-way

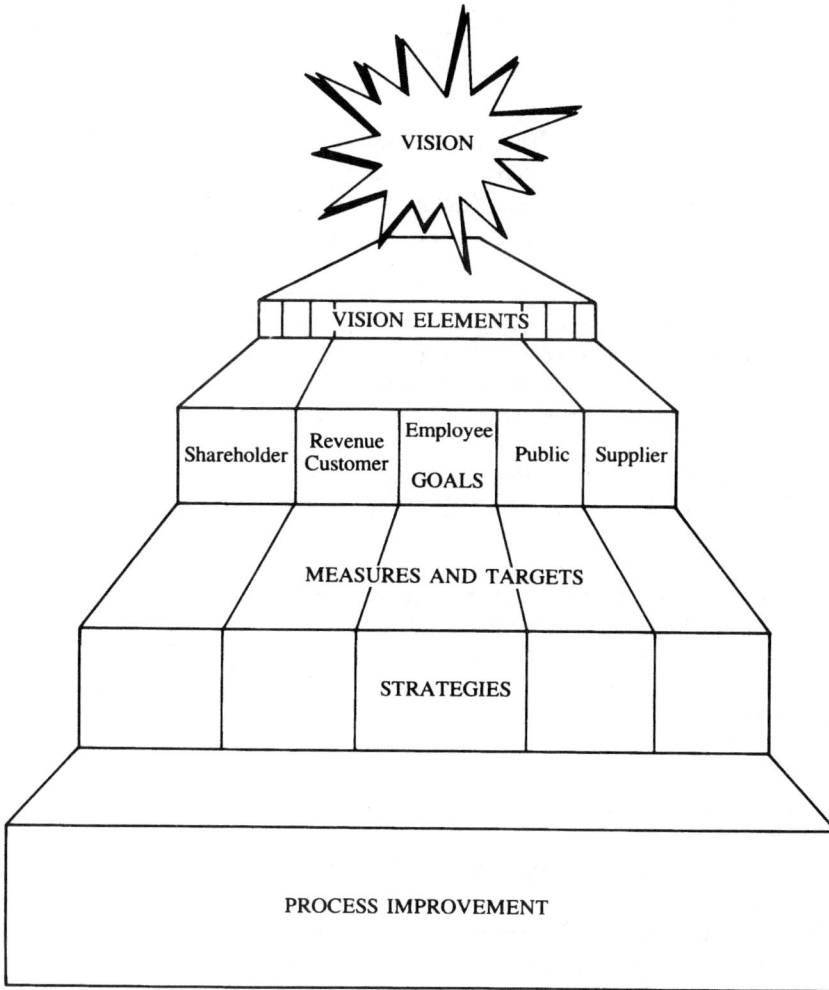

**Figure 16.1** *Goal deployment at Exxon Chemical*

communication, on data and information, on the 'how' rather than the 'what', and on effective teamwork.

There are three key attributes of the 'new' goal deployment process in Exxon Chemical. Firstly, it drives towards the organization's mission/vision of the future. Secondly, the goals are made both challenging and achievable by two-way communication and dialogue. Finally, the goals are measurable and measurement is used to prioritize improvement effort and communicate progress.

## Why do it?

### *It is part of TQM*

Exxon Chemical believe that one of their critical aims is to progress towards a TQM system, and that having a process by which business strategy is deployed throughout the organization is a vital need. As a framework for TQM, the Malcolm Baldrige Award Criteria (1993) state under Category 3.0 – Strategic Quality Planning:

> examine the company's planning process and how all key quality requirements are integrated into overall business planning. Also examine the company's short and longer term plans and how quality and operational performance requirements are deployed to all work units.

The European Foundation for Quality Management Model for Self-Appraisal contains under 2.0 – Policy and Strategy:

> How policy and strategy are based on the concept of TQ.
> How policy and strategy are the basis of business plans.
> How policy and strategy are regularly reviewed and improved.

These requirements can be covered by an effective goal deployment process.

### *It can be motivational*

Goal deployment has provided a focus for Exxon Chemical. It has disciplined management to think out the strategic direction clearly and to translate it into language that the rest of the organization can understand. It has also provided a means for the organization to align and prioritize their activities. In studying job characteristics for motivation at work, Hackman and Oldham (1975) identified three critical psychological states. For people to be motivated they need to experience the feeling that:

- their work is meaningful;
- they are responsible for the outcome of their work;
- they have knowledge of the actual results of their work.

The goal deployment process has helped to support these feelings in Exxon Chemical. Goal deployment indicates to people how they fit into the scheme of things and how their efforts align with and impact on the company's strategic goals, thus making their work more meaningful. The measurement and communication of progress inherent in policy deployment give them both ownership for their efforts and knowledge of results. Overall, goal deployment provides criteria for evaluating work and for rewarding and recognizing achievement.

### Why did Exxon Chemical get into it?

There were two influences involved in launching a goal deployment process within Exxon Chemical: one from general thinking about TQM and the other coming more specifically from use of the Baldrige framework.

In general terms, the company came to the view that Total Quality could be seen as three interlocking circles (Figure 16.2). One circle is about teams, people and culture; the second is about work, processes and systems; and the third is about vision, direction and measurement. Since 1986, the company had been putting most effort and attention into circles 1 and 2. It was becoming clear that they needed to put more effort into circle 3. This management view was supported by conclusions drawn from worldwide employee surveys.

More specifically, the worldwide and regional business management teams completed a gap analysis against the Baldrige TQM framework. This highlighted that the organization assembled large amounts of data, a lot of which it did not use, and that the company had a vision but no effective trendline measures of progress towards it. A combination of these views and conclusions signalled the need for a coherent set of goals and strategies which would provide organizational direction and a framework to which people could align.

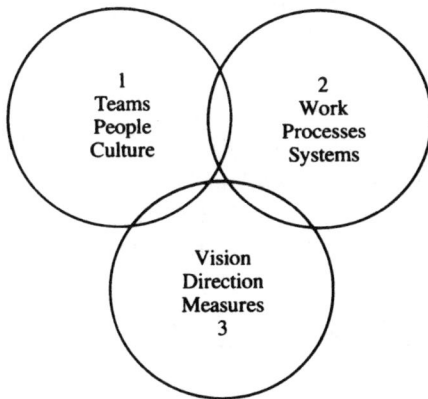

**Figure 16.2** *The three interlocking circles of total quality at Exxon Chemical*

## How to do it

### *Definitions and criteria*

There are a number of different terminologies used by different organizations around goal deployment. For the purposes of this case study, the following terms have been adopted by Exxon Chemical:

### *Vision (or mission)*

A vivid picture of an ambitious, desirable and future state. Its purpose is to inspire and act as a guide for decision-making and planning. It should be:

- memorable;
- involving;
- aligned with company values;
- linked to customer needs;
- a stretch, but not impossible;
- short, clear and communicable;
- within a 5-year horizon.

### *Goal (or critical success factor)*

A result, milestone or checkpoint in the future which will indicate significant progress towards the vision. Achieving a collection of four to six goals would realize the vision. A goal should be:

- measurable;
- critical for success;
- aggressive, benchmarked targets;
- specific.

### *Strategy (or critical process)*

A specific, medium or long-term plan for making progress towards a goal. A strategy should have the same attributes as a goal but should be more specific and action-oriented. Together a set of strategies, if successfully pursued, will impact the goal measure and eventually achieve the goal.

### *Creating a vision of the future*

In Exxon Chemical the goal deployment process started at the top, where the senior management team created a vision for their organization. They took into account the external environment, the capability of the organization and the desired state versus the competition. The vision was checked against the criteria stated above.

Creating a vision for the organization which is clear and inspiring for people is not easy. However, compared with implementing the changes necessary to achieve it, the Exxon Chemical team felt that it was the simplest step of all!

A technique used by the company to help create the vision (Tichy and Devanna, 1986) was for some senior people to write an article about the company to appear in their favourite business journal 5 years from now. Another version of the same technique was to describe a video documentary made in the future about the successes of the organization. This type of technique was powerful in freeing people from stylized business format and encouraged them to think in creative, journalistic terms about their vision of the future. The composers of the vision were few in number. It is difficult to create a vision by committee. The more people that are involved, the longer and less clear the vision. Faced with a vision which is too long, it becomes necessary to break it down into themes. In Exxon Chemical it was important to identify:

- Organizational themes.
- Individual themes.
- Business themes.

The vision needed to impact on the organization and it needed to wake people up! Without awareness of the need for change, the organization would not have changed: no awareness + no pain + no opportunities = no change.


## Setting high-level goals

The top management in Exxon Chemical set a number of goals which, when achieved, would realize the vision. It was helpful to consider the stakeholders in the organization (for example, revenue customers, employees, general public, suppliers, shareholders, etc.) when focusing on the goals. Each goal had a measure. Eventually each measure had a target. These targets were challenging, yet achievable. The organization aspired to be world-class and the targets needed to be benchmarked against world leaders.

The goals themselves became a concise statement which caught people's attention and started the process of communication. This concise statement was backed up with clarifying descriptions, measurements, responsibilities and targets. Measurement was the real key. People in the organization reacted well to understanding what was important enough to be measured by the top management:

- 'What gets measured gets managed'
- 'He who is measured, manages'.

The high-level goals were regarded as a set, together with all of their key measures, and checked against the vision and the values of the organization. The following checklist of questions were used:

- If we achieve the targets/measures, will we have realized the vision?
- Do the goals/measures cover areas not stated in the vision?
- Is the voice of the customer apparent?
- Are the future needs of the other stakeholders in the organization reflected?
- Is it all compatible with the core values of the organization?

The top management team now needed to gain buy-in and involvement from the organization, starting with the next level down. This started a process called 'catch-ball', a two-way iterative process which ensured the cascade or deployment into the organization. The next-level-down management group took the goals and measures developed by the top team and developed a set of strategies to achieve the goals. If they were unable to set strategies to impact the measures given, then this was a point for feedback. In turn, for each of their key strategies, which should collectively achieve the goals and the vision, the management set measures and targets (Figure 16.3).

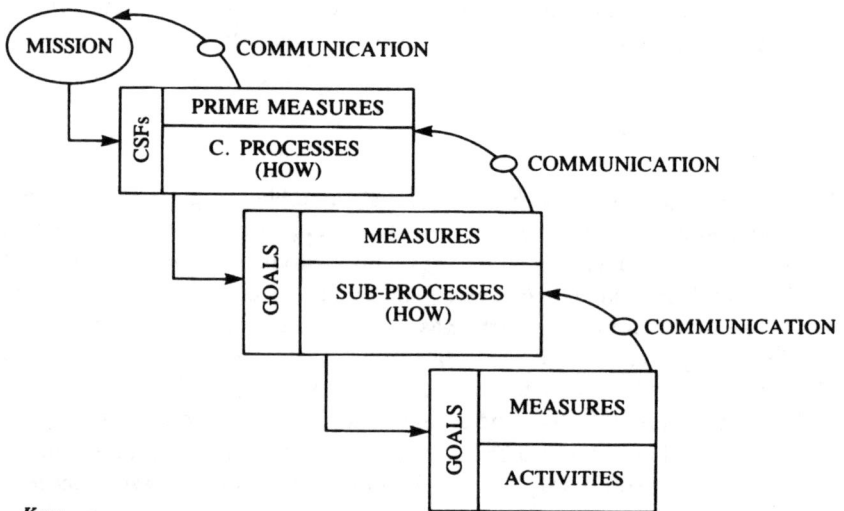

Key:
CSFs Critical success factors

**Figure 16.3** *Goal translation process*

The 'catch-ball' process was the reality check. It required two-way communication and developed a dialogue throughout the organization about the goals, measures and strategies. The strategies of one layer of management became the goals of the next level down. The next level down undertook the goals from above and decided if and how they could achieve them. This was an iterative and often frustratingly long process requiring good communication, dialogue and the ability to be flexible. Managers were prepared to change their goal or measure or target, since they had asked for feedback on them.

### Getting buy-in

Management took the responsibility to communicate the goals. When setting the goals and measures they often found it useful to identify a single 'goal-owner' for each goal. In this role a person owned the goal for the management team and coordinated the initial development and review. In communicating the goals further down into the organization, however, it became more important that the whole management team owned all the goals.

The cascade process eventually reached the 'sharp-end' level where real products or services for outside customers were produced. At this point, ownership and responsibility for the business processes which deliver the organization's goods or services were taken. Here it was important to recognize ongoing business process needs and existing improvement efforts. This was done by developing a matrix (similar to the Quality Function Deployment technique) to align existing activities/processes and improvement programmes with the goals (Figure 16.4). This helped to identify:

- which were the activities/work processes critical to attaining the goals;
- which of the existing improvement activities were already aligned with the goals;
- which goals were not going to be achieved without realigning effort;
- how to prioritize the improvement effort.

### Communicating progress

The central thrust of effective goal deployment in Exxon Chemical was to enhance the quality of the information available to enable the right people to make the right business decisions, at the right time. The measures generated at each level in the organization were designed to be useful to

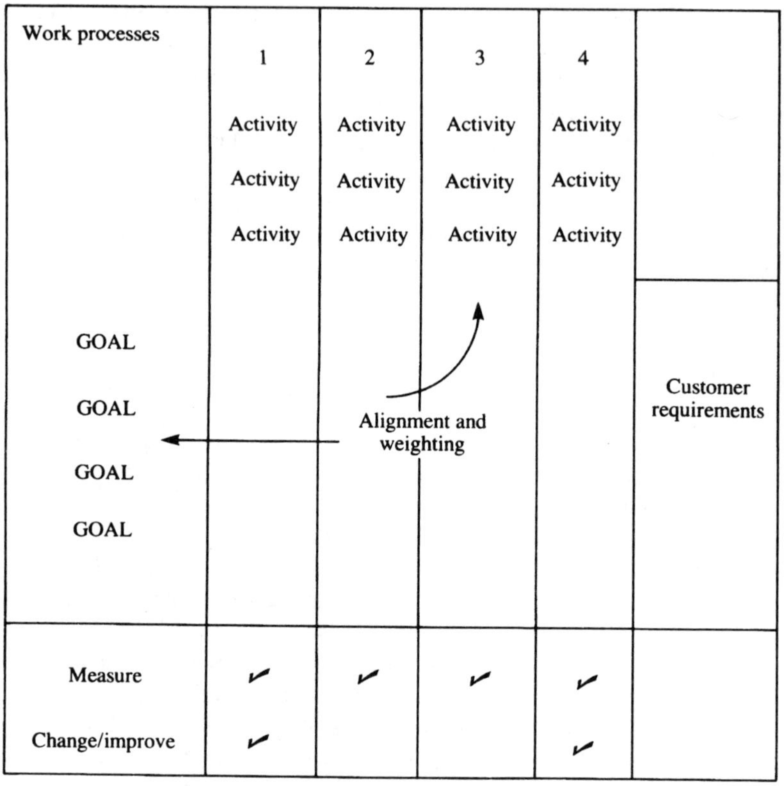

| Work processes | 1 | 2 | 3 | 4 | |
|---|---|---|---|---|---|
| | Activity | Activity | Activity | Activity | |
| | Activity | Activity | Activity | Activity | |
| | Activity | Activity | Activity | Activity | |
| GOAL<br><br>GOAL<br><br>GOAL<br><br>GOAL | | Alignment and weighting | | | Customer requirements |
| Measure | ✓ | ✓ | ✓ | ✓ | |
| Change/improve | ✓ | | | ✓ | |

**Figure 16.4** *Aligning work processes*

them and necessary for them to prioritize their efforts and improvement plans.

The measures were also used to communicate progress. This was done in several ways, for example, reports, newsletters and stewardship meetings. Additionally, they used what they called interactive quality stations. A quality station in Exxon Chemical is a place to display goals and strategies, measure progress and communicate about the ongoing improvement effort. The stations also helped to recognize people for their achievement and encouraged improvement ideas. Generally, a quality station was located at some central meeting place frequented by the group. The goals were displayed together with the updated measures and improvement plans. Extensive use was made of pictures, charts and graphs and plenty of room was provided for suggestions and ideas. A quality station is a good tool but it needs the necessary ongoing maintenance: 'Don't create your quality station and then ignore it!'

## Some pitfalls

The following lessons have been learned by Exxon Chemical in their goal deployment process.

### *A powerless vision*

A vision or mission can be worthless. It adds no value if it is overambitious and seen to be impossible to achieve by the people. Similarly, it adds no value if it is uninspiring and offers no challenge at all.

A vision generated by a committee can be too detailed and too long.

The vision needs to be tested. It is necessary to get feedback on a vision before it is set in stone by the senior management team. Focus groups, using people from a wide cross-section of the organization, were a good method of getting feedback in Exxon Chemical. The feedback was structured with questions such as:

- What do I like/dislike about it?
- What does it mean to me?
- What themes or aspects are missing?
- How could it be improved?

### *Overambition*

The goals must be deployed with a sense of urgency but also with regard to resources and to the pace at which the organization can accept change. Some prioritization of goals and strategies will be necessary.

A useful concept incorporated into the prioritization process in Exxon Chemical was the universal application of measurement. So, for example:

Priority 1 = measure and improve.

These were areas of strategy that were the key to business needs, where early success was critical. They were selected for early attention and focus.

Priority 0 = measure and maintain.

These were areas of strategy that were the key to success but early improvement was not so critical. However, it was important that the existing standard of achievement was maintained. The vital activity here then was to measure performance and maintain it.

This universal application of performance measurement, independent from priority, made a real difference in how the deployment process was perceived and in its practical implementation. It was recognized that the company did not require a plate-spinning exercise, where some plates are kept spinning whilst others crash to the ground. What was needed was all plates to be kept spinning, but some much faster than others!

### Top-down

It is important to recognize the difference between traditional top-down management by objectives and goal deployment. Goal deployment also starts top-down but relies on a cascade of bottom-up feedback processes to achieve alignment throughout the organization:

| *Management by objectives* | *Goal deployment* |
| --- | --- |
| Focus on results | Focus on results through improving the process |
| Top-down | Top-down and bottom-up alignment |
| Focus on who | Focus on how |
| Individual responsibility | Group/team responsibility |
| Work harder | Work smarter |
| Targets/incentives | Realistic measures |
| Who failed? | How can we improve? |
| Manage by dilemma | Prioritize effectively |

### Bolt-on

Goal deployment should not be perceived as a bolt-on appendage to other company planning systems, for example, strategic quality planning.

In Exxon Chemical, goal deployment encompassed the central and single planning system of the business. This implied two important requirements:

1 The deployed goals, measures and strategies needed to be carefully thought through and of high quality, which took time and management effort.
2 If the alignment process worked, then people would use the goals to prioritize their work. To avoid the negative impact on motivation of realigning people, the goals needed to be long-term and sustainable.

## Not invented here

One of the symptoms of empowerment, freedom and diversity, within the goal deployment process, is the strong desire of management and leaders to have their own version of the goals. This sometimes led to a pedantic demand for unnecessary changes to the wording of a goal just to reflect ownership. An example was:

Company level:   Be the preferred supplier.
Regional level:   Be the supplier of choice.

Generally, this limited differentiation was not helpful. It tended to reduce credibility and led to people wasting effort in trying to analyse what the differences actually meant. Usually it meant that the regional manager simply wanted to be different. Often there was no added value in changing the goal or the measures or strategies from one level to the next. Sometimes people asked what added value a management level was providing!

In translating higher-level goals, especially at senior/middle management levels, it was useful to ask the following sorts of questions:

● Do we agree with the higher-level goals, measures and strategies or not? Are they practical, challenging, viable, etc.? If not, then feedback up recommended changes (catch-ball).
● Do we need, as a management group, to translate these goals? If not, then let us adopt them as they are.
● What value do we add? How is our business/culture different and how should we change the 'what' into 'how'? How can we add value by changing the higher-level goals into our own-level version?
● Have we checked, with the next level down, their views and comments?

## Change management

Effectively deploying a set of challenging goals and aligning and motivating people to improve and prioritize their process of work imply change. To succeed, it was important to recognize which elements of change management and awareness of the process of change and transition would be important.

Some fundamental elements of the process of change in Exxon Chemical were:

● The need for change most often comes from outside the organization.
● No need, no pain, no awareness produces no change.
● People do not universally resist change; however, lack of involvement, freedom and choice generates resistance.

- Visioning is easy, implementing is tough.
- Goals and strategy must come first; changes in structure, system and cultural norms come next.
- Complaints during transition are good and a sign of progress.
- Recognize, grieve for and celebrate what was good.
- Three more keys to organizational change:
    communication,
    communication,
    communication.


## Benefits and results

The effort required to deploy goals effectively throughout the Exxon Chemical company has been large. The results, however, are multifaceted and substantial and there has been a significant bottom-line payoff.


### *Benefits for the organization*

Goal deployment has disciplined the organization to focus on the long term and identify its key challenges. It has facilitated two-way communication throughout the organization, and provided a framework for decision-making and prioritizing work. It has brought the vision into reality and shown clearly a pathway or staircase for the organization to tread, which will take it towards its vision.

For the management of the organization it has provided a way of educating the workforce about the business and about what is important for the future. It has provided the boundaries and signposts to the pathway forward.

In recent years, a lot of debate has occurred within Exxon Chemical on the subject of empowerment of the workforce. Management have been more or less comfortable with the prospect of unleashing the creativity and resourcefulness of their people, dependent on the culture of their particular part of the organization and the stage or extent of their change process. In the early stages of TQM, for instance, it was important for people to grapple with their work processes, align with their customers and achieve early improvement success. At this stage it was fairly low-risk to empower the workforce to get on with it. There was so much improvement to make in the high-impact, easy-to-do category that almost wherever they focused their attention it added value. In the subsequent stages of TQM, however, improvements became more significant. The potential improvements were larger, having critical impact on the business but needing significant resources to accomplish. In these conditions it was still important to empower the people and seek their creative innovation, but it became more important to provide a focus, a priority and a direction for these more significant improvement efforts. Goal deployment has provided this aligning framework in Exxon Chemical.

### Benefits for the people

Goal deployment has indicated to people the role they play and how their efforts are reflected in the achievement of the vision. It has allowed them to context, prioritize their work, and has provided a basis for recognition. It has also provided opportunity for them to contribute and become involved.

Goals, once deployed, have made life generally simpler at Exxon Chemical, and certainly made reporting simpler. Goal deployment has also simplified meetings and reviews by providing a recognized agenda and common language. It has also made leadership more obvious and facilitated followership. This is the concept of upward empowerment. For any worker, if his/her boss has made it crystal-clear, through a goal deployment process, what the measures of success are, the worker can think about how he/she can facilitate success for the boss, how he/she can empower the boss.

## Goal deployment in Exxon Chemical

The most senior management group within Exxon Chemical, the Executive Committee, developed a set of goals and measures for the four stakeholders in the chemical company:

1 the shareholder.
2 the public.
3 the employees.
4 the revenue customer.

These were consistent with Exxon's vision to be the best (petro) chemical company.

Each of the company's business groups and functions took these goals and measures and, through the iterative catch-ball process, developed their own compatible business visions and goals.

The Basic Chemicals business group worldwide management team, for example, developed their own vision 'BC 2000', linked to the company core values. Basic Chemicals Americas and Europe took this vision, and the Exxon Chemical Company goals, and developed a set of aligned regional goals, measures and strategies. Each manufacturing site took the regional strategies and developed their own site goals, measures and strategies. Finally, each working group took the site strategies and developed their own improvement plans. An example of a specific goal deployment was:

| | |
|---|---|
| Exxon Chemical Company/ Basic Chemicals | Be the preferred supplier. |
| Basic Chemicals Europe | By having high-quality partnerships with all internal and external customers, always meet or exceed agreed requirements. |
| Marketing operations | Review Basic Chemicals Europe performance yearly with all customers. Track performance versus agreed requirements. Ensure multilevel contact to maintain the continuity and breadth of our customer relationship. Measure customer satisfaction index. |
| Manufacturing plant | Measures: product quality capability. shipping reliability. customer service satisfaction. |

### Specific examples of results

The big impacts of a goal deployment process on a worldwide basis take time to come to fruition. The very nature of the process is long-term. The Exxon Chemical company had always been data-driven, but the deployment process took, on average, about a year to effectively reach the sharp-end or 'shop floor'. The full impact of the process has yet to be fully measured, but it is possible to detect and measure significant improvements at the lower levels in the organization, as people's energy is focused on the goals:

### Example 1 – Manufacturing

| | |
|---|---|
| Company goal | Create the highest shareholder value in our industry. |
| Business group | Be a major source of earnings growth, maintain a competitive return and be a model of operating integrity. |

Regional group   Be the lowest-cost supplier and a leader in the use of feed stocks, hardware and technology and drive quality to the bottom line.

Site group   Reduce fixed and allocated costs versus total erected cost (TEC – project cost) from 25 to 20% in 1 year.

By focusing on the process of how engineering was actually carried out, the organizational structure, and the distribution of costs, the project group was able to reduce engineering costs, on average, to 16% of TEC during the following year. Their ultimate target is 8%, derived from an internal and external benchmarking study.

The group manager stated in his annual report:

> It was our second year of systematic performance measurement in all our areas of responsibility. The focus on a small number of key improvement items resulted in major progress in these areas.

## Example 2 – Marketing and Sales

Regional group   Improve speed of response to customer.

Area group   Focus on improving our customer complaints management process.

The area sales group completed a goal translation process. They did this by building an alignment matrix of their regional goals against their major work processes. This identified that their complaints management process was critical to several of the goal strategies and measures developed at a regional level. They started to measure complaints overdue, analysed by sales area. This was plotted at a quality station in their group meeting room. Complaints overdue dropped from an average of 25 per month over 3 months to less than 5 over 2 months.

The same group also identified receivables as a critical area. They developed a measure of total cash overdue on a monthly basis and plotted this. Focus in this area reduced overdues by at least $0.5m for the group as a whole.

## Example 3 – Manufacturing

Company   Be our customers' preferred supplier.

Regional   Track our performance against agreed requirements and systematically eliminate non-conformances.

Plant   Improve customer satisfaction.

As part of their goal translation effort, the plant group identified several key areas and developed statistical measures which included:

- product quality capability index;
- planned production deviation;
- shipping reliability index.

These are 'traditional' quality assurance measures. In addition, they identified some other customers. These were people and groups in their regional headquarters and venture partners headquarters who had specific requirements for information. They identified the necessary attributes, timing and format for this information. This covered a wide range of daily to monthly performance and planning statistics and information transmitted via a number of different media. They created a charter which defined the specific requirements of this information system as seen through the eyes of their customers. They developed a measurable index of performance against this charter.

Performance increased from 40 to 98% compliance throughout the year. Since this almost met their target of 100%, one of their actions for the following year was to talk to this set of customers about more stretching targets for the future.

### Goal deployment outlook

Within Exxon Chemical the goal deployment process has set challenging goals, measures and targets. The deployment has helped to identify key processes, especially those processes which run through all business groups and/or across business groups and functions which are in need of change. Goal deployment has set the criteria for picking out these key processes. With these identified and, through use of tools like benchmarking, work process restructuring and redesign, it has been possible to progress with major improvement and change projects, which have company-, regional- or business-group-wide implications. Several of these major change projects have been identified and are in progress. This wider application represents the combination of TQM, goal deployment and business process re-engineering (Figure 16.5).

## Acknowledgement

This is from a case study by Alan Randall, Exxon Chemical.

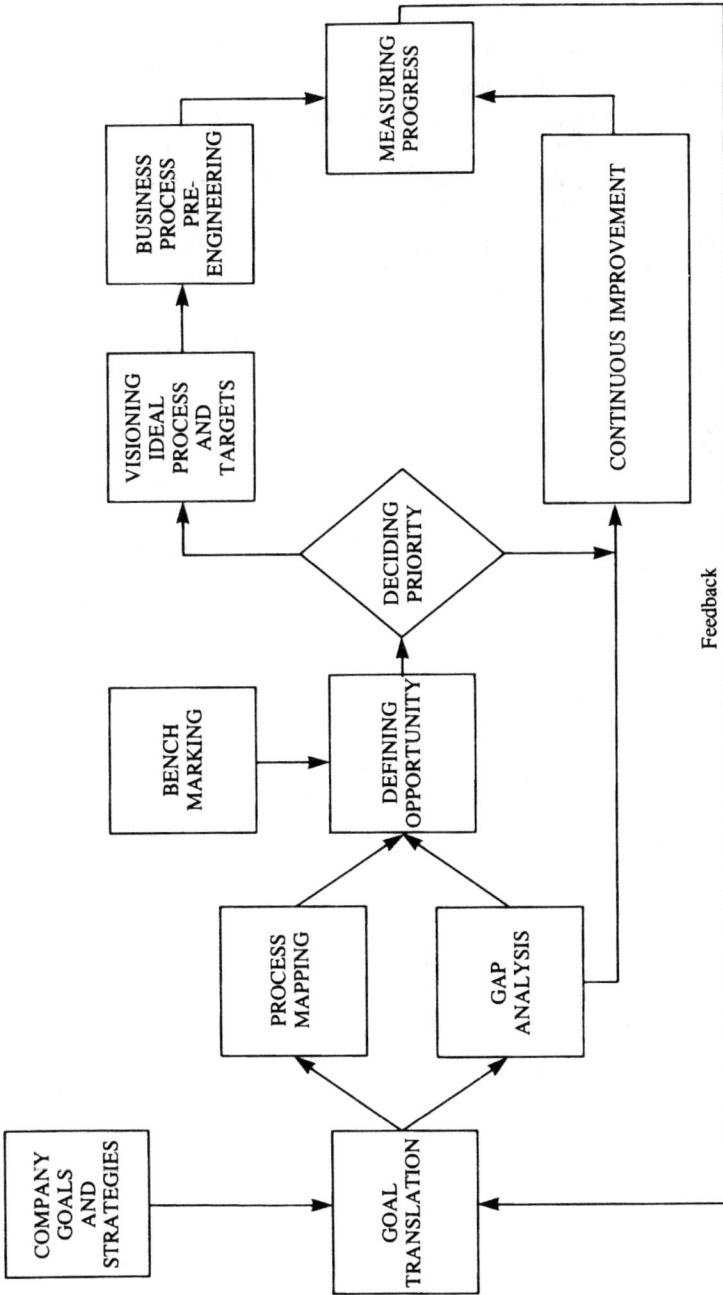

**Figure 16.5** *TQM implementation framework*

## Bibliography

Baldrige, M., *National Quality Award Criteria*, The American Society for Quality Control, Milwaukee, WI, 1993.

Burke, and Spencer, *Interpretation and Industry Comparisons*, Warner Burke, Pelham, NY, 1990.

Hackman, and Oldham, *Development of the job diagnostic survey. Journal of Applied Psychology*, **60**, 1975.

Savage, P. *Who Cares Wins*, Mercury Books, London, 1987.

Tichy, N. M. and Devanna, M. A. *The Transformational Leader* John Wiley, New York, 1986.

*Total Quality Management: The European Model for Self-Appraisal*, European Foundation for Quality Management, Brussels, 1994.

Whiteley, R. C. *The Customer Driven Company*, Business Books, London, 1991.

# 17 Implementing TQM at the University of Bradford Management Centre

## Introduction

The University of Bradford's Management Centre is one of Europe's oldest and largest business schools. The Management Centre pursues an extensive programme of research that has earned an international reputation in many fields of study. It is a fully integrated business school, providing comprehensive and innovative programmes of management education for undergraduates, postgraduates and postexperience students. The interaction of students, experienced managers and staff, with diverse educational and industrial backgrounds, provides a stimulating and creative environment.

The Management Centre has a matrix structure with eight Professors, responsible for the subject groups of Economics, Financial Management, Credit Management, International Business, Marketing, Organization Behaviour, Production and Operations Management, and TQM, whilst non-professorial Programme Chairs manage the undergraduate, postgraduate (MBA), full-and part-time, doctoral, and executive development (EDP) programmes. There is also a Director and Assistant Director of the Centre who are both Professors. The Director, Assistant Director, Programme Chairmen, and some Professors also sit on an Executive Committee, which is the decision-making body of the Management Centre.

There are approximately 80 full-time equivalent academic and related staff, 50 non-academic staff, 500 undergraduates, 300 full-time and part-time MBA students, and 30 doctoral students on site. Almost 2000 executives and managers from industry, commerce and the public sector pass through the EDP each year on various types of short-course programmes, including the executive MBA.

The Management Centre is part of the University of Bradford, although it is physically separated from the main campus. It is set in a pleasant site of approximately 13 acres with a mixture of historically old and new buildings.

The establishment of the industry-funded European Centre for Total Quality Management (ECTQM) in 1987 was a major innovation. The ECTQM is actively involved in research, teaching and advisory work in all areas of quality management. A wide range of students, including those on EDPs, experience TQM training and education at Bradford. The Centre is a member of the European Foundation for Quality Management (EFQM) and the TQM group are involved in many EFQM activities.

In the summer of 1990 it was decided to introduce TQM into the Management Centre itself using the expertise of the European Centre for TQM. The 1990s is a very challenging phase in the life of the Management Centre. Business schools generally operate in an increasingly competitive environment and the Management Centre's future success will depend on the commitment of all its staff to the improvement of its key processes.

## Awareness and organization for TQM

The then nine Professors held two TQM Strategic Planning Workshops in December 1990 and January 1991 to examine the feasibility of introducing TQM into the Management Centre.

A model of TQM (Figure 17.1), developed at the ECTQM, was adopted for implementation at the Management Centre. This conceptual model views the

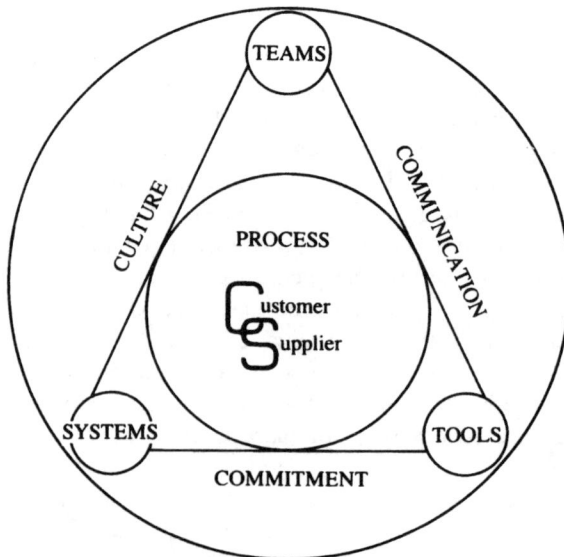

**Figure 17.1** *The 'Bradford' TQM model*

customer–supplier relationship and the processes that link them as being a core value of TQM. Continuous improvement of processes to deliver increasing customer satisfaction is central to the TQM philosophy. To achieve this there are certain requirements that must be in place. A commitment to a culture of continuous improvement is an essential element and this is facilitated by effective two-way communications. Actual process improvement is achieved by teams that are supported by good systems and use the tools of TQM.

The consensus view was that TQM at the Centre should involve:

- Everyone striving to meet customer requirements – internally and externally.
- Managing business processes.
- Continuous improvement in everything we do.
- Open, good communications.
- Participative management style and involvement of everyone.
- Documented, auditable systems for the way we do things.
- Teamwork, built around our processes.
- Training and education in the identification of processes and the tools and techniques of improvement.
- Empowering people to act wherever improvements can be made.

It was recognized that the necessary culture change would happen slowly and that the Management Centre's Total Quality Culture would not be built overnight. There was a strong belief among the Professors that the TQM approach could be used at the Centre in a disciplined approach to never-ending improvement.

It was also recognized that to devise and implement a TQM process takes considerable time and dedication and it must be given the status of an executive project. It was also essential that any TQM initiatives be fully integrated into the Management Centre's operating philosophy and management systems. The Professors suggested to the Executive Committee that the Centre should embark seriously on a TQM implementation programme, but pointed out that the commitment would be continually questioned and be weakened – perhaps destroyed – by the failure of the senior management to support the initiatives.

## Implementing the TQM programme

### *The Quality Council*

It was decided that a Quality Council (QC) should be formed to guide the TQM process. The QC's role is described below.

*Purpose*

To evolve the Centre's culture into one of Total Quality, thereby ensuring that we identify, understand, and achieve our mission.

*Charter and responsibilities*

The members of the QC were drawn from various levels in the organization. It works within the strategic framework laid down by the Professors and the Executive Committee. The membership is the Director, two Professors (including the Professor of TQM as facilitator, and chairperson) two Programme Chairmen, a lecturer, a secretary and a computer officer (technician).

Their responsibilities include:

● Updating the mission statement.
● Identifying the critical success factors.
● Providing overall strategic direction on TQM for the Management Centre.
● Establishing plans for TQM implementation.
● Setting up Process Quality Teams and Quality Action Teams to make improvements.
● Reviewing progress and plans for quality improvement.
● Revising plans for the development of TQM and process improvement.

The QC does not act as a senior problem-solving group. It holds meetings monthly, following the meeting of the Executive Committee to review quality strategy, implementation, progress and improvement.

The first tasks of the QC was to review the previous mission statement. It was found to contain suitable components for the development of a new mission statement, and the Critical Success Factors (CSFs). The CSFs are the key factors that an organization must have to achieve its mission. They are the building blocks of the mission. These were set down as follows, including a list of stakeholders.

*Mission statement*

● To be a growing centre of excellence in teaching and research in the disciplines of management.
● To improve the practice of management, worldwide.

*Critical Success Factors*

1 We must have a University Funding Council (UFC) research rating of 5.
2 We need a demonstrably excellent reputation for an innovative practical approach.
3 We must have products and services which meet current and future market needs.
4 We need financial independence.
к 5 We need an excellent infrastructure.
6 We must have a stimulating and rewarding work environment.
7 We must achieve a critical mass of quality staff.
к 8 We need quality inputs.

These were deemed to be all *necessary* and together *sufficient* for the mission to be achieved. Some are directly measurable (e.g. UFC research rating); some are aspirations, hopes or fears.

*Stakeholders*

These are:

1 Students.
2 Staff:
   (a) academic.
   (b) others.
3 State.
4 Industry/business/public organizations.
5 Professions.
6 The University.

Current Aims were derived from the mission and CSFs as follows:

1 *Stakeholders*: To achieve a UFC research rating of 5 in 1993. To improve the management processes in the external world by research, teaching and advisory work.
2 *Customers*: To be the number one UK business school, in terms of the services and products offered to targeted markets.
3 *Employees*: To be a total quality business school which fully involves and develops all employees. This would revolve around never-ending improvement of processes to meet customers' requirements completely. To empower employees and teams to act in making continuous improvements.

The QC also identified 28 critical processes. These are the activities which must be carried out especially well in order for the CSFs to be achieved. The Council then produced a process quality matrix in order to prioritize critical processes for improvement. This identifies which processes have a high impact on each CSF. Again the necessary and sufficiency rule applies. The matrix also showed the subjective quality ranking given by the Council to each process on the scale:

A    Excellent performance
B    Good performance
C    Fair performance
D    Bad performance
E    Embryonic processes

A second matrix showed the results of this work – a plot of the quality of each process against the number of CSF imports. Shaded zones of the matrix gave the critical processes in most urgent need of attention, i.e. those processes offering the greatest opportunity.

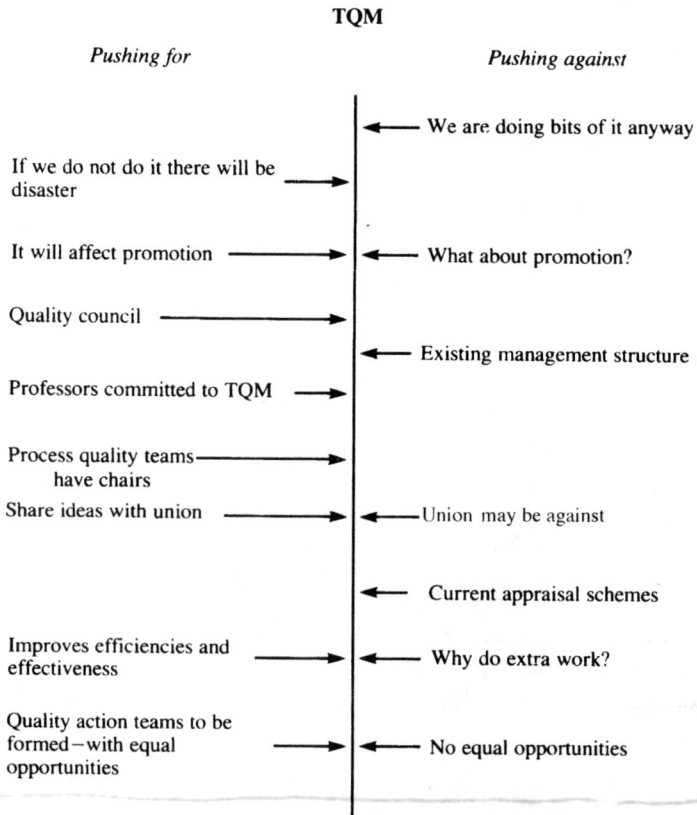

**TQM**

*Pushing for*                                              *Pushing against*

◄——— We are doing bits of it anyway

If we do not do it there will be disaster ———►

It will affect promotion ———►     ◄——— What about promotion?

Quality council ———►

◄——— Existing management structure

Professors committed to TQM ——►

Process quality teams——— have chairs ———►

Share ideas with union ———►     ◄———Union may be against

◄——— Current appraisal schemes

Improves efficiencies and effectiveness ———►     ◄——— Why do extra work?

Quality action teams to be formed – with equal opportunities ———►     ◄——— No equal opportunities

**Figure 17.2** *The pressures for and against TQM: force-field analysis*

All 28 processes were grouped under seven headings and these main groupings given generic titles. Seven Process Quality Teams were set up to manage these processes. The critical processes and quality/impact matrix are shown in Appendix A and B. The QC prepared a force-field diagram for the pressures for and against TQM at the Management Centre (Figure 17.2).

## Teamwork for quality improvement

Involvement in quality improvements was cascaded down through the organization using a structured team approach involving Process Quality Teams (PQTs) and Quality Action Teams (QATs).

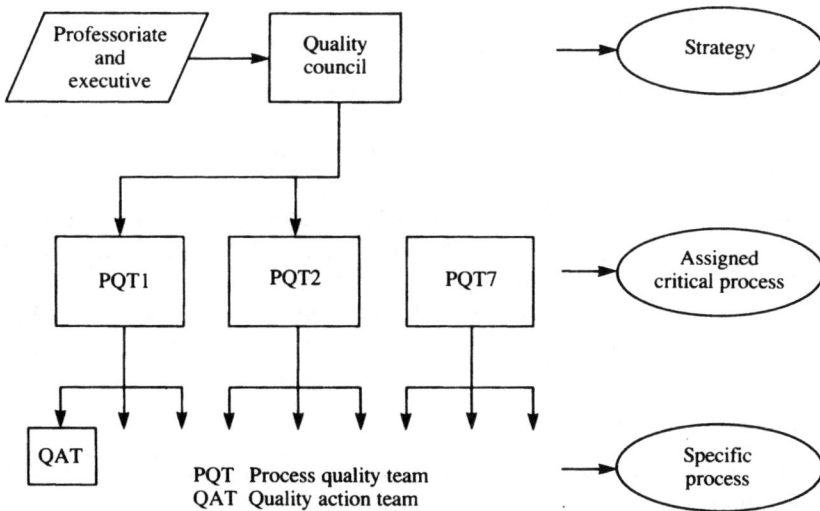

**Figure 17.3** *Organization for TQM*

This teamwork structure, which is shown in Figure 17.3, ensures the widest possible involvement in the TQM process and its effective implementation. The role of these teams is described below.

### Process Quality Teams

The PQTs own and manage the process improvements.

*Purpose*

To define certain business processes and to set them up to run perfectly. Each PQT Chair will form a team of approximately eight staff. Their responsibilities will include:

- Breaking down and describing the assigned critical processes.
- Prioritizing and selecting processes for improvement.
- Setting up QATs.
- Reviewing and supporting QAT activity.

### Quality Action Teams

The detailed improvements will be carried out by QATs.

*Purpose*

To define and improve a particular process assigned by a PQT.

*Composition*

Six to 10 members of staff, selected by a Team Leader, representing all those involved in the assigned process. The team leader will be selected and asked by the PQT to form the team, preferably using a flowchart of the process. It is hoped that every employee at the Management Centre will be involved in quality improvement through a QAT (or PQT) at some point.

*Responsibilities include:*

- Drawing a flowchart of the process to identify its customers and suppliers.
- Identifying measurement points.
- Measuring and comparing results with requirements.
- Improving the process and documenting it.

## The TQM survey

It was agreed at the senior level that only by measurement would people know when the Centre had succeeded in its mission and in meeting its aims. To measure that start point, a survey of the staff's perceptions of quality at the Management Centre was carried out. The survey addressed all the key areas of the Bradford TQM model.

A summary of the survey findings as reported back to the Management Centre staff is shown below.

### External customers

Although we believe we know who are our customers (75% agree or strongly agree), we do not generally believe that we are completely clear about what are our customer's requirements (72%). There is some level of disagreement amongst ourselves about whether we:

1 are *good at keeping up* with the changing needs of our customers;
2 *respond better to customers'* problems now than a *year ago*;
3 are *better than our competitors* at giving customers what they want;
4 work to improve our ability to *measure* how well we meet customer requirements;
5 are *committed* to serving customer needs.

This may reflect our different individual areas of activity – executive development, postgraduate, undergraduate, doctoral, marketing, finance, quality, etc. The overall medians of this group of questions, however, suggest some dissatisfaction with our performance here. One quite negative point is that we are not strong on detection and correction – 73% of respondents disagree with the statement that we do whatever it takes to satisfy a dissatisfied customer. In quality management this is not even 'right second time', and it may be costing us a fortune in lost business.

### Internal customer–supplier relationships

There is a split in the Centre with regard to:

1 knowing the *standards* required;
2 *other people/groups creating unnecessary work*;
3 *work* received from others being *correctly done*;
4 *internal customers* receiving equal treatment to external customers.

*Feedback*, however, seems to be a problem for the majority, with 74% feeling that they do not get information about problems with their work in sufficient time to deal with them, and 66% suggesting that their group does not receive feedback from other groups or course managers about how well their requirements are met. Perhaps we need something in addition to the simple questionnaires completed by students (or delegates) who attend our courses and programmes.

## Staff involvement, development and reward

There are some very positive pointers here; 84% believe that efforts to improve quality are recognized by their boss, 59% of respondents are asked about their ideas for improvement, and 72% feel their boss encourages full use of their skills and abilities. On the negative side, however, 68% feel they do not get the training they need to improve the quality of their work, and 75% are not always provided with what they need to do their job correctly. This is probably linked to the fact that 75% do not feel that doing good work is rewarded and 67% say that the Management Centre is not committed to the development of its people.

A change is clearly needed here if quality improvement is to stand a chance at the Centre. It is nice to know, however, that 63% of the respondents take pride in the place!

## Systems, tools/techniques and teams

One or two highlights here are that 88% of the respondents do not feel that senior staff have established a clear policy and strategy to improve quality (yet!). Clearly people cannot wait for TQM to do this!

On the prevention versus detection issue, we are well over to the detection side of things, with 86% saying that we do not prevent problems before they happen and 78% agreeing that we often make the same mistakes twice in the Centre.

There is a big cry for better and well-documented systems: 97% of respondents say that our system and procedures are not well-documented and up to date. We also do not have records which clearly demonstrate the extent to which we meet customer requirements, according to 79% of respondents.

This is clearly an area which requires massive improvement, particularly if we aspire to BS5750/ISO9000 (Quality Systems) certification, which is rapidly gaining ground in the education sector.

With regard to *data collection* and *measuring the capability* of our processes and *performance*, we do not feel that we are doing very well here. In all, 76% believe we do not present data in a clear and meaningful way, and that we do not always analyse the collected data and information so that appropriate action can be taken. Even without this type of analysis taking place:

- 75% of respondents believe that our system, procedures and processes are not capable of meeting our customers' requirements.
- 71% disagree with the statement that we have means of knowing the causes of our performance variation.

- 87% do not believe we understand and measure our process capabilities.
- 69% think we act on hunches.
- 85% do not agree that we keep accurate records of how quality has improved.
- 88% do not believe we have consistent standards for measuring quality.

This lack of a systematic approach to quality performance measurement and information is directly against what we preach to our customers, but then 72% do not agree that we accept work only when we know we can deliver the customer's requirements.

Teamwork at the Management Centre also gets a bad rating: not a lot of teamwork in handling problems (65%), missed opportunities, room for improvement. Lack of coordination (89%) and lack of trust and dependence on each other (68%) are the negative aspects of this data, but responses to the other teamwork questions showed something of a split in opinion.

Generally speaking, many positive things were revealed in this survey, e.g. people taking a pride in the Management Centre, but the survey also highlighted many areas for improvement. Deficiencies in teamwork, communication, systems and measurement were identified. The most alarming statistic was that 88% of the respondents did not feel that the senior staff had established a clear policy and strategy to improve quality. Clearly this illustrated that the ground was fertile for a TQM initiative.

## The TQM training programme

The TQM training programme commenced in June 1991 with a teamwork workshop for the Executive Committee and the Professoriate (Figure 17.4). The senior team profile had previously been exposed to the Myers-Briggs Type Indicator (MBTI), which is a psychological measure that attempts to explain the central aspects of people's personality, both to the individuals themselves and to their colleagues. An understanding of the MBTI measures helps to promote effective teamwork. This profile was reviewed at the workshop together with the TQM concepts and models. The action plan for implementation of TQM at the Management Centre was also reviewed.

All staff have also taken part in a series of 1-day workshops which were led by the Professor of TQM and facilitated by members of his department.

The objectives of the workshops were:

- to enable staff to share information on their work and associated quality problems;
- to develop the staff's understanding of the concept of TQM;
- to have fun;
- to start building more effective teamwork for quality improvement.

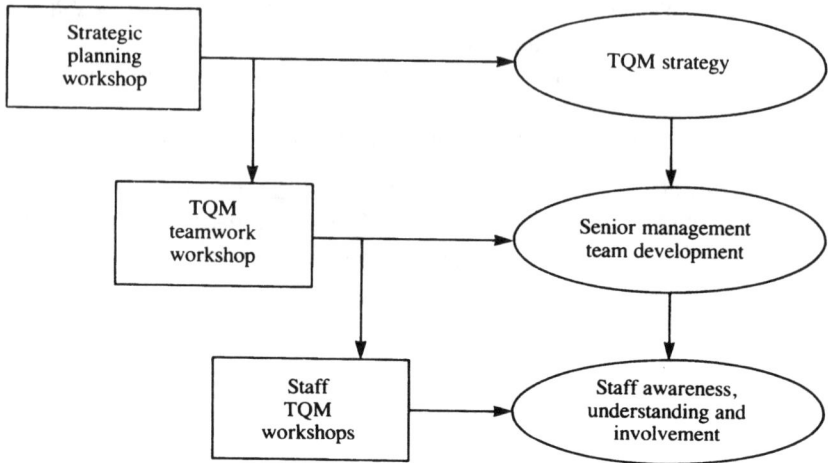

**Figure 17.4** *The training programme*

The outcome of these workshops was that staff were encouraged to participate in the TQM process at the individual and team level. The team approach to continuous improvement, described above, was launched by the QC, once a core of staff had been trained. All staff were asked to do some work on improvement immediately on an individual basis, using the tools and techniques of TQM learnt on their workshops.

Further training on process improvement methods was provided to the individual teams on an 'as-needed' basis. It was expected, however, that academic staff at a management centre should be familiar with techniques such as flow-charting, force-field analysis, Pareto analysis, brainstorming, cause-and-effect analysis, and the use of simple data presentation methods.

## The way ahead

The first phase of the TQM programme was concerned with obtaining the commitment of the Professoriate and Executive Committee to the principles of TQM. This commitment to TQM has been reinforced by the following statement from the Director of Bradford Management Centre, Professor David Weir:

> We are entering a very challenging competitive phase in the life of the Centre, and we are committed to creating a quality environment. Our success over the next few years depends on our ability to liberate the enormous positive energy within the Centre to meet our customers' requirements. Universities, old and new, all over the UK, Europe and the world, will have to adopt never-ending

quality improvement processes to succeed. We want to be one of the first departments to use TQM to gain a clear competitive advantage over our competitors.

A strategy for implementing TQM was developed at a strategic planning workshop. A team-building workshop was used to weld the Professoriate and Executive Committee into an effective senior management team. A QC has been formed to guide the programme. The commitment to TQM was communicated to all the Management Centre's staff through a series of TQM workshops. The development of a TQM culture has started to evolve.

How will the necessary improvements be effected in these areas? Some of the 'harder' tools and techniques of TQM will undoubtedly be called into play. The role of quality management systems such as ISO9000 can make a significant contribution to improvement. The review of existing formal and informal procedures and the adoption of best practices is a fundamental step in the TQM process. It is important to produce a documented system of what is actually done. The danger in all improvement activities is that people prefer to improve processes first before writing down what is done. This results in an indisciplined approach and progress is usually not sustained. Measurement and recording systems required by a good-quality system will also result in more effective operations. Many organizations in the educational sector are considering the contribution of ISO9000 to quality improvement. At the March 1993 QC meeting it was decided to begin the process of registering the Management Centre's quality system for independent third-part certification to ISO9000.

The combined effects of good systems and people working in teams using the tools and techniques of TQM sustain the process of continuous improvement. The PQTs and QATs are empowered to drive the improvement process forward. The results of many team projects have been implemented, e.g. the new induction process.

Initiating and sustaining a TQM programme in a large and well-established academic institution raises many interesting questions. Hopefully, the TQM initiative at Bradford is fully integrated into the Management Centre's operating philosophy and management systems. The TQM awareness level of all staff has been developed by a systematic training programme. As the programme evolves, further development of the Quality Model may be required. The contribution to quality improvement of the various elements of the European Quality Model will be evaluated. The ultimate success of the programme will depend upon people working effectively together, with the shared values of TQM, to achieve the shared aims critical to the future of the Bradford Management Centre. However, some significant milestones have already been passed. In 1992 the Management Centre achieved one of its major critical success factors, namely a research rating of 5.

# Appendix A: Critical processes owned by Process Quality Teams (PQTs)

The 28 critical processes at the Management Centre have been grouped under the various PQTs as follows:

| Critical process number | Critical Success Factor/ quality rank | |
|---|---|---|
| | | *Teaching and Staff Development PQT* |
| 1* | 3E | Reward groups and individuals for performance |
| 4 | 5C | Develop teaching performance |
| 5 | 5C | Develop staff |
| 7 | 6B | Recruit and retain top-quality researchers and teachers |
| 14* | 5D | Communicate and involve people within the Centre |
| 26* | 8E | Manage ownership of the mission |
| | | *Strategic Planning PQT* |
| 2 | 5C | Introduce a strategic planning process |
| 8* | 5D | Measure and control performance |
| 21* | 6E | Research market place for requirements |
| 27 | 5C | Manage new business development |
| | | *Research and Dissemination PQT* |
| 3 | 5B | Obtain research funding |
| 6 | 5B | Convert research into publications |
| 19* | 5E | Provide direct advice to improve management (do consulting) |
| 28 | 5B | Conduct research |
| | | *Corporate Development PQT* |
| 9 | 5C | Recruit quality students |
| 13 | 7B | Form international alliances |
| 18* | 4E | Create business relationships with alumni |
| 27 | 5C | Manage new business development |

| Critical process number | Critical Success Factor/ quality rank | |
|---|---|---|
| | | *External Networks, Information and Promotion PQT* |
| 10* | 5D | Advertise and promote the Centre's activities |
| 11* | 7E | Undertake regular competitor analysis |
| 12* | 7C | Manage external winning relationships |
| 17* | 6C | Communicate externally |
| | | *Facilities Development PQT* |
| 20* | 6D | Have fun |
| 22 | 5C | Research technological innovations |
| 24 | 2D | Make the Management Centre beautiful |
| 25 | 4C | Have appropriate course materials |
| | | *Finance PQT* |
| 15 | 5B | Manage University relationship (negotiate terms with) |
| 16 | 7B | Invest in infrastructure |
| 23* | 7C | Generate general income |

*Processes in most urgent need of attention (shaded zone in Appendix B).

# Appendix B: Critical processes – impact/quality matrix

COUNT

| | E | D | C | B | A | COUNT | |
|---|---|---|---|---|---|---|---|
| | 26 | | | | | 8 | HIGH IMPACT |
| | 11 | | 12 | 23 | 13 | 16 | 7 | |
| | 24 | 20 | 17 | | 7 | | 6 | |
| | 19 | 8 10 / 14 | 2 4 / 5 9 / 22 27 | 3 6 / 15 28 | | 5 | |
| | 18 | | 25 | | | | 4 | |
| | 1 | | | | | | 3 | |
| | | 24 | | | | | 2 | |
| | | | | | | | 1 | LOW IMPACT |

E   D   C   B   A

LOW QUALITY                              HIGH QUALITY

1 etc. Process 1 etc.

# Index

# TOTAL QUALITY MANAGEMENT
## Second Edition

## JOHN OAKLAND
### Exxon Professor Total Quality Management
### Bradford Management Centre

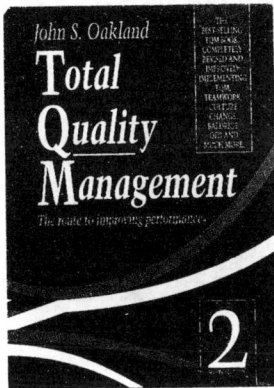

John S. Oakland

**Total Quality Management**

*The route to improving performance*

2

This second edition of the best-selling book on TQM has been largely rewritten and restructured around a new model of TQM.

No matter what your organization does, TQM 2 will help you develop, integrate and sustain TQM and continue improvement as part of your organization's strategy. Some of the major points are:

★ It emphasises more on the integration of TQM into the strategy of the business

★ 10 points for senior management to aid them in their thinking on commitment, culture and communication issues

★ Material on assessing quality systems

★ Chapters on communications and the quality strategy

★ Plus many more exciting new changes.

PROFESSOR OAKLAND aims to show managers how to implement a Total Quality Management strategy throughout all their activities and thereby achieve top quality performance overall, not just in product or service quality.

*"Directors and managers in diverse organizations will be able to help TQM within their own operations after reading this book"*
WORDS OF PRAISE ABOUT THE FIRST EDITION FROM QUALITY TODAY

CONTENTS INCLUDE:
UNDERSTANDING QUALITY; ORGANIZATION FOR QUALITY; PLANNING FOR QUALITY 1 - FLOW CHARTING, QUALITY PLANNING AND JIT; PLANNING FOR QUALITY 2 - PURCHASING, RELIABILITY AND MAINTENANCE; DESIGN FOR QUALITY; CONTROL OF QUALITY; TEAMWORK FOR QUALITY; IMPLEMENTATION OF TQM.

0 7506 0993 1   HARDBACK   316PP   234 x 156MM   1993   £30.00

Available from all good booksellers, or in case of difficulty please phone our direct order line on (0933) 410511 with your credit card details ready.

# MANAGEMENT TEAMS:
## Why they Succeed or Fail

## R M Belbin

A management team can combine all qualities necessary for success which one individual alone cannot possess. Dr Belbin has identified eight key team-roles which are essential to effectiveness, and each of which is associated with a particular type of personality. He assesses the roles of leadership and creativity in a team; and he shows how team size and physical environment can influence effectiveness.

*"It should be read by all who have responsibility and authority for guiding organizations in their selection of management teams."*
PERSONNEL MANAGEMENT

CONTENTS INCLUDE:
*INTRODUCTION; A STUDY OF TEAMS; HOW IT ALL BEGAN; TEAMS CONTAINING SIMILAR PERSONALITIES; TEAM LEADERSHIP; UNSUCCESSFUL TEAMS; WINNING TEAMS; DESIGNING A TEAM; A SELF-PERCEPTION INVENTORY; GLOSSARY; FURTHER READING..*

0 7506 0253 8    PAPERBACK    192PP    216 x 138MM    1984    £17.95

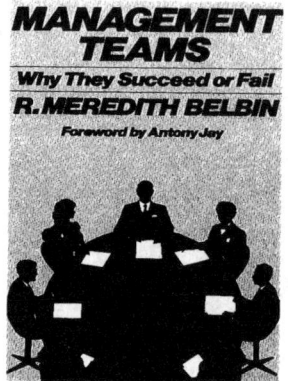

# TEAM ROLES AT WORK

## R M Belbin

This is a follow up to the highly successful book above. In this new book Dr Belbin develops his ideas further, using feedback gained through the users of this work. An overview of the development of team roles is given and various operational strategies are laid out which provide ideas and techniques that can be learned to advantage.

CONTENTS INCLUDE:
*THE PREHISTORY OF TEAM ROLES; EMERGENCE OF A TEAM-ROLE LANGUAGE; INTERPERSONAL; CHEMISTRY AT WORK; A STRATEGY FOR SELF-MANAGEMENT; MANAGING SUCCESSION; THE FUTURE SHAPE OF ORGANIZATION.*

0 7506 0925 7    PAPERBACK    160PP    234x156MM    1993    £17.95

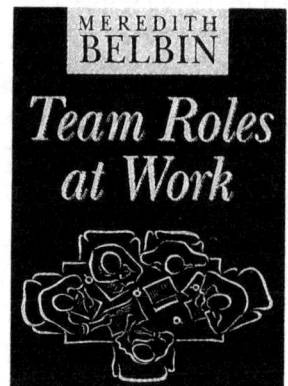

*Available from all good booksellers, or in case of difficulty please phone our direct order line on (0933) 410511 with your credit card details ready.*

# STRATEGIC MANAGEMENT
## A PC Based Approach

### PATRICK MCNAMEE
*Professor of International Business, University of Ulster*

## A FREE DISK IS INCLUDED WITH THIS BOOK

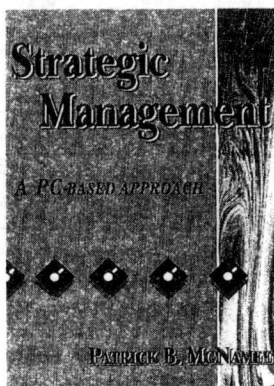

The practice of strategic management is not easy. However, the aim of this book is to make its use more widespread. This straightforward guide to practical strategic management also includes a disk to carry out all the calculations in the text, enhancing the understanding and use of management skills.

After reading this book the reader will be familiar with the core concepts in strategic management, have a good knowledge of the language of strategy and have the computing skills to develop planning models.

CONTENTS INCLUDE:
*STRATEGIC MANAGEMENT: THE CONCEPT AND A MODEL; ANALYSING THE ENVIRONMENT; THE PRODUCT MARKET PORTFOLIO; DEVELOPING STRATEGIES; COMPUTER MODELLING OF NEW STRATEGIES; EVALUATION AND CONTROL; DEVELOPING AND WRITING A STRATEGIC PLAN; INDEX*

0 7506 0505 7    1993    PAPERBACK    272PP    234 x 156MM    £19.95

*Available from all good booksellers, or in case of difficulty please phone our direct order line on (0933) 410511 with your credit card details ready.*

# FROM TIN SOLDIERS TO RUSSIAN DOLLS
## Creating Added Value Through Services

## SANDRA VANDERMERWE
### Professor of International Marketing and Services, IMD, Lausanne

This book is based on several years research into how companies can gain and maintain customers by adding value through first class service.

★ The "tin soldiers" of the title reflects the product focused attitudes and systems of many companies up until the late 1980's. Immersed in technical innovations and many manufacturing efficiencies they somehow forgot the customer.

★ The "Russian doll" image reflects the new customer focused company which sees its people, processes and core markets as a whole, made up of interconnected and interdependent parts.

from **Tin Soldiers** to **Russian Dolls**

Creating added value through services

Sandra Vandermerwe

The author examines why this is happening and what manufacturers and service companies can do to adapt their structures, skills and strategies to compete by adding value through service.

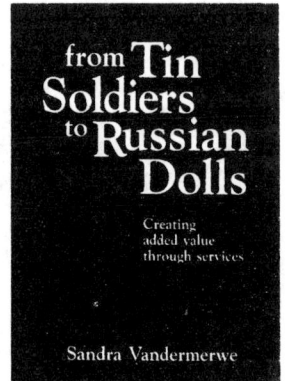

*"This book aims to change your whole way of thinking about customers, markets, and organizations. Be prepared for a fundamental mindshift on how to run your business in the coming century."*
PHILIP KOTLER

*"Should be compulsory reading in business schools."*
PAUL STONEHAM

CONTENTS INCLUDE:
INTRODUCTION; PRODUCTS, TIN SOLDIERS AND MATTER; THE MARKET POWER IS IN THE SERVICES BECAUSE THE VALUE IS IN THE RESULTS; BUILDING SERVICE INTENSIVE NETWORKS; MANAGING THE STEPPING-STONES TO CUSTOMER SATISFACTION; MAKING SERVICES PAY THEIR WAY; LOOKING AHEAD AND BEYOND.

0 7506 0974 5   HARDBACK   256PP   234 X 156MM   53 LINE ILLUSTRATIONS   1993   £25.00

*Available from all good booksellers, or in case of difficulty please phone our direct order line on (0933) 410511 with your credit card details ready.*